EVERY BELIEVER'S PROPHECY GUIDE

The Prophetic Destiny of Judah and Israel and The Kingdom of God

Essential Revelation for End-time Saints

ELIHU BEN EPHRAIM

WESTBOW
PRESS®
A DIVISION OF THOMAS NELSON
& ZONDERVAN

WestBow Press books may be ordered through booksellers or by contacting:

WestBow Press
A Division of Thomas Nelson & Zondervan
1663 Liberty Drive
Bloomington, IN 47403
www.westbowpress.com
1 (866) 928-1240

ISBN: 978-1-9736-2326-7 (sc)
ISBN: 978-1-9736-2327-4 (e)

Library of Congress Control Number: 2018903186

Print information available on the last page.

WestBow Press rev. date: 3/28/2018

EVERY BELIEVER'S PROPHECY GUIDE

THIS **ABSOLUTELY ESSENTIAL REVELATION** OF THE
PROPHETIC ROAD MAP WILL EQUIP THE END-TIME SAINTS
TO SEE WHERE THEY ARE IN PROPHECY AND ENABLE
THEM TO EASILY RECOGNISE THE MANY FALSE CHRISTS AND
FALSE PROPHETS WHO WILL COME IN JESUS' NAME
WITH LYING SIGNS AND WONDERS TO DECEIVE
IF POSSIBLE EVEN THE ELECT IN
THE LATTER DAYS

A NEVER-BEFORE PRESENTATION OF **ALL** THE PROPHETIC
SCRIPTURES WRITTEN BY THE PROPHETS AND
THE APOSTLES THAT PERTAIN TO THE
KINGDOM OF JUDAH, THE **KINGDOM OF ISRAEL,** AND
THE KINGDOM OF GOD

ARRANGED IN A **COMPREHENSIVE CHRONOLOGICAL
COLLATION,** TOGETHER WITH THE HISTORICAL
FULFILMENT OF THOSE PROPHESIED EVENTS THAT
HAVE ALREADY PASSED, THIS STUDY REVEALS WITH
CLARITY **THE DIVINE DESTINY** OF THESE **THREE
KINGDOMS** FROM ABRAHAM RIGHT THROUGH
THE TIME OF THE GENTILES, CULMINATING WITH THE
END OF THE AGE

**LEAVE THE INTERPRETATIONS AND OPINIONS OF MAN
BEHIND AND DISCOVER FOR YOURSELF THAT
THE SCRIPTURES ACTUALLY SPEAK FOR THEMSELVES**

Dedication

In memory of my dear wife Rosalie

A beloved disciple of Jesus Christ

Thank you Lord for all the years

When you gave her

When you gave her to me

Now my Lord I freely let her go

For she is yours she is yours

For Eternity

Acknowledgements and Thanks

A very special thanks to my friends and family who volunteered to become members of my editing team. Of special note are: Shannon, Greg, Nova and Abi, with the Pedantic Award going to Jude. Despite their busy lives they managed to do a stellar job. Their critical input helped tremendously both in the presentation of the information and in the very necessary and tedious work of proof reading. I would also like to acknowledge the input from everyone else who offered their comments both written and in conversation, it was all useful. Love, joy, peace and multiple thanks to all.

Contents

Preface

This book is a full on Bible Study. It has a story but it is no novel. It is absolutely loaded with Scripture so take your time to process the contents. Unless otherwise indicated, all Scripture quotations are from the King James Version of the Bible as I have been constrained by copyright and publishing considerations. It's not always the easiest version to read so you may like to read along with your preferred translation. My personal preference is the New King James Version which you will notice I have often quoted. Here is a list of the Bible Versions I have used with their respective abbreviations:

KJV   King James Version
NKJV   New King James Version
DRA   Douay-Rheims 1899 American Edition
MEV   Modern English Version
YLT   Young's Literal Translation
GNT   Good News Translation
ICB   International Children's Bible
ESV   English Standard Version
NIV   New International Version
ISR   Institute for Scripture Research
CEB   Common English Bible

I have given the source of my information by citations in the text, so there will be no separate bibliography, nor the clutter of footnotes. I am of course confident that everything I have written is thoroughly researched and accurate, however I am human. Therefore, I have taken up this saying that I heard somewhere, "I am convinced that I am right, but I am also convinced that I could be wrong."

I have come to believe that the searching and confirming exercise is healthy for the soul and therefore I encourage each individual to personally validate. In this modern day, practically everything can be researched online by simply typing the subject of interest into your favourite search engine, click and "hey presto", dozens of sites with which one can be informed. (Warning: eat the fish and spit out the bones.) In the process you will definitely find some scholars who completely disagree with me. Check them out and trust in the Lord to lead you into all truth. When in doubt, let God be true and every man a liar.

You will notice a different style of approach to the subject matter in the various chapters. This is due to the nature of the common misconceptions certain passages of Scripture have historically been subjected to. Sometimes it's just a matter of the particular passage of Scripture being overlooked and all that's required is to bring it into focus. Another time it is ignorance of the relevant history. On occasion I have found it necessary to get pedantic about the laws of grammar that have been abused which has on occasion caused complete misunderstanding. A common problem has been the lack of care to note the context. And then there is an awareness of the Gospel that is often required in order to discern the metaphorical language used by the original writer. In particular there are several passages where Scripture is required to interpret the Scripture. So along with the presentation of the prophecies, each chapter has unintentionally become its own lesson in rightly handling the Word of God.

Approach this study prayerfully and don't just take my word for anything. Allow the Holy Spirit to lead you into the truth of His Word so that at the end of the day you will not be saying, "So and so says this", but will be able to say with assurance, "Thus says the LORD". Get out your pen and get ready to make some notes in your Bible.

There are some supplementary articles to be found in the Appendix which I suggest you read as you are prompted to as you go through the study, as that would be the appropriate time; or leave them till you have finished all the chapters. I would discourage you from reading these items beforehand, as some of what is found there may not be easy to understand if you have not first read the information in the main body of this book.

No apology is given for the use of the Queen's English. I am sure that despite the occasional slight difference in spelling and grammar, my dear friends and fellow believers in North America will still be able to understand, though on occasion I might drift into some 'down under' expression which even Her Majesty will just have to bear with. If Her Majesty gets to read this book (I hope she does) I trust that she will understand and realise that in my heart she has all the respect that her position deserves. OK Mate, let's get on with it.

Love, joy and peace to you in Jesus Name.

Introduction

A significant portion of the Holy Scriptures is devoted to prophecy. Some say a little over a quarter, others say as much as a third. I've never counted, but I can testify that there are literally hundreds and hundreds of verses that are clearly prophetic. Many of these prophecies are predicting and describing the coming of the Lord Jesus Christ, some are directed at various Gentile nations, and others relate to specific individuals. Setting these aside, we find that the remainder of the prophetic writings can be placed into three categories: those concerning the Kingdom of Judah, those concerning the Kingdom of Israel, and those concerning the Kingdom of God. The Scriptures that speak of the prophetic destinies of these three kingdoms are scattered throughout the Bible like pieces of a jigsaw in a children's playroom, making it almost impossible to apprehend a coherent prophetic picture.

In this book I have gathered up the fragments of the prophetic jigsaw puzzle and put them together in a Comprehensive Chronological Collation so that men and women of God can readily see precisely what the Word of God actually says about these kingdoms.

It's amazing how clear God's picture of the latter days leading toward the end of the age becomes when ALL the verses that speak of the individual destinies of these kingdoms are arranged in an orderly fashion. It's also amazing how many prevalent contemporary end-time theories are completely overturned in the light of His Word.

Where appropriate, those prophecies which have already been fulfilled with the passing of time are presented with their corresponding historical records. Ignorance concerning which prophecies have been fulfilled has caused confusion regarding what events are yet to come. False prophets and teachers can lead people astray by asserting things are going to happen that have already come to pass. We will be better equipped to discern with clarity the signs of the times during the latter days if we have both the prophetic Scriptures and sufficient historical knowledge with which to ascertain what is past and what we can expectantly wait for. This book will provide both.

I have chosen to allow the Word of God to speak for itself by restricting my comments to highlighting what has actually been said in God's Word. Some passages of Scripture have suffered from a history of serious misinterpretation and I've found the need from time to time to be a bit pedantic pointing out the details. With careful attention to what is actually written and using Scripture to interpret Scripture, I believe I have been enabled to avoid giving my own ideas. On the rare occasion where I have offered my opinion, it is only where the subject matter is a moot point and/or of little consequence and I have been careful to make it understood when it is but my conjecture.

The student of eschatology is presently confronted with a multitude of end-time theories: pre-tribulation, mid-tribulation, post-tribulation, pre-millennial, post-millennial, a-millennial, futurist, historicist, full or partial preterist, hyper-literal or allegorical interpretations and the list goes on . . . With the variations within each particular school of thought we probably find that there are over a hundred different scenarios offered up as truth, if not more. Therefore, if you happen to align yourself with any one of the eschatological viewpoints, you will automatically find yourself in disagreement with over ninety percent of the Christian Community. This ought not to be.

If we take the incredible leap of faith and actually believe that God has His own interpretation and all other theories are but "private interpretations" (2 Peter 1:20), we can then look to the Lord to show us how we can recognize the interpretations of man, discern the doctrines of demons, and come to the understanding of what is really the Word of the Lord. Thankfully, God has not left us to our own devices on this most important subject. He has given us clear instructions in His Word as to how we are to approach the Holy Scriptures in order to receive the message they contain.

Again, a leap of faith. If we actually follow His instructions on how we are to handle His Word, we will be enabled to understand the intended meaning thereof. This requires a humble heart and a teachable mind with which we will find that the Scriptures end up speaking for themselves. We will be delivered from the multiple deceptions that presently prevail and we will come to the place where we realize that the Word of God is **not to be interpreted, rather it is to be believed.** And if we come to His Word as little children and simply believe it, we will eventually understand it.

So that you may have confidence to pursue this journey through the Prophetic Scriptures with me, I have included the methodology wherewith I have approached this most controversial of subjects. What follows is a short teaching on the subject of Biblical Comprehension which includes a collection of the relevant verses from the Bible that instruct us how to handle His Word. This will also serve as a demonstration of my manner of presentation. I have called this teaching:

Twelve Rules for Handling God's Word

Rule Number One:

Do not add or take from His Word.

Proverbs 30:6 NKJV
Do not add to His words, lest He rebuke you, and you be found a liar.

Deuteronomy 12:32 NKJV
Whatever I command you, be careful to observe it; you shall not add to it nor take away from it.

1 Corinthians 4:6 NKJV
. . . that you may learn in us not to think beyond what is written . . .

Don't even think beyond what is written. WOW. This requires us to pay attention to details and not be careless in our reading of the Word. Restraining ourselves from leaving out uncomfortable truths that do not conform to our preconceived theological perspective would be a practical application of this rule.

Rule Number Two:

Have two or three witnesses.

Matthew 18:16 NKJV
. . . by the mouth of two or three witnesses every word may be established.

2 Corinthians 13:1 NKJV
By the mouth of two or three witnesses every word shall be established.

Deuteronomy 19:15 NKJV
. . . by the mouth of two or three witnesses the matter shall be established.

This rule admonishes us not take one verse or passage on its own to make a doctrine from. As you may be aware, many heresies are based on isolated passages or single verses from the Bible.

Rule Number Three:

Get all the Scriptures on the subject.

Proverbs 18:13 NKJV
He who answers a matter before he hears it, it is folly and shame to him.

Ecclesiastes 12:13 NKJV
Let us hear the conclusion of the whole matter:

2 Timothy 3:16 NKJV
All Scripture is given by inspiration of God, and is profitable for doctrine, for reproof, for correction, for instruction in righteousness,

Without the whole counsel of God on any subject we can easily come to wrong conclusions. In this study you will be presented with many commonly overlooked Scriptures that have been ignored by contemporary prophecy teachers. Failing to present all the prophetic Scriptures concerning the latter days has resulted in many false teachings about the end of the age.

Rule Number Four:

Do not attempt to interpret God's Word. Simply believe the plain reading.

2 Peter 1:20 NKJV
. . . no prophecy of Scripture is of any private interpretation,

2 Peter 3:16 NKJV
. . . untaught and unstable *people* twist to their own destruction, as *they do* also the rest of the Scriptures.

Deuteronomy 29:29 NKJV
The secret *things belong* to the Lord our God, but those *things which are* revealed *belong* to us and to our children forever,

Obviously there are passages that are highly symbolic and for us to understand the meaning we would have to have an interpretation. However, this is where many people stumble. Attempting to interpret any vision or dream, metaphoric passage or parable from God's Word that does not have an interpretation given in the Word itself is a sure way to open the door to private interpretations.

If God hasn't given the meaning in His Word, leave it alone! Remember, it is His prerogative to keep some things to Himself. "The secret things belong the Lord our God." It is the things that are revealed that are for us. Our response is not to interpret His Word, but to understand and believe it, or should I say: believe it, then you will understand it.

There is a huge difference between interpreting God's Word and understanding God's Word. People who interpret God's Word are lacking wisdom, therefore they lack understanding

Proverbs 4:7 NKJV
Wisdom is the principal thing; therefore get wisdom. And in all your getting, get understanding.

To speculate on the meaning of a symbolic passage of Scripture may be acceptable in some circumstances, provided we do not become dogmatic about our musings and attempt to make doctrine from it. This tendency to interpret God's Word is THE major stumbling block to understanding what it is that He actually intends for us to comprehend. As Joseph said when presented with a dream:

Genesis 40:8 NKJV
Do not interpretations belong to God?

Rule Number Five:

Do not take a verse out of context.

This rule is actually covered in the above but for clarification I have added it as a rule on its own. The tendency to take verses out of context is something I call Cut and Paste Theology. (Since taking up this phrase I have discovered others use it too.) With it you can even 'prove' that suicide is how we are to reckon ourselves dead to sin. Matthew 27:5 says that Judas hung himself and Luke 10:37 says that we should do likewise.

One of the primary laws of comprehension used in language translation is that the meaning of anything is found in its context. That's how you learnt your mother tongue. Therefore, do not take any verse or passage out of its historical and grammatical context and thereby alter its meaning. This would result in a twisting of the Scriptures and as they say, "A text out of context has become a con and not a text." Remember how the devil tempted Jesus with out of context Scripture quotations.

Rule Number Six:

The hidden meaning does not negate the plain reading.

This rule may seem obscure, but it has implications as to how we understand many prophecies. For example: the promise concerning Samson becoming a Nazarite in Judges 13:5 is fulfilled in the natural during his lifetime AND it is also applied to Jesus being brought up in Nazareth in Matthew 2:23. The fulfilment in the life of Jesus does not negate the fulfilment in the life of Samson. And so it is with many other Scriptures.

Another example of this principle is found in this verse: "Out of Egypt I called my son." (Hosea 11:1) In its natural context it applies to Israel and in particular the leading tribe of Ephraim. Yet in Matthew 2:15 we find it applied to Jesus as a child with Joseph and Mary returning from Egypt after having fled there from the evil plans of King Herod.

In the course of this study, we will come across some promises made to Abraham and to the children of Israel that have dual meanings in the Word: one meaning for his natural descendants and another meaning for those who follow in his faith. What we must remember is that whilst the spiritual hidden meaning is revealed in the New Covenant and is positively okay to be applied to the people of faith, the natural prophetic proclamation still stands and will also most certainly come to pass.

Rule Number Seven:

Do not expect a dual fulfilment unless God indicates it is so in the Word.

This is the inverse of the previous rule. Not all prophecies have dual fulfilments. False prophets abound and one of the ways they deceive is to pronounce dual fulfilments for things that God has not revealed are so. The legitimate dual fulfilments are revealed as such by Scripture, not by man. Some prophecy pundits have gone so far as to declare that there is a law of dual or multiple fulfilment. This idea makes the way for all sorts of proclamations that are just not true. Here's just one example that completely refutes that so called law: The prophecies about Jesus coming and His death being a once and for all sacrifice for sin definitely have no dual fulfilment.

It is acknowledged that God may 'quicken' a verse to you concerning a situation, even out of context for you personally, but that is not a licence to extrapolate doctrine or prophecy.

Rule Number Eight:

Scripture interprets Scripture.

This rule is likewise covered above, but again for clarification it is added as a rule on its own.

2 Peter 1:20 NKJV
Knowing this first, that no prophecy of Scripture is of any private interpretation,

2 Timothy 3:16 NKJV
All Scripture is given by inspiration of God, and is profitable for doctrine, for reproof, for correction, for instruction in righteousness . . .

Combining 2 Timothy 3:16 with 2 Peter 1:20 reveals this important rule for our consideration. If a Scripture is not understood, and there is a need to be taught its meaning, allow the rest of Scripture to bring the understanding. Sooner or later, if you stay in His Word with the Holy Spirit leading you into the Truth, you will get the revelation that you desire. All Scripture is suitable for doctrine; that is teaching. So let ALL Scripture teach us what Scripture means. If this one rule was adhered to it would put away most, if not all, of the present day deceptions.

Rule Number Nine:

Let the witness of history confirm prophecy.

Jeremiah 28:9 NKJV
As for the prophet who prophesies of peace, when the word of the prophet comes to pass, the prophet will be known as one whom the Lord has truly sent.

Deuteronomy 18:22 NKJV
When a prophet speaks in the name of the Lord, if the thing does not happen or come to pass, that *is* the thing which the Lord has not spoken; the prophet has spoken it presumptuously; you shall not be afraid of him.

To discover which prophecies have or have not been fulfilled requires us to do the necessary historical research. With the aid of the internet this is no longer a major difficulty. This book will assist anyone who wants to follow through by bringing attention to historical events that can then be searched for online. I realise many will simply take my word for it, but I do encourage personal verification.

When I was at school, I never had any interest in history and did not consider it a worthwhile subject for me to study. Once I became a Christian and discovered that the Bible is entirely rooted in history, my attitude towards this subject completely changed. I found that an accurate knowledge of history is absolutely essential for one to ascertain what has been fulfilled and what is yet to come. The testimony of history is God's 'acid test' on prophecy. When history and prophecy kiss, you get reality.

Rule Number Ten:

Make Jesus the Cornerstone.

Ephesians 2:20 NKJV
... the foundation of the apostles and prophets, Jesus Christ Himself being the chief corner*stone* ...

Whilst this study is more or less chronological in its presentation, it is entirely based on what Jesus said in the Gospel accounts. Jesus Himself had to show the disciples on the road to Emmaus all the things that the prophets had said regarding His first coming. What He said opened their eyes. In like manner, the prophecies given by Jesus in the Gospels and the proclamations of the Apostles in the Letters will shine the necessary light on the prophetic Scriptures that speak of Judah, Israel and the Kingdom of God. Very difficult, if not impossible, trying to do it the other way around. It is like putting the prophetic cart before the horse.

Many people have misunderstood prophecies because they were not able to shine the full light of the Gospel onto what they were reading. If there is confusion concerning what it means to be crucified with Christ, to be a new creation in Christ, to be made the righteousness of God in Christ, to be dead to sin and alive to God, then the light of the Gospel is not yet shining fully into the heart and mind.

A proper understanding of the Gospel and all that it has done for the man or woman of God, who has been born again, will preclude certain assumptions being made about the nature and destiny of the Kingdom of God and its manifestation in this earth and age. In like manner, this understanding will also keep us from deceptions regarding the fulfilment of God's promises for the Kingdom of Judah and the Kingdom of Israel.

This is probably the most important rule of all in understanding God's Word. First let Christ be the Cornerstone of our whole being and then Jesus can be the Cornerstone of our prophetic understanding. Amen.

Rule Number Eleven:

Know that God does not contradict Himself or His Character.

Numbers 23:19 ESV
God is not man, that he should lie, or a son of man, that he should change his mind.

James 1:17 NKJV
... the Father of lights, with whom there is no variation or shadow of turning.

If we have an understanding of a particular verse or passage that doesn't fit with other passages on the same subject, it is our understanding that has to change. The Spirit of God who inspired the Scriptures is the same yesterday, today and forever. As a new believer, one of the first things that I realised about the Kingdom of God was that it was completely logical and without contradiction.

Rule Number Twelve:

Speak the Truth in Love.

This rule I have inserted is not so much to do with how we understand God's Word, but how we deliver it. However, if we are lacking in our delivery, it will affect our ability to understand.

1 Corinthians 13:1-2 NKJV
Though I speak with the tongues of men and of angels, but have not love, I have become sounding brass or a clanging cymbal. 2 And though I have *the gift of* prophecy, and understand all mysteries and all knowledge, and though I have all faith, so that I could remove mountains, but have not love, I am nothing.

Ephesians 4:15 NKJV
. . . but, speaking the truth in love, may grow up in all things into Him who is the head—Christ—

James 1:22 NKJV
But be doers of the word, and not hearers only, deceiving yourselves.

It is simply not good enough for us to speak the truth. If we try to convey the Word of God to those around us without the fruit of love, we actually become an unpleasant noise and a stumbling block to that very same truth. And as the above verse points out, if we fail to become doers of the Word by not speaking the truth in love, we ourselves will become deceived. Want to avoid deception? Be sure to walk in love.

With the Twelve Rules for Handling God's Word, the diligent disciple can approach the subject of prophecy with confidence and not be deceived. I believe it's time for some 'let us' salad.

Let us not add to the plain meaning of the Word. Let us not try interpreting the Word according to our own understanding and end up twisting the Scriptures. Let us gather all the Scriptures on the matter and thereby avoid jumping to wrong conclusions by failing to hear the whole story. At a minimum; let us have two or three witnesses to establish any doctrine. Let us also be careful to examine Scriptures in the light of the context wherein they are found. And to establish whether we are to expectantly look to the future for the fulfilment of a prophecy, let us consider the historical records and see if the prediction has already come to pass. Let us make the words of Jesus the foundation of all our knowledge and let us always be ready to grow in our understanding, especially when we find what appears to be a contradiction. Let us not lean on our own understanding and read into God's Word things He has not put there. And last but not least, let us speak the Word in LOVE. You will find that I have been diligent to hold fast to these precepts.

We may never get to know every little detail about the times to come. Nevertheless, as God's people we can know the necessary basics of His latter day road map sufficiently well to keep us from being blown about by the many winds of doctrine which have been and will be unleashed to deceive, if possible, the very elect (Matthew 24:24). In the Synoptic Gospels, where we find the bulk of Jesus' prophetic statements, Matthew and Mark record these words: "Take heed that no man deceive you." And Luke says similarly: "Take heed lest any man deceive you."

Praise the Lord, the darkness of confusion and deception flees at the light of His Word. God's Word speaks and we can simply say AMEN. Through this comprehensive Bible Study, the student of eschatology will have a better understanding of God's purposes and plans concerning the Kingdom of God, the Kingdom of Judah and the Kingdom of Israel. Consequently, you will be well equipped to recognize the many false prophets and false teachers that Jesus said would abound in the last days. What's more, you will not be relying on the words of any teacher, and certainly not me, but you will have the Prophetic Word of God confirmed in your hearts by the Holy Spirit. This will enable you to pray according to the will of God concerning the fulfilment of His plan to not only bring forth a great harvest out from among the Gentiles, but also to gather the descendants of Abraham, Isaac and Jacob into the Promised Land AND into the Kingdom of God during the latter days before the end of the age.

Because of the busyness of raising a family and being generally active in the work of the Lord, this project has taken me several years to complete and was initially begun only to satisfy my own quest for truth. I did not set out to write a book. In the course of my study of God's Word, I had discovered with various subjects that it was absolutely necessary to have the full counsel of God on any matter before the whole truth could be readily understood. Confronted with a myriad of different end-time theories, I decided to apply this principle of "getting all the verses on a subject" to the study of prophecy in the belief that God was not the author of all the confusion and that if I followed His instructions He would lead me into the truth.

As I continued to grow in understanding, I eventually became convinced that what I was discovering was not solely for my own benefit. As I did not want to reinvent the wheel, I searched online to see if anyone had already published anything like what I was envisioning and found to my surprise that there was nothing on the market.

I then found myself gifted with the opportunity and the ability to sit at this keyboard for hours on end and doggedly tap away, mostly with two fingers. During the process I became amazed at how it was all coming together: certain snippets of information would somehow just get stumbled upon; a revelation of His Word would come to me in the middle of the night; a discussion with another saint would correct my thinking; an amazing 'coincidence' which upon reflection let me know that the Hand of God was upon the whole process; and eventually this book emerged.

As the story from the Scriptures was unfolding and I was searching for a name for this work, I was going to call this revelation of God's plan by a rather cryptic title: **The Lion and The**

Unicorn on the Road to Zion. However, I was persuaded that it might give the impression of a fantasy and frustrate God's purpose in having me prepare this study by taking away from the seriousness of the subject. But now it seems okay to present this alternative title as a mystery, a riddle to be solved along the way. God willing, in the midst of this study you will get to identify the Lion and the Unicorn on the Road to Zion and accompany them on their journey if you have not already done so. You may even find yourself riding on the back of the Unicorn.

I hope you will enjoy reading and learning what God's Word has to say about Judah, Israel and the Kingdom of God as much as I have in producing it. It is my desire that it may enlighten the eyes of your understanding to God's incredibly glorious plan for His people in the latter days and at the same time prepare your hearts for the trials of faith that are to be endured before the end of the age.

Chapter One

The Patriarchal Prophecies

The Lion and the Unicorn on the Road to Zion is the mostly forgotten story of the prophesied destiny of two kingdoms that have a future rendezvous with the Kingdom of God. Many will readily identify the Lion, but most will have no idea about the Unicorn. How it could have been forgotten and why it got forgotten when there is so much said about it in the pages of God's Word is beyond me. Perhaps it is simply because: "For everything there is a season" (Ecclesiastes 3:1).

In this chapter you will find God's promises made to the patriarchs that have set the course of history right through to the latter days. The destiny of the descendants of Abraham, Isaac and Jacob is the central and most important piece of the eschatology puzzle, without which fully ninety percent of end-time prophecy cannot be correctly understood. That estimation might seem rather audacious, but when this study has been completed, you may even consider it an understatement.

This prophetic destiny is first revealed in Chapter 12 of Genesis where Abraham is chosen by God to be the father of many nations. Through Abraham and Sarah the whole world would be blessed by the bringing forth of both the Lion and the Unicorn.

Abraham and Sarah were at this time known as Abram and Sarai.

Genesis 12:1-3
Now the Lord had said unto Abram, Get thee out of thy country, and from thy kindred, and from thy father's house, unto a land that I will shew thee: 2 And I will make of thee a great nation, and I will bless thee, and make thy name great; and thou shalt be a blessing: 3 And I will bless them that bless thee, and curse him that curseth thee: and in thee shall all families of the earth be blessed.

Genesis 13:16
And I will make thy seed as the dust of the earth: so that if a man can number the dust of the earth, then shall thy seed also be numbered.

Genesis 15:3-5
And Abram said, Behold, to me thou hast given no seed: and, lo, one born in my house is mine heir. 4 And, behold, the word of the Lord came unto him, saying, This shall not be thine heir; but he that shall come forth out of thine own bowels shall be thine heir. 5 And he brought him forth

abroad, and said, Look now toward heaven, and tell the stars, if thou be able to number them: and he said unto him, So shall thy seed be.

The promises or prophecies given to Abraham by God are: He will become a great nation; His name shall be great; He will be a blessing; Blessed be everyone who blesses him; Cursed be everyone who curses him; In him all families of the earth will be blessed; His descendants shall be as uncountable as the stars in heaven; His descendants will be as uncountable as the dust of the earth.

At this point in time, Abram and Sarai could not see how these promises would come to pass so they made their own plan.

Genesis 16:3-4
And Sarai Abram's wife took Hagar her maid the Egyptian, after Abram had dwelt ten years in the land of Canaan, and gave her to her husband Abram to be his wife. 4 And he went in unto Hagar, and she conceived: and when she saw that she had conceived, her mistress was despised in her eyes.

Genesis 16:10-12
And the angel of the Lord said unto her, I will multiply thy seed exceedingly, that it shall not be numbered for multitude. 11 And the angel of the Lord said unto her, Behold, thou art with child and shalt bear a son, and shalt call his name Ishmael; because the Lord hath heard thy affliction. 12 And he will be a wild man; his hand will be against every man, and every man's hand against him; and he shall dwell in the presence of all his brethren.

The promises to Ishmael through Hagar are: He will be a wild man; His hand shall be against every man; Everyman's hand will be against him; He will dwell in the presence of all his brethren; He will multiply exceedingly.

However, God was about to make it clear that the promises concerning Abram's descendants were going to be fulfilled through his wife. In doing so He also changed their names to Abraham and Sarah.

Genesis 17:1-7
And when Abram was ninety years old and nine, the Lord appeared to Abram, and said unto him, I am the Almighty God; walk before me, and be thou perfect. 2 And I will make my covenant between me and thee, and will multiply thee exceedingly. 3 And Abram fell on his face: and God talked with him, saying, 4 As for me, behold, my covenant is with thee, and thou shalt be a father of many nations. 5 Neither shall thy name any more be called Abram, but thy name shall be Abraham; for a father of many nations have I made thee. 6 And I will make thee exceeding fruitful, and I will make nations of thee, and kings shall come out of thee. 7 And I will establish my covenant between me and thee and thy seed after thee in their generations for an everlasting covenant, to be a God unto thee, and to thy seed after thee.

Genesis 17:15-22
And God said unto Abraham, As for Sarai thy wife, thou shalt not call her name Sarai, but Sarah shall her name be. 16 And I will bless her, and give thee a son also of her: yea, I will bless her, and she shall be a mother of nations; kings of people shall be of her. 17 Then Abraham fell upon his face, and laughed, and said in his heart, Shall a child be born unto him that is an hundred years old? and shall Sarah, that is ninety years old, bear? 18 And Abraham said unto God, O that Ishmael might live before thee! 19 And God said, Sarah thy wife shall bear thee a son indeed; and thou shalt call his name Isaac: and I will establish my covenant with him for an everlasting covenant, and with his seed after him. 20 And as for Ishmael, I have heard thee: Behold, I have blessed him, and will make him fruitful, and will multiply him exceedingly; twelve princes shall he beget, and I will make him a great nation. 21 But my covenant will I establish with Isaac, which Sarah shall bear unto thee at this set time in the next year. 22 And he left off talking with him, and God went up from Abraham.

In the process Ishmael receives these blessings through Abraham: He will become a great nation; He shall beget 12 princes.

Abraham himself receives further blessings which include: Abraham shall have a son by his wife and will name him Isaac; Abraham will become the father of many nations; Kings will come from him; He will be exceedingly fruitful; The everlasting covenant will be established through Isaac. In due time, God fulfils His promise to Abraham to bring forth a child through Sarah.

Genesis 21:1-3
And the Lord visited Sarah as he had said, and the Lord did unto Sarah as he had spoken. 2 For Sarah conceived, and bare Abraham a son in his old age, at the set time of which God had spoken to him. 3 And Abraham called the name of his son that was born unto him, whom Sarah bare to him, Isaac.

And the blessings upon Sarah are: She will be blessed; She will be a mother of nations; Kings of peoples will come from her.

Genesis 22:17
. . . in blessing I will bless thee, and in multiplying I will multiply thy seed as the stars of the heaven, and as the sand which is upon the sea shore; and thy seed shall possess the gate of his enemies;

Abraham again receives promises: His descendants shall multiply as the stars in heaven and the sand on the sea shore; His descendants shall possess the gates of their enemies.

Isaac receives the promise of the Birthright Blessing; Ishmael does not. Ishmael receives his own promises from God, but not those promised to Abraham and Sarah. God confirms the Birthright Blessings to Isaac after Abraham dies.

Genesis 26:3-5
Sojourn in this land, and I will be with thee, and will bless thee; for unto thee, and unto thy seed, I will give all these countries, and I will perform the oath which I sware unto Abraham thy father; 4 And I will make thy seed to multiply as the stars of heaven, and will give unto thy seed all these countries; and in thy seed shall all the nations of the earth be blessed; 5 Because that Abraham obeyed my voice, and kept my charge, my commandments, my statutes, and my laws.

God said to Isaac: I will be with you; I will give you all these lands; I will make your descendants multiply as the stars of heaven; In your seed, all nations of the earth will be blessed. Hidden in these blessings given to Abraham and Isaac is the Promise of the Seed through whom all nations shall be blessed. Isaac marries Rebekah who receives more promises.

Genesis 24:67
And Isaac brought her into his mother Sarah's tent, and took Rebekah, and she became his wife; and he loved her: and Isaac was comforted after his mother's death.

Genesis 24:60
And they blessed Rebekah, and said unto her, Thou art our sister, be thou the mother of thousands of millions, and let thy seed possess the gate of those which hate them.

The New King James gives it more literally regarding the number of the descendants.

Genesis 24:60 NKJV
. . . *The mother of* thousands of ten thousands . . .

The promises to Rebekah are: Her descendants will possess the gates of their enemies; Rebekah will be the mother of thousands of ten thousands. One thousand times one thousand equals one million, so I wonder how many tens of millions are intended in this promise?

Isaac and Rebekah have twin boys: Esau and Jacob; Esau being the firstborn.

Genesis 25:23
And the Lord said unto her, Two nations are in thy womb, and two manner of people shall be separated from thy bowels; and the one people shall be stronger than the other people; and the elder shall serve the younger.

Genesis 25:24-26
And when her days to be delivered were fulfilled, behold, there were twins in her womb. 25 And the first came out red, all over like an hairy garment; and they called his name Esau. 26 And after that came his brother out, and his hand took hold on Esau's heel; and his name was called Jacob: and Isaac was threescore years old when she bare them.

Genesis 25:29-34

And Jacob sod pottage: and Esau came from the field, and he was faint: 30 And Esau said to Jacob, Feed me, I pray thee, with that same red pottage; for I am faint: therefore was his name called Edom. 31 And Jacob said, Sell me this day thy birthright. 32 And Esau said, Behold, I am at the point to die: and what profit shall this birthright do to me? 33 And Jacob said, Swear to me this day; and he sware unto him: and he sold his birthright unto Jacob. 34 Then Jacob gave Esau bread and pottage of lentiles; and he did eat and drink, and rose up, and went his way: thus Esau despised his birthright.

Oh boy, that first phrase really got me: Jacob sod pottage! How English has changed. It means he cooked a stew. But concerning the destiny we are focusing on, it is the last phrase that is significant: Esau despised his birthright and as a consequence, Jacob received the Birthright Blessing from his father, Isaac:

Genesis 27:27-29

And he came near, and kissed him: and he smelled the smell of his raiment, and blessed him, and said, See, the smell of my son is as the smell of a field which the Lord hath blessed: 28 Therefore God give thee of the dew of heaven, and the fatness of the earth, and plenty of corn and wine: 29 Let people serve thee, and nations bow down to thee: be lord over thy brethren, and let thy mother's sons bow down to thee: cursed be every one that curseth thee, and blessed be he that blesseth thee.

Jacob received the Birthright Blessing: May the Lord give you of the dew of heaven and the fatness of the earth; And plenty of grain and wine; Let people serve you; Many nations will bow down to you; Be master over your brethren; Let your mother's sons bow down to you; Cursed be everyone who curses you; Blessed be those who bless you.

Esau also received promises, but not the Birthright Blessing, because he despised it earlier.

Genesis 27:39-40

And Isaac his father answered and said unto him, Behold, thy dwelling shall be the fatness of the earth, and of the dew of heaven from above; 40 And by thy sword shalt thou live, and shalt serve thy brother; and it shall come to pass when thou shalt have the dominion, that thou shalt break his yoke from off thy neck.

The promises to Esau were: Dwell in the fatness of the earth and with the dew of heaven from above; He shall live by his sword; Serve his brother (Jacob); Break his yoke from his neck.

God foresaw, even in the womb, that Esau would despise his birthright and so the Birthright Blessing of Abraham came upon Jacob. Jacob marries two sisters: Leah and Rachel. From them and their two maidservants, Bilhah and Zilpah, Jacob has 12 sons. The Birthright Blessing begins to unfold.

Genesis 35:23-26
The sons of Leah; Reuben, Jacob's firstborn, and Simeon, and Levi, and Judah, and Issachar, and Zebulun: 24 The sons of Rachel; Joseph, and Benjamin: 25 And the sons of Bilhah, Rachel's handmaid; Dan, and Naphtali: 26 And the sons of Zilpah, Leah's handmaid: Gad, and Asher: these are the sons of Jacob, which were born to him in Padanaram.

These are the sons listed in order from oldest to youngest: Reuben, Simeon, Levi, Judah, Dan, Naphtali, Gad, Asher, Issachar, Zebulun, Joseph, Benjamin.

God changes Jacob's name to Israel.

Genesis 35:10
And God said unto him, Thy name is Jacob: thy name shall not be called any more Jacob, but Israel shall be thy name: and he called his name Israel.

Most people recognise the Birthright Blessing being passed from Abraham to Isaac to Jacob. However, the blessing can be traced further as we shall see. God gives Joseph, the eldest son of Rachel, dreams of greatness.

Genesis 37:5-11
And Joseph dreamed a dream, and he told it his brethren: and they hated him yet the more. 6 And he said unto them, Hear, I pray you, this dream which I have dreamed: 7 For, behold, we were binding sheaves in the field, and, lo, my sheaf arose, and also stood upright; and, behold, your sheaves stood round about, and made obeisance to my sheaf. 8 And his brethren said to him, Shalt thou indeed reign over us? or shalt thou indeed have dominion over us? And they hated him yet the more for his dreams, and for his words. 9 And he dreamed yet another dream, and told it his brethren, and said, Behold, I have dreamed a dream more; and, behold, the sun and the moon and the eleven stars made obeisance to me. 10 And he told it to his father, and to his brethren: and his father rebuked him, and said unto him, What is this dream that thou hast dreamed? Shall I and thy mother and thy brethren indeed come to bow down ourselves to thee to the earth? 11 And his brethren envied him; but his father observed the saying.

Joseph is sold into slavery by his brothers.

Genesis 37:28
Then there passed by Midianites merchantmen; and they drew and lifted up Joseph out of the pit, and sold Joseph to the Ishmaelites for twenty pieces of silver: and they brought Joseph into Egypt.

However, God exalts Joseph to the highest rank in Egypt.

Genesis 41:39-40

And Pharaoh said unto Joseph, Forasmuch as God hath shewed thee all this, there is none so discreet and wise as thou art: 40 Thou shalt be over my house, and according unto thy word shall all my people be ruled: only in the throne will I be greater than thou.

In Egypt Joseph had two sons: Ephraim and Manasseh.

Genesis 41:50-52

And unto Joseph were born two sons before the years of famine came, which Asenath the daughter of Potipherah priest of On bare unto him. 51 And Joseph called the name of the firstborn Manasseh: For God, said he, hath made me forget all my toil, and all my father's house. 52 And the name of the second called he Ephraim: For God hath caused me to be fruitful in the land of my affliction.

Jacob then conveys the Birthright Blessing through Joseph to Ephraim and Manasseh. Ephraim is given the greater blessing.

Genesis 48:5

And now thy two sons, Ephraim and Manasseh, which were born unto thee in the land of Egypt before I came unto thee into Egypt, are mine; as Reuben and Simeon, they shall be mine.

Genesis 48:12-20

And Joseph brought them out from between his knees, and he bowed himself with his face to the earth. 13 And Joseph took them both, Ephraim in his right hand toward Israel's left hand, and Manasseh in his left hand toward Israel's right hand, and brought them near unto him. 14 And Israel stretched out his right hand, and laid it upon Ephraim's head, who was the younger, and his left hand upon Manasseh's head, guiding his hands wittingly; for Manasseh was the firstborn. 15 And he blessed Joseph, and said, God, before whom my fathers Abraham and Isaac did walk, the God which fed me all my life long unto this day, 16 The Angel which redeemed me from all evil, bless the lads; and let my name be named on them, and the name of my fathers Abraham and Isaac; and let them grow into a multitude in the midst of the earth.

17 And when Joseph saw that his father laid his right hand upon the head of Ephraim, it displeased him: and he held up his father's hand, to remove it from Ephraim's head unto Manasseh's head. 18 And Joseph said unto his father, Not so, my father: for this is the firstborn; put thy right hand upon his head. 19 And his father refused, and said, I know it, my son, I know it: he also shall become a people, and he also shall be great: but truly his younger brother shall be greater than he, and his seed shall become a multitude of nations. 20 And he blessed them that day, saying, In thee shall Israel bless, saying, God make thee as Ephraim and as Manasseh: and he set Ephraim before Manasseh.

The significance of that statement in Genesis 48:19 from the above passage is completely overlooked by most Christians. This promise that was given to Ephraim, concerning his seed becoming a multitude of nations, is the key that unlocks the door to understanding God's plan for the latter days.

Genesis 48:22
Moreover I have given to thee one portion above thy brethren, which I took out of the hand of the Amorite with my sword and with my bow.

Genesis 49:22-26
Joseph is a fruitful bough, even a fruitful bough by a well; whose branches run over the wall: 23 The archers have sorely grieved him, and shot at him, and hated him: 24 But his bow abode in strength, and the arms of his hands were made strong by the hands of the mighty God of Jacob; (from thence is the shepherd, the stone of Israel:) 25 Even by the God of thy father, who shall help thee; and by the Almighty, who shall bless thee with blessings of heaven above, blessings of the deep that lieth under, blessings of the breasts, and of the womb: 26 The blessings of thy father have prevailed above the blessings of my progenitors unto the utmost bound of the everlasting hills: they shall be on the head of Joseph, and on the crown of the head of him that was separate from his brethren.

Joseph's sons get the Birthright Blessings, but the Sceptre went to Judah who is also likened unto a lion in this prophecy of Jacob.

Genesis 49:8-10
Judah, thou art he whom thy brethren shall praise: thy hand shall be in the neck of thine enemies; thy father's children shall bow down before thee. 9 Judah is a lion's whelp: from the prey, my son, thou art gone up: he stooped down, he couched as a lion, and as an old lion; who shall rouse him up? 10 The sceptre shall not depart from Judah, nor a lawgiver from between his feet, until Shiloh come; and unto him shall the gathering of the people be.

This separation of the Sceptre from the Birthright is also recorded later in Chronicles.

1 Chronicles 5:1-2
Now the sons of Reuben the firstborn of Israel, for he was the firstborn; but forasmuch as he defiled his father's bed, his birthright was given unto the sons of Joseph the son of Israel: and the genealogy is not to be reckoned after the birthright. 2 For Judah prevailed above his brethren, and of him came the chief ruler; but the birthright was Joseph's.

Judah was to bring forth the "chief ruler" otherwise known as the Messiah and as we saw above, the Sceptre would not depart from Judah. However, the Scripture says plainly that the Birthright belongs to Joseph. Here we have Moses who also prophecies concerning the sons of Joseph.

Deuteronomy 33:16-17
And for the precious things of the earth and fulness thereof, and for the good will of him that dwelt in the bush: let the blessing come upon the head of Joseph, and upon the top of the head

of him that was separated from his brethren. 17 His glory is like the firstling of his bullock, and his horns are like the horns of unicorns: with them he shall push the people together to the ends of the earth: and they are the ten thousands of Ephraim, and they are the thousands of Manasseh.

Moses likens the sons of Joseph to horns of unicorns, and prophecies the "blessing upon the head of Joseph". For more on unicorns, see the article: I Believe in Unicorns in the Appendix.

Ephraim and Manasseh were also given the privilege to be named Israel/Jacob, Abraham and or Isaac, so that throughout the Scriptures we often find Joseph or Ephraim referred to as Israel or Jacob and vice versa.

Genesis 48:16
The Angel which redeemed me from all evil, bless the lads; and let my name be named on them, and the name of my fathers Abraham and Isaac; and let them grow into a multitude in the midst of the earth.

The destiny of the sons of Joseph and the destiny of Judah were established forever in these passages from Genesis. **It is God Himself who has spoken through the Patriarchs who watches over His Word to see to it that it does not return to Him void.** (Isaiah 55:11) What He has said He will perform. As we continue in this study, we will see the kiss of history upon these words of prophecy.

Though there were later promises that were associated with the giving of the Law (with the Covenant that was made through Moses) which were conditional upon the obedience of the children of Israel, the Birthright Blessings and the Promise of the Sceptre given through Jacob were not conditional and are guaranteed by God Himself and for this we are to be thankful. Had it depended upon the righteousness of the descendants for these prophecies to be fulfilled, the promise of the coming King through Judah would never have come to pass.

Galatians 3:15-18 NKJV
Brethren, I speak in the manner of men: Though *it is* only a man's covenant, yet *if it is* confirmed, no one annuls or adds to it. 16 Now to Abraham and his Seed were the promises made. He does not say, "And to seeds," as of many, but as of one, "And to your Seed," who is Christ. 17 And this I say, *that* the law, which was four hundred and thirty years later, cannot annul the covenant that was confirmed before by God in Christ, that it should make the promise of no effect. 18 For if the inheritance *is* of the law, *it is* no longer of promise; but God gave *it* to Abraham by promise.

A word of caution: The Holy Spirit is the only one with the prerogative to inject hidden meanings into the original text as He has done through Paul with this passage from Galatians. We are not to take it as a cue to use our own initiative and make a practice of taking verses out of context for ourselves. Amen.

Whilst the above passage is speaking of one particular promise (that of Christ), Galatians 3:16 encourages us to believe that all the promises of God made before the law will surely come to pass, including those given to Ephraim.

Unfortunately, this very same verse has been seriously misused and has become the foundation for a theory now known as Replacement Theology. This theory espouses the idea that all the promises to Abraham are fulfilled in Christ and that they are now to be applied to Spiritual Israel (the Church) and not to Natural Israel. Whilst there are promises that are applied to a Spiritual Israel, this theology fails to account for the fact that the Birthright Blessings of Abraham, Isaac and Jacob were given to the sons of Joseph, and are consequently completely separate from the Sceptre promises concerning Christ that were given to Judah. Replacement Theology overlooks the fact that the Seed that came through Judah has nothing to do with the seed that was to come through Ephraim, just as it has nothing to do with seed that came through Ishmael. Praise be to our God who fulfils ALL His promises to all the seed. Hallelujah!

Romans 11:29 NKJV
For the gifts and the calling of God *are* irrevocable.

Most scholars have no problem believing that the promises to Ishmael have most certainly come to pass. They look at the situation in the Middle East and commiserate among themselves about what Abraham and Sarah's decision has brought forth. By way of reminder, here are the promises made to the three different seeds. First we have the promise concerning the seed of Hagar, her son Ishmael.

Genesis 16:10-11
And the angel of the Lord said unto her, I will multiply **thy seed** exceedingly, that it shall not be numbered for multitude. 11 And the angel of the Lord said unto her, Behold, thou art with child and shalt bear a son, and shalt call his name Ishmael; because the Lord hath heard thy affliction. (Emphasis mine)

Then, in the passage from Galatians we have the hidden promise of the Seed that was to come through Judah which we all appreciate as being fulfilled in Christ.

Galatians 3:16 NKJV
Now to Abraham and his Seed were the promises made. He does not say, "And to seeds," as of many, but as of one, "And to **your Seed**," who is Christ. (Emphasis mine)

And then we have the promises concerning the seed that was to come from Ephraim.

Genesis 48:17-19
And when Joseph saw that his father laid his right hand upon the head of Ephraim, it displeased him: and he held up his father's hand, to remove it from Ephraim's head unto Manasseh's head. 18 And Joseph said unto his father, Not so, my father: for this is the firstborn; put thy right hand

upon his head. 19 And his father refused, and said, I know it, my son, I know it: he also shall become a people, and he also shall be great: but truly his younger brother shall be greater than he, **and his seed** shall become a multitude of nations. (Emphasis mine)

It needs to be emphatically stated that the seed of Ephraim is not the Seed fulfilled in Christ; that Seed came through Judah. The importance and significance of the Birthright Promise is absolutely critical for us to acknowledge, for without the awareness of the Promises of God regarding the Birthright, one simply cannot get an accurate understanding of the Latter Days. This truth will become increasingly apparent as this study continues.

And so we have the Patriarchal Prophecies wherein we find assurance from God concerning both the Sceptre and the Birthright. We have the birth of the Lion and the birth of the Unicorn and the promises of God for them both. The Lion being Judah and the Unicorn being Joseph, in particular the horns being his sons. The Sceptre was granted to Judah and the Birthright Blessing of greatness and fruitfulness was granted to Joseph's sons: Manasseh was promised to become a great nation and Ephraim was to become greater by becoming a multitude, or company of nations.

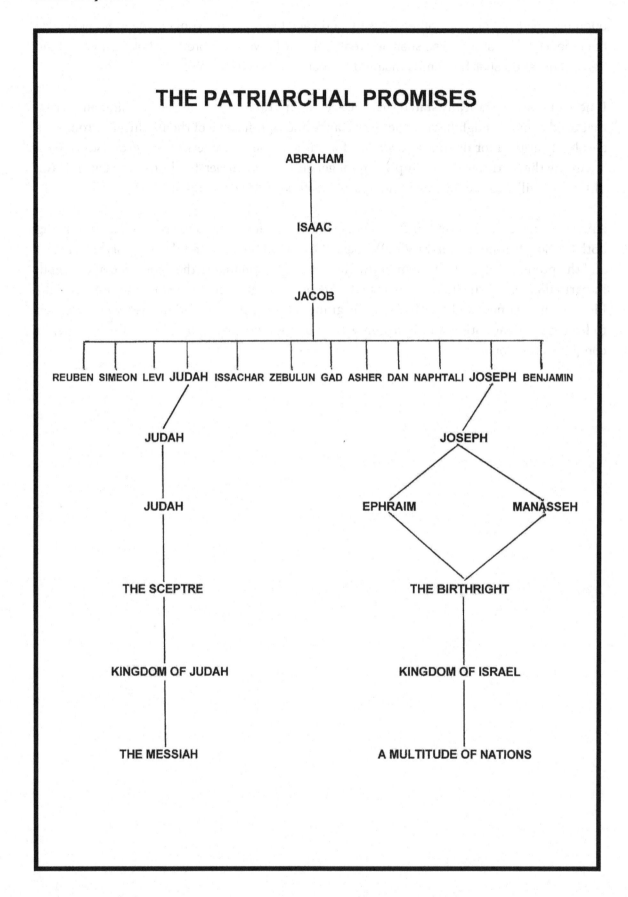

THE PATRIARCHAL PROMISES

ABRAHAM

ISAAC

JACOB

REUBEN SIMEON LEVI JUDAH ISSACHAR ZEBULUN GAD ASHER DAN NAPHTALI JOSEPH BENJAMIN

JUDAH

JUDAH

THE SCEPTRE

KINGDOM OF JUDAH

THE MESSIAH

JOSEPH

EPHRAIM   MANASSEH

THE BIRTHRIGHT

KINGDOM OF ISRAEL

A MULTITUDE OF NATIONS

Chapter Two

A Tale of Two Kingdoms

It is the presumption of this author that the reader has read their Bible and is somewhat familiar with the following biblical history. After Joseph's death, the Children of Israel became slaves in Egypt. Later they were led out of Egypt under Moses and wandered in the desert for 40 years. The Children of Israel were then brought into the Promised Land under Joshua. The Tribes of Israel eventually became one nation under King Saul and King David, occupying most of the territory promised to Abraham, Isaac and Jacob.

After the reign of David's son King Solomon, the tribes were split into two kingdoms: ten tribes to Israel and two tribes to Judah. Israel was the Northern Kingdom, headed by the tribe of Ephraim with their capitol in Samaria. Judah was the Southern Kingdom, headed by the tribe of Judah with their capitol in Jerusalem. Because Joseph had received the double blessing, both of Joseph's sons, Ephraim and Manasseh, received an inheritance as individual tribes. Even though they are always referred to as the 12 tribes, there are actually 13 tribes, with the Northern Kingdom of 10½ tribes and the Southern Kingdom of 2½ tribes. The tribe of Levi was scattered throughout both kingdoms, although after a very short time the majority of the Levites returned to join with Judah and Benjamin when the new king of Israel removed them from their ministry and installed his own priesthood to serve his golden calves which he had set up (2 Chronicles 11:13-16).

The people of the Northern Kingdom are Children of Israel and are biblically referred to as the Kingdom of Israel, and the people of the Southern Kingdom, although they are also Children of Israel, they are biblically referred to as the Kingdom of Judah. The term 'Jews' is the name given to those who are of the Kingdom of Judah. Only the Children of Israel of the Southern Kingdom are Jews. All Jews are Children of Israel, but not all Children of Israel are Jews.

In this part of the study we will examine the Scriptures that delineate between Judah and Israel and thereby be enabled and enlightened to follow their individual destinies. Under the reign of King David, God's promise to give the land of the Canaanites to the descendants of Abraham would seem to have been fulfilled, and for a time the Promised Land was mostly under their control. Yet when David had conquered all his enemies and the Lord had given him peace and he was contemplating building a house for the Lord, the prophet Nathan came to him. Amongst other words came this promise concerning Israel:

2 Samuel 7:10
Moreover I will appoint a place for my people Israel, and will plant them, that they may dwell in a place of their own, and move no more; neither shall the children of wickedness afflict them any more, as beforetime.

Here we have Israel in the Promised Land, with Judah, and the Lord is saying through the prophet to David that He "will appoint a place for my people Israel" and that they "may dwell in a place of their own."

Even before the Children of Israel were divided into two kingdoms, God was making reference in the Scriptures to the reality of the two houses: Judah AND Israel, the Lion and the Unicorn. These two verses illustrate this distinction being made:

1 Samuel 11:8
And when he numbered them in Bezek, the children of Israel were three hundred thousand, and the men of Judah thirty thousand.

Joshua 11:21
And at that time came Joshua, and cut off the Anakims from the mountains, from Hebron, from Debir, from Anab, and from all the mountains of Judah, and from all the mountains of Israel: Joshua destroyed them utterly with their cities.

The following verses all make reference to Judah and Israel as separate entities **before** the days of them being separated from one another: 1 Samuel 17:52; 18:16; 2 Samuel 2:10; 3:10; 5:5; 11:11; 12:8; 19:11,40,41,42,43; 20:2; 21:2; 24:1,9; 1 Kings 1:35; 2:32; 4:20,25.

God had a purpose and a plan to fulfil all his promises to the sons of Jacob and to the sons of Joseph whom Jacob had adopted to be called by his name. The Birthright Blessing, that was taken from Reuben because he defiled his father's bed, was placed upon Ephraim who would also be called Israel (Genesis 48:16). The Destiny of the Birthright Blessing and the Destiny of the Sceptre Promise were always in God's mind and His individual plans for them were beginning to unfold. So after Solomon did great evil in the sight of the Lord, God began the process of separating Israel from Judah.

1 Kings 11:11-13
Wherefore the Lord said unto Solomon, Forasmuch as this is done of thee, and thou hast not kept my covenant and my statutes, which I have commanded thee, I will surely rend the kingdom from thee, and will give it to thy servant. 12 Notwithstanding in thy days I will not do it for David thy father's sake: but I will rend it out of the hand of thy son. 13 Howbeit I will not rend away all the kingdom; but will give one tribe to thy son for David my servant's sake, and for Jerusalem's sake which I have chosen.

1 Kings 11:29-36

And it came to pass at that time when Jeroboam went out of Jerusalem, that the prophet Ahijah the Shilonite found him in the way; and he had clad himself with a new garment; and they two were alone in the field: 30 And Ahijah caught the new garment that was on him, and rent it in twelve pieces: 31 And he said to Jeroboam, Take thee ten pieces: for thus saith the Lord, the God of Israel, Behold, I will rend the kingdom out of the hand of Solomon, and will give ten tribes to thee: 32 (But he shall have one tribe for my servant David's sake, and for Jerusalem's sake, the city which I have chosen out of all the tribes of Israel:) 33 Because that they have forsaken me, and have worshipped Ashtoreth the goddess of the Zidonians, Chemosh the god of the Moabites, and Milcom the god of the children of Ammon, and have not walked in my ways, to do that which is right in mine eyes, and to keep my statutes and my judgments, as did David his father. 34 Howbeit I will not take the whole kingdom out of his hand: but I will make him prince all the days of his life for David my servant's sake, whom I chose, because he kept my commandments and my statutes: 35 But I will take the kingdom out of his son's hand, and will give it unto thee, even ten tribes. 36 And unto his son will I give one tribe, that David my servant may have a light alway before me in Jerusalem, the city which I have chosen me to put my name there.

1 Kings 12:12-24

So Jeroboam and all the people came to Rehoboam the third day, as the king had appointed, saying, Come to me again the third day. 13 And the king answered the people roughly, and forsook the old men's counsel that they gave him; 14 And spake to them after the counsel of the young men, saying, My father made your yoke heavy, and I will add to your yoke: my father also chastised you with whips, but I will chastise you with scorpions. 15 Wherefore the king hearkened not unto the people; for the cause was from the Lord, that he might perform his saying, which the Lord spake by Ahijah the Shilonite unto Jeroboam the son of Nebat.

16 So when all Israel saw that the king hearkened not unto them, the people answered the king, saying, What portion have we in David? neither have we inheritance in the son of Jesse: to your tents, O Israel: now see to thine own house, David. So Israel departed unto their tents.

17 But as for the children of Israel which dwelt in the cities of Judah, Rehoboam reigned over them.

18 Then king Rehoboam sent Adoram, who was over the tribute; and all Israel stoned him with stones, that he died. Therefore king Rehoboam made speed to get him up to his chariot, to flee to Jerusalem. 19 So Israel rebelled against the house of David unto this day.

20 And it came to pass, when all Israel heard that Jeroboam was come again, that they sent and called him unto the congregation, and made him king over all Israel: there was none that followed the house of David, but the tribe of Judah only.

21 And when Rehoboam was come to Jerusalem, he assembled all the house of Judah, with the tribe of Benjamin, an hundred and fourscore thousand chosen men, which were warriors, to fight

against the house of Israel, to bring the kingdom again to Rehoboam the son of Solomon. 22 But the word of God came unto Shemaiah the man of God, saying, 23 Speak unto Rehoboam, the son of Solomon, king of Judah, and unto all the house of Judah and Benjamin, and to the remnant of the people, saying, 24 Thus saith the Lord, Ye shall not go up, nor fight against your brethren the children of Israel: return every man to his house; for this thing is from me. They hearkened therefore to the word of the Lord, and returned to depart, according to the word of the Lord.

Interestingly, when Solomon's son Rehoboam sought to squash the apparent rebellion led by Jeroboam, the prophet declared, "Thus saith the Lord, 'Ye shall not go up, nor fight against your brethren the children of Israel: return every man to his house; for this thing is from me.'" To help with remembering who was with who when referring to Rehoboam and Jeroboam, try this: Jeroboam Jilted Judah AND Remember Rehoboam Remained. Or more simply: Jeroboam Jumped Rehoboam Remained.

Yes, the dividing of the children of Israel into two kingdoms was of the Lord. And from that time on Judah and Israel have been two separate entities. In the Scriptures, Israel is sometimes referred to as Ephraim and sometimes as Joseph. This is because the descendants of Joseph became the leading and dominant tribe of the Kingdom of Israel. Occasionally when the context indicates, they were also referred to as Jacob. The following Scripture references are instances where Israel and Judah, or Ephraim and Judah, or Joseph and Judah are juxtaposed in the Word of God, clearly indicating that they are two separate 'kingdoms' or 'houses'.

Joshua 11:21; 1 Samuel 11:8; 17:52; 18:16; 2 Samuel 2:10; 3:10; 5:5; 11:11; 12:8; 19:11,40,41,42,43; 20:2; 21:2; 24:1,9; 1 Kings 1:35; 2:32; 4:20,25; 12:17,20,21; 15:9,17,25,33; 16:8,23,29; 22:2,10,29,41,51; 2 Kings 3:1,9; 8:16,25; 9:21; 13:1,10,12; 14:1,9,11,12,13,15,17,23,28; 15:1,8,17,23,27,32; 17:1,13,18,19; 18:1,5; 22:18; 23:22,27; 1 Chronicles 5:17; 9:1; 13:6; 21:5; 28:4; 2 Chronicles 10:17; 11:1,3; 13:15,16,18; 15:9; 16:1,11; 18:3,9,28; 20:35; 21:13; 23:2; 24:5,6,9; 25:17,18,21,22,23,25,26; 27:7; 28:19,26; 30:1,6,25; 31:1,6; 32:32; 34:9,21; 35:18,27; 36:8; Psalms 76:1; 114:2; Isaiah 5:7; 7:1; 11:12; 48:1; Jeremiah 3:8,11,18; 5:11; 9:26; 11:10,17; 12:14; 13:11; 23:6; 30:3,4; 31:23,27,31; 32:30,32; 33:7,14; 36:2; 50:4,20,33; 51:5; Lamentations 2:5; Ezekiel 9:9; 25:3; 27:17; 37:16,19; Daniel 9:7; Hosea 1:1,11; 4:15; 5:5; 8:14; 11:12; Amos 1:1; Micah 1:5; 5:2; Zechariah 1:19; 8:13; 11:14; Malachi 2:11.

I could almost guarantee that you did not look up and read through the above list . . .
(: -)

There are about 180 references in the Scriptures that speak on this subject; about 160 are mentioned above. (I checked a lot of these, but have not double checked all of these myself, so I hope there are no typographical errors amidst that list) There are also other Scriptures that speak of Israel or Jacob, and the historical and Scriptural context refers not to the House of Judah, but to the House of Israel. It has already been noted that some of the above Scriptures identify the two separate houses of the Children of Israel even before they were divided from each other.

Confusion and ignorance about the Two House Reality abounds and some of that confusion is because there are also many references to Jacob and Israel in the Word of God that are inclusive of Judah. That said, there are zero examples of Judah being spoken of when it is to include the Ten Tribes of Israel. When the Scriptures speak of Judah, they never mean Jacob. Even though the mention of Jacob sometimes includes Judah, this can be discerned by the context. The presence of such verses in Scripture does in no way nullify the reality of God dealing with the two kingdoms individually.

A myth about their later amalgamation is also prevalent, driven by the mystery of their whereabouts. Further confusion has been added recently since the Jews that have returned to the Holy Land have named their nation Israel, when world leaders at the time were expecting them to call the new born nation Judea. Perhaps this was unintentionally prophetic.

In the books of 1 Kings and 2 Kings, along with 1 Chronicles and 2 Chronicles, we find the history of the separated kingdoms: the House of Israel in the north; the House of Judah in the south, each with their distinctive ruling dynasties. Again and again the prophets consistently maintained this distinction and tailored their messages to either the Kingdom of Israel or the Kingdom of Judah (and sometimes both). During this period of time several wars were fought between them.

1 Kings 15:16
And there was war between Asa and Baasha king of Israel all their days.

Asa was king of Judah.

2 Kings 14:12-13
And Judah was put to the worse before Israel; and they fled every man to their tents. 13 And Jehoash king of Israel took Amaziah king of Judah, the son of Jehoash the son of Ahaziah, at Bethshemesh, and came to Jerusalem, and brake down the wall of Jerusalem from the gate of Ephraim unto the corner gate, four hundred cubits.

2 Kings 16:5
Then Rezin king of Syria and Pekah son of Remaliah king of Israel came up to Jerusalem to war: and they besieged Ahaz, but could not overcome him.

2 Chronicles 13:15-17
Then the men of Judah gave a shout: and as the men of Judah shouted, it came to pass, that God smote Jeroboam and all Israel before Abijah and Judah. 16 And the children of Israel fled before Judah: and God delivered them into their hand. 17 And Abijah and his people slew them with a great slaughter: so there fell down slain of Israel five hundred thousand chosen men.

My goodness, that's half a million slain. No wonder the animosity continued to prevail.

2 Chronicles 25:13

But the soldiers of the army which Amaziah sent back, that they should not go with him to battle, fell upon the cities of Judah, from Samaria even unto Bethhoron, and smote three thousand of them, and took much spoil.

2 Chronicles 25:21-24

So Joash the king of Israel went up; and they saw one another in the face, both he and Amaziah king of Judah, at Bethshemesh, which belongeth to Judah. 22 And Judah was put to the worse before Israel, and they fled every man to his tent. 23 And Joash the king of Israel took Amaziah king of Judah, the son of Joash, the son of Jehoahaz, at Bethshemesh, and brought him to Jerusalem, and brake down the wall of Jerusalem from the gate of Ephraim to the corner gate, four hundred cubits. 24 And he took all the gold and the silver, and all the vessels that were found in the house of God with Obededom, and the treasures of the king's house, the hostages also, and returned to Samaria.

2 Chronicles 28:6,8

For Pekah the son of Remaliah slew in Judah an hundred and twenty thousand in one day, which were all valiant men; because they had forsaken the Lord God of their fathers.

8 And the children of Israel carried away captive of their brethren two hundred thousand, women, sons, and daughters, and took also away much spoil from them, and brought the spoil to Samaria.

Isaiah 7:1

And it came to pass in the days of Ahaz the son of Jotham, the son of Uzziah, king of Judah, that Rezin the king of Syria, and Pekah the son of Remaliah, king of Israel, went up toward Jerusalem to war against it, but could not prevail against it.

Judah and Joseph, the Jews and the Joes, have been at odds with each other for a long time. It's a family feud and it's not over yet. From the time of the Patriarchs, through the division of the kingdoms after Solomon: two houses, two kingdoms, two destinies. At this point in this study, the Lion and the Unicorn are still occupying the Promised Land but they are at enmity with each other.

Chapter Three

Israel's Exile

Although the history of both Israel and Judah are very similar in that they both ended up being banished from the Promised Land because of their unfaithfulness, the fulfilment of the promised Birthright Blessings to Ephraim and the fulfilment of the Sceptre Promises to Judah meant that their histories would ultimately be different.

Israel was taken into captivity by the Assyrians about 745BC, however, it wasn't until about 573BC that Judah was taken into captivity by the Babylonians. The Jews returned from their captivity after 70 years and their final dispersion, at that point of time, was about 600 years in the future when Jerusalem was destroyed by the Romans in 70AD. Because they mostly kept their identity and customs in the nations where they found themselves, we have little problem recognizing their presence and have ample historical records to trace the migrations of the Jews. For the most part they refrained from inter-marrying with the Gentiles (some definitely did intermarry) and thus they are mostly relatively easy to identify. We will cover their story more fully later.

But the scattering of Israel is not so well known. Apart from a very small minority (perhaps representatives of every tribe), the ten tribes of Israel never returned to their homeland. In the final years of Israel's presence in the Promised Land, God sent His prophets to His people to warn of the consequences of their wickedness. Israel would be punished and suffer greatly as a nation for their apostasy. They would be scattered among the nations and would become for a considerable time just like the rest of the nations, worshipping false gods and committing all manner of evil. Because they went away from the Lord and forsook the laws and customs delivered to them by Moses and took on the worship of other gods and the customs of the Gentiles, God declared that for this period of time they were not His people (Hosea 1:9). Whatever happened to them has been shrouded in mystery and it has been theorised that they were completely assimilated amongst the Gentiles and are no longer to be accounted for as an entity. This theory however, would make God a liar and nullify His promises to the sons of Joseph. Let us follow the last traces of them in the Word of God and discover further prophecies regarding their future.

1 Chronicles 5:26
And the God of Israel stirred up the spirit of Pul king of Assyria, and the spirit of Tilgathpilneser king of Assyria, and he carried them away, even the Reubenites, and the Gadites, and the half tribe of Manasseh, and brought them unto Halah, and Habor, and Hara, and to the river Gozan, unto this day.

This was the first of the Assyrian deportations.

2 Kings 17:5-6
Then the king of Assyria came up throughout all the land, and went up to Samaria, and besieged it three years. 6 In the ninth year of Hoshea the king of Assyria took Samaria, and carried Israel away into Assyria, and placed them in Halah and in Habor by the river of Gozan, and in the cities of the Medes.

These areas are in the region north and west of Nineveh, in an area now referred to as Upper Mesopotamia in modern Turkey.

2 Kings 17:16-18
And they left all the commandments of the Lord their God, and made them molten images, even two calves, and made a grove, and worshipped all the host of heaven, and served Baal. 17 And they caused their sons and their daughters to pass through the fire, and used divination and enchantments, and sold themselves to do evil in the sight of the Lord, to provoke him to anger. 18 Therefore the Lord was very angry with Israel, and removed them out of his sight: there was none left but the tribe of Judah only.

2 Kings 17:21-23
For he rent Israel from the house of David; and they made Jeroboam the son of Nebat king: and Jeroboam drave Israel from following the Lord, and made them sin a great sin. 22 For the children of Israel walked in all the sins of Jeroboam which he did; they departed not from them; 23 Until the Lord removed Israel out of his sight, as he had said by all his servants the prophets. So was Israel carried away out of their own land to Assyria unto this day.

The Assyrians began a program of population replacement.

2 Kings 17:24
And the king of Assyria brought men from Babylon, and from Cuthah, and from Ava, and from Hamath, and from Sepharvaim, and placed them in the cities of Samaria instead of the children of Israel: and they possessed Samaria, and dwelt in the cities thereof.

2 Kings 17:41
So these nations feared the Lord, and served their graven images, both their children, and their children's children: as did their fathers, so do they unto this day.

These people brought into the Land of Israel by the Assyrians served their own gods and made sacrifices to the God of Israel as well after an Israelite was sent to them because of their fear of lions attacking them (2 Kings 17:25-33). They became known as the Samaritans and were despised by the Jews. The feelings were mutual and the Samaritan's unfavourable attitude to the Jews is recorded in the books of Ezra and Nehemiah. Records are scant with regards to the Ten Tribes from this point on and we have but a few definitive details with which to trace their history.

A few years after the removal of the Kingdom of Israel from the Land, the Assyrians began to attack the Kingdom of Judah during the reign of King Hezekiah. This is recorded in 2 Kings 19 and 2 Chronicles 32. In answer to King Hezekiah's prayers, God destroyed 185,000 of the Assyrian army overnight and thus the power of the Assyrians was seriously broken. Around this time the Babylonian Empire was on the rise and this is mentioned in 2 Kings 20:12-19. Hezekiah's great grandson Josiah, another godly king of the Jews, held a massive Passover feast where it is mentioned that some of Israel attended (2 Chronicles 35:18-19). These details enable us to see that the Israelites recovered at least a measure of freedom after their captivity and some took opportunity to return to the Promised Land and lived among the pagans that the Assyrians had placed there. The majority, however, remained in the area north of the Euphrates, and as opportunity provided they migrated to the land between the Caspian Sea and the Black Sea in proximity to the Caucasus Mountains. More on this later.

The Israelites who returned to Samaria were also referred to as Samaritans by the Jews. In Jesus' time, we have the story of the Samaritan woman at the well (John 4:1-42), which tells of a resident from a village in Samaria who identified herself as a descendant of Jacob. So the term Samaritan refers to both Assyrian imports and returned Israelites and without the context of who is being referred to it is difficult to know who's who. Sometimes it is simply impossible to discern. In the New Testament, Jesus mentions the Twelve Tribes in Matthew 19:28 and Luke 22:30. One member of the tribe of Asher is mentioned in Luke 2:36, so it seems possible that others may have also joined themselves with the Jews. Paul speaks of them in Acts 26:7 and James addresses his letter to them (James 1:1). More on this later.

Isaiah 14:24-25
The Lord of hosts hath sworn, saying, Surely as I have thought, so shall it come to pass; and as I have purposed, so shall it stand: 25 That I will break the Assyrian in my land, and upon my mountains tread him under foot: then shall his yoke depart from off them, and his burden depart from off their shoulders.

From the Bible we can deduce that approximately 120 years after the captivity of Israel (2 Kings Chapters 17-25), the Assyrians were defeated by the Babylonians. Initially a great multitude of Israelites became free at the onset of the Babylonian period as the above verse implies; the yoke of slavery was removed. Many migrated north (you'll read more on that later), some returned to the Holy Land, but most came under Babylonian oppression as the new regime established their control.

Let's now look at some other prophetic proclamations concerning this period of time with regard to the Kingdom of Israel.

Hosea 1:9-10
Then said God, Call his name Loammi: for ye are not my people, and I will not be your God. 10 Yet the number of the children of Israel shall be as the sand of the sea, which cannot be measured

nor numbered; and it shall come to pass, that in the place where it was said unto them, Ye are not my people, there it shall be said unto them, Ye are the sons of the living God.

Hosea 3:4
For the children of Israel shall abide many days without a king, and without a prince, and without a sacrifice, and without an image, and without an ephod, and without teraphim:

Hosea 5:7
They have dealt treacherously against the Lord: for they have begotten strange children: now shall a month devour them with their portions.

Ezekiel 4:13
And the Lord said, Even thus shall the children of Israel eat their defiled bread among the Gentiles, whither I will drive them.

Ezekiel 12:16
But I will leave a few men of them from the sword, from the famine, and from the pestilence; that they may declare all their abominations among the heathen whither they come; and they shall know that I am the Lord.

Ezekiel 20:23
I lifted up mine hand unto them also in the wilderness, that I would scatter them among the heathen, and disperse them through the countries;

Hosea 8:8
Israel is swallowed up: now shall they be among the Gentiles as a vessel wherein is no pleasure.

Ezekiel 11:16
Therefore say, Thus saith the Lord God; Although I have cast them far off among the heathen, and although I have scattered them among the countries, yet will I be to them as a little sanctuary in the countries where they shall come.

Amos 9:8-9
Behold, the eyes of the Lord God are upon the sinful kingdom, and I will destroy it from off the face of the earth; saving that I will not utterly destroy the house of Jacob, saith the Lord. 9 For, lo, I will command, and I will sift the house of Israel among all nations, like as corn is sifted in a sieve, yet shall not the least grain fall upon the earth.

So then, we see that God promised to reduce them to a remnant, and then He would make them a multitude. To begin with they were destroyed as a nation and they were taken as slaves. But as time went on they found their freedom and went on to become as the sand of the sea, a number that none can count. And a time would come when they would be known as "sons of the Living God" (Hosea 1:10).

Before the Babylonians destroyed the Jewish Temple, they had taken many Jews captive and left the city as a puppet state. During this time, Ezekiel, who apparently had some liberty under the Babylonian captivity, prophesies against representatives of the House of Israel who had entered Jerusalem and joined with the remnant of Judah in their abominations, that they would be destroyed and scattered when Nebuchadnezzar finally destroyed the city during the time of King Zedekiah.

Ezekiel 12:1-10
The word of the Lord also came unto me, saying, 2 Son of man, thou dwellest in the midst of a rebellious house, which have eyes to see, and see not; they have ears to hear, and hear not: for they are a rebellious house.

3 Therefore, thou son of man, prepare thee stuff for removing, and remove by day in their sight; and thou shalt remove from thy place to another place in their sight: it may be they will consider, though they be a rebellious house. 4 Then shalt thou bring forth thy stuff by day in their sight, as stuff for removing: and thou shalt go forth at even in their sight, as they that go forth into captivity. 5 Dig thou through the wall in their sight, and carry out thereby. 6 In their sight shalt thou bear it upon thy shoulders, and carry it forth in the twilight: thou shalt cover thy face, that thou see not the ground: for I have set thee for a sign unto the house of Israel.

7 And I did so as I was commanded: I brought forth my stuff by day, as stuff for captivity, and in the even I digged through the wall with mine hand; I brought it forth in the twilight, and I bare it upon my shoulder in their sight. 8 And in the morning came the word of the Lord unto me, saying, 9 Son of man, hath not the house of Israel, the rebellious house, said unto thee, What doest thou? 10 Say thou unto them, Thus saith the Lord God; This burden concerneth the prince in Jerusalem, and all the house of Israel that are among them.

The "prince in Jerusalem" mentioned here is the last king to reign over Judah: King Zedekiah. Being designated 'prince' and not 'king' reflects his position as an appointed king by the Babylonians. Jeconiah, the actual king, was in captivity in Babylon and Zedekiah was his uncle. Ezekiel never called Zedekiah 'king'. That aside, we take note that among the Jews in Jerusalem were some members of the house of Israel (Ezekiel 12:10).

Ezekiel 12:11-28
Say, I am your sign: like as I have done, so shall it be done unto them: they shall remove and go into captivity. 12 And the prince that is among them shall bear upon his shoulder in the twilight, and shall go forth: they shall dig through the wall to carry out thereby: he shall cover his face, that he see not the ground with his eyes. 13 My net also will I spread upon him, and he shall be taken in my snare: and I will bring him to Babylon to the land of the Chaldeans; yet shall he not see it, though he shall die there. 14 And I will scatter toward every wind all that are about him to help him, and all his bands; and I will draw out the sword after them.

15 And they shall know that I am the Lord, when I shall scatter them among the nations, and disperse them in the countries. 16 But I will leave a few men of them from the sword, from the famine, and from the pestilence; that they may declare all their abominations among the heathen whither they come; and they shall know that I am the Lord.

17 Moreover the word of the Lord came to me, saying, 18 Son of man, eat thy bread with quaking, and drink thy water with trembling and with carefulness; 19 And say unto the people of the land, Thus saith the Lord God of the inhabitants of Jerusalem, and of the land of Israel; They shall eat their bread with carefulness, and drink their water with astonishment, that her land may be desolate from all that is therein, because of the violence of all them that dwell therein. 20 And the cities that are inhabited shall be laid waste, and the land shall be desolate; and ye shall know that I am the Lord.

21 And the word of the Lord came unto me, saying, 22 Son of man, what is that proverb that ye have in the land of Israel, saying, The days are prolonged, and every vision faileth? 23 Tell them therefore, Thus saith the Lord God; I will make this proverb to cease, and they shall no more use it as a proverb in Israel; but say unto them, The days are at hand, and the effect of every vision. 24 For there shall be no more any vain vision nor flattering divination within the house of Israel. 25 For I am the Lord: I will speak, and the word that I shall speak shall come to pass; it shall be no more prolonged: for in your days, O rebellious house, will I say the word, and will perform it, saith the Lord

26 Again the word of the Lord came to me, saying. 27 Son of man, behold, they of the house of Israel say, The vision that he seeth is for many days to come, and he prophesieth of the times that are far off. 28 Therefore say unto them, Thus saith the Lord God; There shall none of my words be prolonged any more, but the word which I have spoken shall be done, saith the Lord God.

Around this time this proclamation by the inhabitants of Jerusalem was recorded.

Ezekiel 11:15
Son of man, thy brethren, even thy brethren, the men of thy kindred, and all the house of Israel wholly, are they unto whom the inhabitants of Jerusalem have said, Get you far from the Lord: unto us is this land given in possession.

And so it was that the majority of those of Israel who had returned then departed to return no more. It is interesting to note that this attitude of the Jews remains to this day. "The Land is ours" is what they say and the idea of Israelites who are not Jews having any claim to the Land is simply not entertained. (Except by a tiny minority)

Zechariah also prophesies against the nations that scattered them.

Zechariah 1:18-21

Then lifted I up mine eyes, and saw, and behold four horns. 19 And I said unto the angel that talked with me, What be these? And he answered me, These are the horns which have scattered Judah, Israel, and Jerusalem. 20 And the Lord shewed me four carpenters. 21 Then said I, What come these to do? And he spake, saying, These are the horns which have scattered Judah, so that no man did lift up his head: but these are come to fray them, to cast out the horns of the Gentiles, which lifted up their horn over the land of Judah to scatter it.

History shows us who the "four horns" are: the Assyrians, the Babylonians, the Medes and the Persians. The Greek Empire, which was divided into four, are the "four carpenters" that effectively crushed all the remnants of these nations when they conquered the Medes and the Persians.

As mentioned above, a significant number of the House of Israel found their freedom when Babylon defeated the Assyrians, thus fulfilling the above mentioned prophecy in Isaiah 14:24-25. Of those who had migrated north, some were called Cimmerians (thought to be a transliteration of Samaritans or Samarians) and later became known as the Scythians. (Perhaps two different groups who migrated at different times. Again, more on this later) However, there were still Israelites dwelling under the dominion of Alexander and his successors during the time of the Greek Empire. These would not gain their independence until the following century with the rise of the Parthian Empire around 203-202BC. Approximately forty years after the Parthians gained their ascendancy and had weakened the Greeks, the Jews led by the Maccabees also broke the yoke of the Greeks and attained their independence for about a hundred years until becoming a vassal state again under Roman dominion and the rise of King Herod the Great. King Herod was not so great in my opinion . . . he was a real bad dude.

The Jewish historian Josephus, writing in the first century AD, recorded that there were *"but two tribes under the dominion of the Romans"*, and that *"the Ten Tribes were beyond the Euphrates and had become a multitude that none could count"* (*Antiquities of the Jews*, 11.5.2). Even though there were a scattering of Israelites of the Northern Kingdom living among the pagans in Samaria, the Jews, who simply lumped them all under the term 'Samaritans' with whom they had no dealings, were clearly aware of where the bulk of their estranged brethren were situated. This historical testimony reveals that the freedom that Israel had gained during the latter time of the Greek Empire was not taken away from them by the Romans who had subjugated the Jews in the land then known as Judea. The phrase, "beyond the Euphrates" mentioned by Josephus, refers to the area between the Black Sea and the Caspian Sea, north of the head-waters of the Euphrates River, a place where we find the Caucasus Mountains which formed a natural barrier easy to defend against the Roman Empire. This mountain range is approximately 1200 kilometres long, averaging around 100 kilometres wide, 180 kilometres at its widest point, has over 2200 glaciers and has very few mountain passes, all of which are at least 3000 metres above sea level (approximately) and can only be traversed at certain times of the year. From the annals of history we find that the Roman Empire never made any significant advances north of this massive range of mountains.

It is interesting how the names of the patriarchs Manasseh and Ephraim also have a prophetic message. Manasseh means forgetfulness and Ephraim means fruitfulness.

Genesis 41:51-52
And Joseph called the name of the firstborn Manasseh: For God, said he, hath made me forget all my toil, and all my father's house. 52 And the name of the second called he Ephraim: For God hath caused me to be fruitful in the land of my affliction.

So it is that Israel, led by the sons of Joseph, were made to forget their Father's house and yet at the same time they were to become fruitful in the land of their affliction. And just as Joseph arose to prominence in Egypt whilst separated from his brethren, the descendants of Joseph were prophesied to become like a "lion among the sheep" (Micah 5:8), and would "push the peoples to the ends of the earth" (Deuteronomy 33:17), and would "possess the gates of their enemies" (Genesis 22:17, 24:60); and receive multiple blessings and abounding riches and be a blessing to all the nations of the earth. At the same time they were lost, they had forgotten their God, and they had forgotten their heritage.

Micah 5:7-9
And the remnant of Jacob shall be in the midst of many people as a dew from the Lord, as the showers upon the grass, that tarrieth not for man, nor waiteth for the sons of men. 8 And the remnant of Jacob shall be among the Gentiles in the midst of many people as a lion among the beasts of the forest, as a young lion among the flocks of sheep: who, if he go through, both treadeth down, and teareth in pieces, and none can deliver. 9 Thine hand shall be lifted up upon thine adversaries, and all thine enemies shall be cut off.

Take note of the details of this particular prophetic statement in Micah just mentioned. Jacob is compared with the Gentile nations and is likened as a lion among the sheep, victorious over them all. Despite the use of the image of a lion, this certainly does not describe Judah down through the ages.

Isaiah 41:8-16
But thou, Israel, art my servant, Jacob whom I have chosen, the seed of Abraham my friend. 9 Thou whom I have taken from the ends of the earth, and called thee from the chief men thereof, and said unto thee, Thou art my servant; I have chosen thee, and not cast thee away. 10 Fear thou not; for I am with thee: be not dismayed; for I am thy God: I will strengthen thee; yea, I will help thee; yea, I will uphold thee with the right hand of my righteousness. 11 Behold, all they that were incensed against thee shall be ashamed and confounded: they shall be as nothing; and they that strive with thee shall perish. 12 Thou shalt seek them, and shalt not find them, even them that contended with thee: they that war against thee shall be as nothing, and as a thing of nought. 13 For I the Lord thy God will hold thy right hand, saying unto thee, Fear not; I will help thee. 14 Fear not, thou worm Jacob, and ye men of Israel; I will help thee, saith the Lord, and thy redeemer, the Holy One of Israel.

15 Behold, I will make thee a new sharp threshing instrument having teeth: thou shalt thresh the mountains, and beat them small, and shalt make the hills as chaff. 16 Thou shalt fan them, and the wind shall carry them away, and the whirlwind shall scatter them: and thou shalt rejoice in the Lord, and shalt glory in the Holy One of Israel.

Deuteronomy 33:17
His glory is like the firstling of his bullock, and his horns are like the horns of unicorns: with them he shall push the people together to the ends of the earth: and they are the ten thousands of Ephraim, and they are the thousands of Manasseh.

As you can see, these proclamations of Isaiah and Moses concerning Ephraim and Manasseh have nothing to do with Judah.

Genesis 22:17
That in blessing I will bless thee, and in multiplying I will multiply thy seed as the stars of the heaven, and as the sand which is upon the sea shore; and thy seed shall possess the gate of his enemies;

These passages all speak of Israel, also known as Jacob, as a dominating force among the nations, something that Judah has never fulfilled in all of history, for the promise was not theirs. Remember, the promise to Ephraim was that his descendants would become a multitude, or company, or commonwealth of nations, depending on your translation. Therefore we should expect to find a people group who have made themselves a multitude of nation states and are a world power and have been, despite their failings, a blessing to all the other nations during their history. There can only be one people group that fits the biblical description. However, the record of their destiny is not complete, the prophets have yet more to say, and we shall have to follow the destiny of the House of Judah before we hear more of the House of Israel.

Chapter Four

Nebuchadnezzar's Dream

In these next two chapters we will be looking at the prophecies in Daniel Chapters 2 and 7 wherein we find no mention of Judah or Israel, which is interesting seeing as this portion of God's Word from Daniel 2:4 through to the end of Chapter 7 was originally written in Aramaic and not Hebrew. Although the Israelite nations are absent from these portions of Scripture, the bigger picture that the dream and visions are symbolic of set the stage wherein the destiny of Judah, Israel and the Kingdom of God is played out. This knowledge will help us in understanding the fulfilment of God's Promises for these three kingdoms.

Because these passages contain much that is highly symbolic, both Chapter 2 and Chapter 7 have had a history of controversy as to their meaning. Both passages speak of the latter days: Daniel Chapter 2 prophesies the procession of the Gentile kingdoms that would rule in the Middle East from Daniel's time and Daniel Chapter 7 gives us insight into what will be prevailing over the whole world prior to the culmination of the Kingdom of God. From both these portions of Scripture we find our first prophetic glimpse of the latter days and the end of the age.

Leaving Chapter 7 for the time being, we shall begin with Daniel addressing King Nebuchadnezzar in reply to his request to understand a great vision he had seen in a dream.

Daniel 2:31-45
Thou, O king, sawest, and behold a great image. This great image, whose brightness was excellent, stood before thee; and the form thereof was terrible. 32 This image's head was of fine gold, his breast and his arms of silver, his belly and his thighs of brass, 33 His legs of iron, his feet part of iron and part of clay. 34 Thou sawest till that a stone was cut out without hands, which smote the image upon his feet that were of iron and clay, and brake them to pieces 35 Then was the iron, the clay, the brass, the silver, and the gold, broken to pieces together, and became like the chaff of the summer threshingfloors; and the wind carried them away, that no place was found for them: and the stone that smote the image became a great mountain, and filled the whole earth.

36 This is the dream; and we will tell the interpretation thereof before the king.

37 Thou, O king, art a king of kings: for the God of heaven hath given thee a kingdom, power, and strength, and glory. 38 And wheresoever the children of men dwell, the beasts of the field and the fowls of the heaven hath he given into thine hand, and hath made thee ruler over them

all. Thou art this head of gold. 39 And after thee shall arise another kingdom inferior to thee, and another third kingdom of brass, which shall bear rule over all the earth.

40 And the fourth kingdom shall be strong as iron: forasmuch as iron breaketh in pieces and subdueth all things: and as iron that breaketh all these, shall it break in pieces and bruise.

41 And whereas thou sawest the feet and toes, part of potters' clay, and part of iron, the kingdom shall be divided; but there shall be in it of the strength of the iron, forasmuch as thou sawest the iron mixed with miry clay. 42 And as the toes of the feet were part of iron, and part of clay, so the kingdom shall be partly strong, and partly broken. 43 And whereas thou sawest iron mixed with miry clay, they shall mingle themselves with the seed of men: but they shall not cleave one to another, even as iron is not mixed with clay. 44 And in the days of these kings shall the God of heaven set up a kingdom, which shall never be destroyed: and the kingdom shall not be left to other people, but it shall break in pieces and consume all these kingdoms, and it shall stand for ever. 45 Forasmuch as thou sawest that the stone was cut out of the mountain without hands, and that it brake in pieces the iron, the brass, the clay, the silver, and the gold; the great God hath made known to the king what shall come to pass hereafter: and the dream is certain, and the interpretation thereof sure.

Let us now be careful as we handle God's Word. Most contemporary prophecy commentators declare that there are four kingdoms mentioned in this passage, the last being Rome which they believe will somehow be reconstructed in the last days. Proponents of this theory interpret the iron of the legs and the iron of the feet and toes from Nebuchadnezzar's dream of the statue to be the continuation of the Roman Empire.

Another popular interpretation also declares that there are four kingdoms, but somehow makes the breakup of Alexander the Great's empire as the fourth Kingdom. The continuation of the Greek culture and language through much of the Roman Empire is offered as 'proof' that the Greek kingdom is still with us.

The key to understanding Daniel's interpretation of the dream requires nothing but a careful attention to detail and a strict adherence to the basic laws of grammar. Now, please forgive me for being a little tedious with this portion of Scripture. There is just so much confusion over the meaning of this passage that I have found it necessary to labour the point somewhat.

When Daniel begins to interpret the dream to Nebuchadnezzar, he addresses the king saying these words, "Thou art this head of gold" (verse 38). We could also write it this way, "You are the golden head." The head is the subject noun and the element of gold is the adjective describing the quality and content of the head.

If we go back to the description of the dream itself we find that each of the five body parts of the statue is a noun (head; chest and arms; belly and thighs; legs; feet and toes) and the elements (gold, silver, bronze, iron and clay) are the descriptive adjectives.

Daniel 2:32-33
This image's head was of fine gold, his breast and his arms of silver, his belly and his thighs of brass, 33 His legs of iron, his feet part of iron and part of clay.

Daniel 2:39
And after thee shall arise another kingdom inferior to thee, and another third kingdom of brass, which shall bear rule over all the earth.

Each body part represents a kingdom. Verse 32 has "his belly and his thighs of brass" and we see in verse 39 it mentions a "third kingdom of brass". The belly and thighs are brass and the third kingdom is brass. Thus the belly and thighs are the kingdom. This is letting us know that the body parts are representing the kingdoms and the elements are serving as adjectives to describe the character and content of the respective kingdoms. The brass is describing the kingdom. This use of the different elements in the form of an adjective is consistent all through the giving of the interpretation.

Daniel 2:40
And the fourth kingdom shall be strong as iron: forasmuch as iron breaketh in pieces and subdueth all things: and as iron that breaketh all these, shall it break in pieces and bruise.

In verse 40 we have the description of the fourth kingdom, where the iron is elaborated on and it is explained that the iron represents strength.

The feet and toes are the last body part to be mentioned and they represent a kingdom that shall be divided.

Daniel 2:41-43
And whereas thou sawest the feet and toes, part of potters' clay, and part of iron, the kingdom shall be divided; but there shall be in it of the strength of the iron, forasmuch as thou sawest the iron mixed with miry clay. 42 And as the toes of the feet were part of iron, and part of clay, so the kingdom shall be partly strong, and partly broken. 43 And whereas thou sawest iron mixed with miry clay, they shall mingle themselves with the seed of men: but they shall not cleave one to another, even as iron is not mixed with clay.

The mixture of iron and clay is more fully explained in verses 41-43 where it is explained that the kingdom's mixture is symbolic of the kingdom's nature being partly strong and partly "broken", or "fragile" as it is otherwise translated.

In every instance the elements (gold, silver, brass, iron and clay) are ALL adjectives within the sentences, describing the qualities of the kingdoms. It is the body parts that are the subject of each sentence and thus are the representatives of each kingdom. To remind us, here is the description of the statue.

Elihu Ben Ephraim

Daniel 2:32-33
This image's head was of fine gold, his breast and his arms of silver, his belly and his thighs of brass, 33 His legs of iron, his feet part of iron and part of clay.

The body of the statue was divided into the following five parts, the head, the chest, the belly and thighs, the legs, and finally the feet and toes; each part representing a kingdom, each with its own description. Five body parts, five kingdoms.

A common objection to the five kingdom paradigm is brought about by the use of the word "Finally" at the beginning of verse 2:40 in three New International Versions of the Bible (NIV, NIRV, NIVUK). I looked up nearly 50 other English versions and no other translation does this. I further discovered that there is no Aramaic word representing "finally" in the original text to support such an addition being made. Check it out in Strong's or any other comprehensive concordance. To me it is obviously an editor's bias toward a four kingdom paradigm that has led to this abuse of God's Word. Incidentally, while the NIV often makes verses easier to read, I have personally found too many problems with its use of what they call "dynamic equivalence" as its method of translation. It really should be regarded as a paraphrase rather than a translation. As a paraphrase I have sometimes found it helpful, but it also has been found to omit many words and important verses found in the KJV and NKJV. In this instance, the most unfortunate addition of the word "finally" to this particular passage has provided a classic example of the NIV's unreliability.

The emphasis many place on the mention of the phrase "the fourth kingdom" in verse 2:40 is also used to support the four kingdom interpretation. They note that the third kingdom is numbered and the fourth kingdom is numbered but no fifth kingdom is numbered. From this they assume there is no fifth kingdom. In placing significance upon the fact that these particular kingdoms are numbered, they fail to account for the fact that the first kingdom is not numbered and neither is the second kingdom. In reality, three out of the five kingdoms are not numbered. Whether the kingdoms were numbered or not clearly has no bearing on their existence.

There is one other complication that as long as I am being pedantic I may as well deal with while we are on this subject. The Hebrew language and the Aramaic from which this passage is translated, do not use the words 'a' and 'the' as we do in English: the 'a' being the indefinite article and the 'the' being the definite article. (Note: Daniel 2:4 right through to Daniel 7:28 was written in Aramaic, not Hebrew)

In the Hebrew and Aramaic languages there are no indefinite articles. Whenever a noun is indefinite, the context defines what is meant. Whether it is the kingdom, a kingdom, this kingdom, that kingdom, etc., is left to editors and translators to determine the meaning from the context. The absence of the article, either indefinite or definite, is apparent when one compares various English translations, for the different translators have chosen a wide variety of pronouns in their rendering of Daniel 2:40-41, many of them even inserting the words "fourth kingdom" into verse 41 when there is nothing in the original to support such

32

an addition. Check it out yourself. Go to biblegateway.com and type in the verse, choose your default Bible translation and when the page comes up, click on the link for all English translations which will be beneath the verse and you will see what I mean. Be sure to do only one verse at a time or the option for all translations will not appear. Check out interlinear renderings also to confirm these findings.

The word 'this' is correctly used by the NIV in verse 2:41, but because they added the word 'finally' to the previous verse they completely changed the meaning. To me it is contrived to present a version that fits with their preconceived interpretation of the end-times. In doing so they have created untold confusion. Most unfortunate. This is heady stuff I know, however, sometimes the truth has to be diligently pursued and every stumbling stone removed. Note, the above is not my opinion, it's simply what I discovered and the evidence is there for all to see. Again, check it out.

That aside, to accept a four kingdom interpretation requires one to ignore the laws of grammar common to all languages and make the iron a kingdom rather than the legs and ignore the fact that the iron is the symbolic descriptive element of the legs, and the iron is but one of two descriptive elements of the final kingdom of feet and toes. The fact that the kingdom represented by the legs, and the kingdom represented by the feet and toes are both described as having the element of iron is coincidental and only descriptive of the reality that they both had the strength that the iron represented. Here's hoping you are not overwhelmed by my pedantics.

The subject of the whole passage of the dream and its interpretation is the procession of the kingdoms which were to follow the reign of Nebuchadnezzar, who is identified as the head and each body part that followed represented the kingdoms that we will now show from the historical record, knowing that the kiss of history upon prophecy is the God given proof of a correct understanding.

Deuteronomy 18:22 NKJV
. . . when a prophet speaks in the Name of the LORD, if the thing does not happen or come to pass, that *is* the thing which the LORD has not spoken; the prophet has spoken it presumptuously . . .

It will become clear that many interpreters of this passage have spoken presumptuously as we will now look at what actually has come to pass.

It has been noted among scholars that Bible prophecies are Middle East centred and indeed they are. It may be debated that perhaps the dream of Nebuchadnezzar is Babylon centred rather than Jerusalem centred and I am inclined to agree. But in reality it becomes a moot point, for as we follow the history we will discover that all the empires as they succeeded each other, conquered and subdued both the city of Babylon and the city of Jerusalem AND the capitol city of the previous empire. So with regard to this prophecy, it really doesn't matter which city is used as the centre as it applies any which way. And besides, we understand that an empire's defeat and final capitulation is complete when its capitol is conquered and its government done away with.

There seems to be total agreement among scholars regarding the procession of the kingdoms: from Babylon, to the Medes and the Persians, to the Greeks. But confusion is apparent when it comes to the Roman Empire and the kingdom that will be present on earth when Jesus returns. We need no longer be subject to ignorance regarding this period of history. It is well documented and supported by both archaeological evidence and ancient writings and, as I have mentioned, the information is now available online via your favourite search engine. Type this link into your browser:

history.com/topics/ancient-history/byzantine-empire

Searching for The History of the Byzantine Empire will provide literally dozens of articles that will also confirm the historical details I am about to share. You may be wondering what on earth the Byzantine Empire has to do with the Roman Empire. That will become apparent as we continue.

As mentioned above, there seems to be total agreement among scholars regarding the procession of the kingdoms: from Babylon, to the Medes and the Persians, and then to the Greeks. For this we have only to look in Daniel Chapter 8 for confirmation. What follows is a brief account of the Roman Empire and its demise condensed from the history links suggested above.

Many prophecy commentators and historians, when they speak of the end of the Roman Empire, refer to the destruction wrought by the European hordes upon the city of Rome in the fifth century as being when this kingdom's rule ended. However, the historical record reveals that well before that event, during the fourth century, the Roman Emperor Constantine, who had taken control of the empire and unified it after a period of civil war, MOVED the capitol city from Rome to a new city that he had built and named after himself. He had taken over a small town called Byzantium on the western shore of the Bosporus Strait, lavishly rebuilt it, fortified it and renamed it Constantinople and it remained the capitol of the Roman Empire for over a thousand years! In its early days Constantinople was known as Nova Roma: which means New Rome.

After Constantine's death (337AD), there was a series of different arrangements, from delegated authorities for the eastern and western portions of the empire, to outright civil war and contested authority, but it was always the Roman Empire. This continuing situation gradually weakened the western portion of the empire, resulting in the city of Rome being plundered in 410AD and again in 455AD and eventually Rome was completely overrun by the Europeans around 476AD. This is the date that most scholars consider to be the end of the Roman Empire, but the truth is, at that time the Roman Empire continued to maintain its rule from its position in the east at Constantinople where its capitol had previously been established for about a hundred and fifty years. It just lost some territory.

At that time the western portion of the Roman Empire was divided up among the various European non Roman powers that had arisen: the Gauls, the Franks, the Germans, the Ostrogoths, the Visigoths, the Vandals, the Burgundians, the Basques, the Saxons, the Celts and others. These powers, with a little alteration to their borders, became the foundation of the present countries that make up modern Europe.

And some years later, around the sixth century, the city of Rome and many other territories were reconquered and remained under Roman control from Constantinople for over two hundred years. Again the European hordes took the city of Rome, but the Roman Empire was still ruled from Constantinople. The power that arose via the Catholic Church from the city of Rome was incidental to the demise of the Roman Empire's hold on the city of Rome and Italy. The European conquerors granted favour to the priesthood who later assumed secular power. They eventually became known as the Holy Roman Empire, however, their institution never was holy, and apart from speaking Latin they never were the Roman Empire. It was another monster altogether, even though it was based in Rome.

As mentioned above, the whole idea of a divided kingdom of east and west comes from segments of the empire's history when it was plagued by civil wars and attempts to take over the empire. There were also times of delegated authority and shared authority. The Church in the East and the Church in the West also became divided over the issue of icons. This and other theological disputes had its effect on the geopolitical scene. Another factor was that the West spoke mostly Latin whereas in the East, Greek was the predominant language of the population, although Latin was the language of the administration and the military until the seventh century. (In the Gospels, the sign placed above Jesus' head on the cross was written in Hebrew, Greek and Latin: Luke 23:38; John 19:20) However, the people still referred to themselves as Roman. For a thousand years (minus 23 years) the Roman Empire was ruled undivided from Constantinople after Rome and the western part of the empire was lost to the Europeans. The name Byzantine Empire was not assigned to the Roman Empire ruled from Constantinople until a French historian coined the term in the sixteenth century. English historical commentators followed suit some time afterward and the term has stuck, probably because the new rulers had by then assumed the name Holy Roman Empire. Thankfully, in this day and age of easy access to information we can overcome this confusion of the historical record.

Another piece of support offered for a divided Roman Empire is the fact that there are two legs in the statue, which people interpret to mean that the kingdom became divided into two. However, it is the previous kingdom, the Greek Empire that is described as the belly and thighs. Besides the fact that God's Word places no significance to the two arms, the ten fingers or the two thighs, if we were to place any significance to these details we would have to assume that the Greek Empire became two rather than four and the Roman Empire began as two and remained two. It's too silly. No matter which way we look at it, the four kingdom theory does not fit.

The final demise of the Roman/Byzantine Empire was not accomplished until 1453 when the Muslim hordes took over the city which they then renamed Islambol, (meaning full of

Islam) and later Stamboul or Instanbul, as it is known today. The entire area remains under Islamic domination to this day in what we now call Turkey which was previously known as the Ottoman Empire which had laid claim to the Islamic Caliphate.

The Muslim Empire, (yes, Islam is more than a religion, it's a theocratic political system) which arose in the area of the ancient Babylonian Empire during the seventh century, had at that time taken control of what was left of Babylon, they had taken possession of Jerusalem and finally the Roman capitol at Constantinople, thus qualifying this kingdom to be recognised as the fifth kingdom in the interpretation of Nebuchadnezzar's dream given to us by the prophet Daniel. Here we find that history and prophecy have kissed.

If we were to accept the four kingdom interpretation of Daniel Chapter 2, we would be faced with the reality of a false prophecy, for history clearly does not bear witness to such a four kingdom scenario. Five kingdoms have reigned in the Middle East and the fifth kingdom is still with us to this day and will be until the return of Christ. Just go and visit the Middle East and you will find, that apart from the nation of Israel, the entire area is dominated by Islam. It certainly isn't ruled by Rome. This kingdom is different from all the other kingdoms that have gone before it, but we will expand more on that later.

In summary: Daniel Chapter 2 serves as a Biblical Timeline of the procession of the kingdoms of the Gentiles that were to rule in the Middle East from the time of King Nebuchadnezzar through to the end of the age. Babylon was conquered by the combined empire of the Medes and the Persians. Next came Alexander the Great who conquered them and established the realm of the Greeks. After his death, the Greek Empire was divided into four among his generals and Greek dominance continued until the rise of the Romans. It was only a few years before the birth of Jesus that the Romans destroyed the final remnant of the Greek Empire which was at that time still ruling in Egypt. Roman dominance over the area of Babylon was accomplished around 116AD under Emperor Trajan, although it was subject to several wars over the following centuries with the expansion and contraction of the Parthian Empire (Modern day Iran). Roman control of Babylonia finally ceased altogether around 640AD when the Muslim Empire began and it has remained under Muslim control ever since. It is unclear whether the city itself was finally utterly destroyed by Romans, Parthians or Muslims. The Muslim Empire expanded rapidly and within a short period of time after taking Babylonia they had also taken over Jerusalem. The Roman Empire, ruled from Constantinople, also went through times of expansion and contraction over the centuries and eventually succumbed to Muslim domination in 1453 when Constantinople was finally conquered. At that time, the Muslim Empire was known as the Ottoman Empire which was the centre of the Islamic Caliphate. Thus we have the history which fits the prophecy.

From the Scriptures:

Daniel describes a statue with five parts, each part with a different composition; 1. The head of gold; 2. The chest and arms of silver; 3. The belly and thighs of brass; 4. The legs of iron; 5. The feet and toes of iron and clay.

History combined with Scripture:

1 The head was Babylon; 2 The chest and arms was the Medes and the Persians; 3 The belly and thighs was Greece; 4 The legs was Rome; 5 The feet and toes is the Islamic Empire.

The fifth kingdom is here now and although it has had times of expansion and contraction over the centuries, it still dominates the Middle East and with the money it now gets from the sale of oil, it is financing its infiltration of the nations at a rapid pace. I don't know if I will see it manifest its full dominion with its ten kings in my time. Somehow I think we've still got too many prophecies to be fulfilled. That final scenario, which will come in its own time, we will read of in our study of Daniel Chapter 7 in the following chapter. In the next few pages I have presented some maps of the Middle East and Europe that illustrate the areas dominated by the various empires we have just been studying.

Babylonian Empire

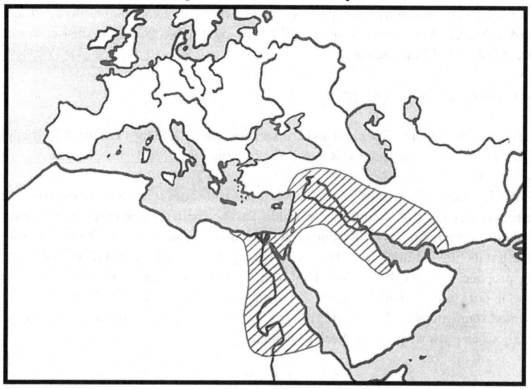

Medes and Persian Empire

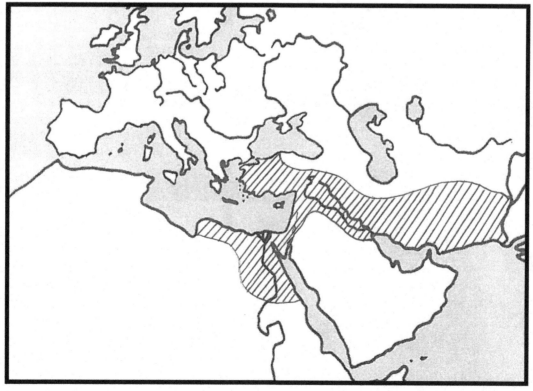

Greek Empire
Showing the four divisions

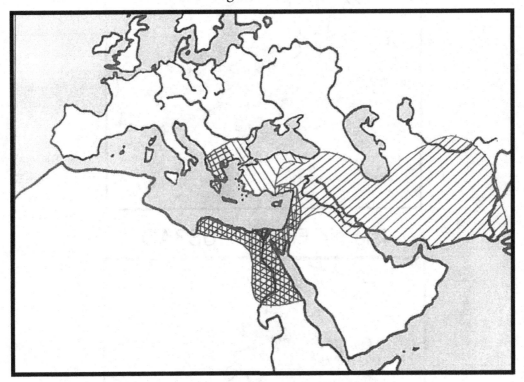

Roman Empire

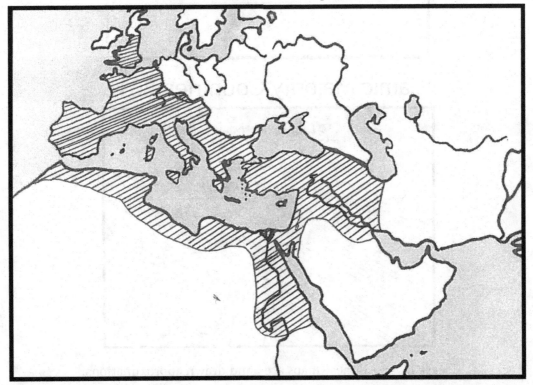

Islamic Empire 750AD

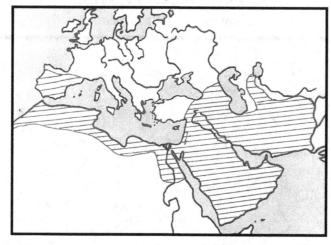

Islamic Empire 1683AD

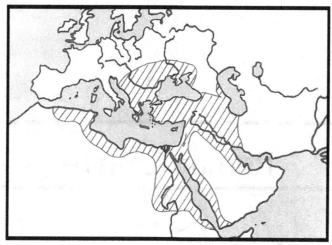

Islamic Majority Countries 2012

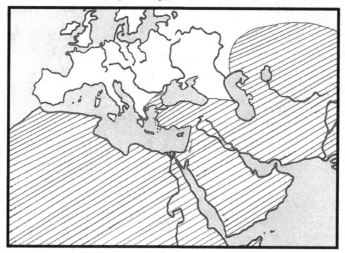

Please Note: All these maps are hand drawn approximations.

Chapter Five

Vision of Four Beasts

Daniel 7:1-28

In the first year of Belshazzar king of Babylon Daniel had a dream and visions of his head upon his bed: then he wrote the dream, and told the sum of the matters. 2 Daniel spake and said, I saw in my vision by night, and, behold, the four winds of the heaven strove upon the great sea. 3 And four great beasts came up from the sea, diverse one from another. 4 The first was like a lion, and had eagle's wings: I beheld till the wings thereof were plucked, and it was lifted up from the earth, and made stand upon the feet as a man, and a man's heart was given to it.

5 And behold another beast, a second, like to a bear, and it raised up itself on one side, and it had three ribs in the mouth of it between the teeth of it: and they said thus unto it, Arise, devour much flesh. 6 After this I beheld, and lo another, like a leopard, which had upon the back of it four wings of a fowl; the beast had also four heads; and dominion was given to it.

7 After this I saw in the night visions, and behold a fourth beast, dreadful and terrible, and strong exceedingly; and it had great iron teeth: it devoured and brake in pieces, and stamped the residue with the feet of it: and it was diverse from all the beasts that were before it; and it had ten horns. 8 I considered the horns, and, behold, there came up among them another little horn, before whom there were three of the first horns plucked up by the roots: and, behold, in this horn were eyes like the eyes of man, and a mouth speaking great things.

9 I beheld till the thrones were cast down, and the Ancient of days did sit, whose garment was white as snow, and the hair of his head like the pure wool: his throne was like the fiery flame, and his wheels as burning fire. 10 A fiery stream issued and came forth from before him: thousand thousands ministered unto him, and ten thousand times ten thousand stood before him: the judgment was set, and the books were opened. 11 I beheld then because of the voice of the great words which the horn spake: I beheld even till the beast was slain, and his body destroyed, and given to the burning flame. 12 As concerning the rest of the beasts, they had their dominion taken away: yet their lives were prolonged for a season and time.

13 I saw in the night visions, and, behold, one like the Son of man came with the clouds of heaven, and came to the Ancient of days, and they brought him near before him. 14 And there was given him dominion, and glory, and a kingdom, that all people, nations, and languages, should serve him: his dominion is an everlasting dominion, which shall not pass away, and his kingdom that which shall not be destroyed.

Daniel's Visions Interpreted

15 I Daniel was grieved in my spirit in the midst of my body, and the visions of my head troubled me. 16 I came near unto one of them that stood by, and asked him the truth of all this. So he told me, and made me know the interpretation of the things. 17 These great beasts, which are four, are four kings, which shall arise out of the earth. 18 But the saints of the most High shall take the kingdom, and possess the kingdom for ever, even for ever and ever.

19 Then I would know the truth of the fourth beast, which was diverse from all the others, exceeding dreadful, whose teeth were of iron, and his nails of brass; which devoured, brake in pieces, and stamped the residue with his feet; 20 And of the ten horns that were in his head, and of the other which came up, and before whom three fell; even of that horn that had eyes, and a mouth that spake very great things, whose look was more stout than his fellows. 21 I beheld, and the same horn made war with the saints, and prevailed against them; 22 Until the Ancient of days came, and judgment was given to the saints of the most High; and the time came that the saints possessed the kingdom.

23 Thus he said, The fourth beast shall be the fourth kingdom upon earth, which shall be diverse from all kingdoms, and shall devour the whole earth, and shall tread it down, and break it in pieces. 24 And the ten horns out of this kingdom are ten kings that shall arise: and another shall rise after them; and he shall be diverse from the first, and he shall subdue three kings. 25 And he shall speak great words against the most High, and shall wear out the saints of the most High, and think to change times and laws: and they shall be given into his hand until a time and times and the dividing of time. 26 But the judgment shall sit, and they shall take away his dominion, to consume and to destroy it unto the end. 27 And the kingdom and dominion, and the greatness of the kingdom under the whole heaven, shall be given to the people of the saints of the most High, whose kingdom is an everlasting kingdom, and all dominions shall serve and obey him.

28 Hitherto is the end of the matter. As for me Daniel, my cogitations much troubled me, and my countenance changed in me: but I kept the matter in my heart.

To begin with, let us have a closer look at these three verses:

7 After this I saw in the night visions, and behold a fourth beast, dreadful and terrible, and strong exceedingly; and it had great iron teeth: it devoured and brake in pieces, and stamped the residue with the feet of it: and it was diverse from all the beasts that were before it; and it had ten horns.

19 Then I would know the truth of the fourth beast, which was diverse from all the others, exceeding dreadful, whose teeth were of iron, and his nails of brass; which devoured, brake in pieces, and stamped the residue with his feet;

23 Thus he said, The fourth beast shall be the fourth kingdom upon earth, which shall be diverse from all kingdoms, and shall devour the whole earth, and shall tread it down, and break it in pieces.

In the vision the fourth beast is said to be devouring and stamping the residue. The Hebrew word *sha'ar* or *shear*; Strong's #7605 and #7606: a remainder, other, remnant, residue, rest. Residue in English also means: that which remains; the remainder; the rest of them; or the others. In the context it refers to the **other** three kingdoms. In verse 23 the term "the residue" is rephrased as ". . . the whole earth" which would clearly include the other kingdoms. There is nothing in the context of this passage to give any indication that the other three beasts conquered or stamped or destroyed each other in a chronological progression. Rather, it indicates that they were all contemporary kingdoms being stamped on by the fourth kingdom.

Consider this verse also:

12 As concerning the rest of the beasts, they had their dominion taken away: yet their lives were prolonged for a season and time.

First of all, we take note that the Hebrew word *shear* is here translated 'rest', the very same word that is used for 'residue'. (It seems to me that English translators use as many different words as possible for the same Hebrew word. Means you have to pay close attention to detail.) When we take into consideration the context of the whole passage, it becomes clear that the fourth kingdom is the instrument that takes away the dominion of the other three kingdoms by "stamping" or "trampling" them and that the existence of those kingdoms remains for a "season and a time", until the coming of The Kingdom of God which shall never be destroyed.

What makes this verse difficult to comprehend is that it comes after the scene before the judgment seat with the Ancient of Days and confusion can arise if we think it's a continuation of the activities before the Throne.

However, when we realise that it is but a change of subject in the narrative beginning with the phrase "As concerning the rest", or "as concerning the residue" as it could be translated, the confusion is removed. These days we would probably say "By the way" rather than "As concerning" to introduce the short statement about the other three kingdoms which the fourth beast tramples. Nevertheless, the rest of the verse makes it clear that the "rest of the beasts" lose their dominion, but remain in existence for "a season and a time".

In the previous chapter when we discussed Daniel Chapter 2, we found the description of the procession of the earthly kingdoms that would follow the reign of Nebuchadnezzar and it is primarily Babylon centred, as the dream was actually given to the king to show him what would follow after his reign. In contrast, the Chapter 7 scenario includes the whole earth and focuses on kingdoms that would have dominion over all mankind.

Let us now let Scripture shine light on this passage of Scripture. These verses from Daniel will give us some insight into the nature of these beast kingdoms.

Daniel 10:13
But the prince of the kingdom of Persia withstood me one and twenty days: but, lo, Michael, one of the chief princes, came to help me; and I remained there with the kings of Persia.

When the angel Gabriel came to Daniel, he mentioned a little of the spiritual battle that he and the angel Michael were involved in. He mentioned the "kings of Persia" and in so doing he calls the ruling powers of darkness kings.

Throughout the long and detailed prophecy in Daniel Chapter 11, that covers a period of about 500 years, there are repeated references to the king of the South and the king of the North (more on them later). Gabriel in his message to Daniel speaks of these two kings in the singular, even while detailing the actions of several Greek leaders that succeeded each other in the natural. As we continue with the following verses it will become increasingly apparent that these kings are spiritual entities that hold sway over the earthly kingdoms.

Ephesians 6:12
For we wrestle not against flesh and blood, but against principalities, against powers, against the rulers of the darkness of this world, against spiritual wickedness in high places.

The apostle Paul refers to these spiritual beings as principalities, powers and rulers of the darkness of this age. Let's get back to Daniel.

Daniel 7:2-3
Daniel spake and said, I saw in my vision by night, and, behold, the four winds of the heaven strove upon the great sea. 3 And four great beasts came up from the sea, diverse one from another.

Daniel 7:16-17
I came near unto one of them that stood by, and asked him the truth of all this. So he told me, and made me know the interpretation of the things. 17 These great beasts, which are four, are four kings, which shall arise out of the earth.

The Hebrew word for 'wind' is also translated 'spirit'. The word is *ruach*, used over forty times in the Hebrew Scriptures in the phrase *Ruach Elohim* which is translated Spirit of God. In a similar passage from the prophet Zechariah, who was a contemporary of Daniel, we find the alternative translation of the Hebrew word *ruach*:

Zechariah 6:5,7
And the angel answered and said unto me, These are the four spirits of the heavens, which go forth from standing before the Lord of all the earth.

7 . . . So they walked to and fro through the earth.

Zechariah tells us there are four spirits of the heavenly spiritual realm. In Daniel 7:2, if we use the alternative translation of *ruach*, we can get some insight into the meaning intended. The four spirits of heaven were stirring up the "sea", which verse 17 interprets as "the earth".

It is clear then, that the 'sea' is the 'sea of humanity' of all the earth that Jesus speaks metaphorically of in His parable of the dragnet (Matthew 13:47-50). From this 'sea', these great beasts arise, which are four 'kings' (Daniel 7:17) and as we have just seen, these 'kings' are the spiritual principalities and powers which hold sway over people and are the enemy with which the angels do battle. By way of reminder, the word 'spirits' in the passage from Zechariah is the exact same Hebrew word that gives us 'winds' in Daniel 7. Here is another Scripture from Hosea that speaks similarly that I believe sheds more light on this subject:

Hosea 13:7-10 NKJV
"So I will be to them like a lion; like a leopard by the road I will lurk; 8 I will meet them like a bear deprived of her cubs; I will tear open their rib cage, and there I will devour them like a lion. The wild beast shall tear them.

9 "O Israel, you are destroyed, but your help is from Me. 10 I will be your King.

These verses in their context are speaking to Ephraim, the leading tribe of the Kingdom of Israel that were to be scattered among the Gentiles, and God was warning them that through these four beasts (lion, leopard, bear and 'wild beast'), they would be afflicted with destruction, yet promising them that He was their help. These beasts were going to be out in the world where Israel was going to be, four beasts that would devour them because of their apostasy even when the Lord was there to be their King and help if they would but turn to Him. God gave them over to their pagan ways and this was the warning of the consequences. Typical Israel, they didn't listen.

The fourth beast is a particularly evil beast indeed and ends up ruling the whole earth and persecuting the saints until the "dividing of time" and is destroyed when Christ shall come to culminate the Kingdom of God. It seems that it is He, and only He, that will conquer this beast.

Daniel 7:9
I beheld till the thrones were cast down, and the Ancient of days did sit, whose garment was white as snow, and the hair of his head like the pure wool: his throne was like the fiery flame, and his wheels as burning fire.

At the beginning of this verse we have the phrase: "thrones were cast down". Most modern translations render this as "thrones set up", or "set in place", or some such phrase. The Hebrew word for cast is *remah* and is used in all the following verses throughout the book of Daniel. (3:6, 11, 15, 20, 21, 24; 6:7, 12, 16, 24; 7:9; 8:7, 12; 11:12). In Chapter 3 it refers to being cast into the fiery furnace. In Chapter 6 it is being cast into the lion's den. With Daniel 8:7 it is the Goat casting down the Ram in the vision. Daniel 8:12 has it as the Sanctuary being cast down. In Daniel 11:12 it is the casting down of tens of thousands by a conquering king. Daniel never used this word as setting something up, it is always used as casting down. I believe the King James Version has it correct and Young's Literal Translation confirms it:

Daniel 7:9 YLT
I was seeing till that thrones have been thrown down, and the Ancient of Days is seated

When Christ comes, the thrones of this final beast kingdom are cast down (and any other thrones) and the beast is defeated, the Ancient of Days will be seated on His Throne, the court shall be seated and the books shall be opened. It looks like Judgment Day when all authorities and powers are made subject unto Him (see also 1 Corinthians 15:25). The saints will inherit the Kingdom that is promised to them and all other kingdoms will be destroyed forever. This is the first look at the Kingdom of God at the end of the age that appears in the Holy Scriptures. Of course, there is much more to say on this matter that we will come to later in this study.

I have offered up some personal insights on the Four Beasts that you might find interesting. **WARNING:** Some of what follows is my opinion.

In Chapter Seven of Daniel, the interpretation of that vision given to us is limited in its details with regard to the identity of the various beasts. Although the fourth beast has more said about it, it is still left somewhat vague as far as who or what this kingdom actually is when it appears on the scene. The only identifying comments are mostly concerned with what the beast actually does; it tramples the rest. And as for the other three beasts, the only comments we have are scant: the leopard beast has dominion given to it and later the three beasts have their dominion taken away and their lives prolonged for a "season and a time".

Many prophecy pundits have theorised that the four beasts in the vision are four successive kingdoms, basically subscribing to the idea that the vision is but a confirmation of their interpretation of Nebuchadnezzar's dream that asserts a four kingdom paradigm. With examination of the details, we discovered that the four kingdom scenario for Daniel Chapter 2 cannot be supported for there are in fact five kingdoms referred to in that dream of the statue, which we found to be confirmed by the testimony of history.

We then discovered in God's Word that there are four spirits in the heavenly realm which go out into all the world (Zechariah 6:5-7; Hosea 13:7-8; Daniel 7:2). Based on the understanding coming from these Scriptures, I believe these four beasts of Daniel Chapter Seven represent the four major spiritual and religious principalities and powers that have dominion over the nations of the whole earth.

It is interesting to note that the entire multitude of all religions outside of the revelation of God found in the Holy Bible can be reduced into four categories. This is because outside of Christ, people have four basic dispositions toward God: 1. They deny His existence, which gives place to Atheism and Pantheism; 2. They make Him just one of many gods, which creates Polytheism; 3. They acknowledge His existence but have no personal relationship with Him and consequently have no idea what He is really like, thus forming Monotheism, of which we find there are two main streams of thought: Deism and Theism; 4. Then there is Anti-Christ, which is singled out from the Monotheistic beliefs because it directly attacks the reality of the Father and the Son with the purpose of eventually presenting another 'Christ'. And so we have these four principalities and powers prevailing over the earth: Atheism; Polytheism; Monotheism; Anti-Christ. Four ruling spirits of the heavenly or spiritual realm.

Let us now take a look at the four beasts in Daniel:

The First Beast: A lion with eagle's wings.

Daniel 7:4 NKJV
The first *was* like a lion, and had eagle's wings. I watched till its wings were plucked off; and it was lifted up from the earth and made to stand on two feet like a man, and a man's heart was given to it.

The First Beast: Atheism

Pantheism and Atheism are two sides of the same coin. Saying that everything is God (Pantheism) is effectively saying there is no God. The thought is, "I'm God, you're God, everyone and everything thing is God." This line of thinking reduces God to nothing that can be related to; some kind of cosmic consciousness without personality. Pantheism is found primarily in the teachings of Buddhism; which is a spiritual form of Atheism. It is also found in the philosophy of the New Age Movement. China, which is predominately Buddhist, finds no problem aligning itself with atheistic communism because it is the same spiritually. Buddhism first arose in southern Nepal and spread rapidly into Asia and India, later into China, Southeast Asia and Sri Lanka, otherwise known as Ceylon. It then declined in India due to the rise of Hinduism and later Islam. Estimates of the world's population of Atheists and Pantheistic Buddhists vary greatly from around 350 million to well over a billion.

The description of it being a lion with wings that are later plucked off, could refer to its powerful and rapid initial growth, it flew, but plucked wings defining its much inhibited proselytization in later years. A man's heart given to it perhaps signifying its humanistic nature, something that developed as it went along. This aspect of Atheism is expressed in the philosophy of Humanism and Communism.

The Second Beast: A bear with ribs in its mouth.

Daniel 7:5 NKJV
"And suddenly another beast, a second, like a bear. It was raised up on one side, and *had* three ribs in its mouth between its teeth. And they said thus to it: 'Arise, devour much flesh!'

The Second Beast: Polytheism.

The primary organised religion that promotes Polytheism is Hinduism, which is a fusion or synthesis of various Indian cultures and traditions, with diverse roots and no founder. Basically a formalization and systemization of the rampant Polytheism that prevailed among the various tribes who worshipped a multitude of gods after the tower of Babel. This 'Hindu Synthesis' developed into the oppressive caste system that prevails throughout India to this day. Estimates of the world population of Hindus is somewhere around one billion. Polytheism includes all the various animalistic cultures around the world.

The bear with three ribs in its mouth that devours much flesh suitably and accurately describes the manner in which the upper caste devours the lower castes in society. In all polytheistic cultures, the priesthood and witch doctors devour the common people through fears and superstitions. The bear having no wings never moved much from where it originated, clings stubbornly to its traditions and is not particularly proselytistic.

The Third Beast: A leopard with four heads and four wings.

Daniel 7:6 NKJV
"After this I looked, and there was another, like a leopard, which had on its back four wings of a bird. The beast also had four heads, and dominion was given to it.

The Third Beast: Monotheism.

This spiritual power includes all monotheistic religions, whether deistic or theistic. Includes, but not limited to, the Sikh and Bahai faiths, and Judaism, but the most dominant manifestation is false Christianity which began to be formed immediately after the apostolic age, though the seeds were being planted even in New Testament times. True Christianity is an ongoing spiritual experience with the Holy Spirit that provides a personal relationship with God through His Son, Jesus Christ. The effect of this beast is always to block, remove or suppresses that reality so that one is simply left with a religion whose adherents are holding fast to a form of godliness that denies the power thereof (2 Timothy 3:5).

Evidence of its foundations being laid can be found in the writings of the 'church fathers', (more on this later) and it was well established and institutionalised by the fourth century during the reign of the Roman Emperor Constantine. There are four main streams, each with their multiple off-spring, and they are: the Roman Catholic Church, the Greek Orthodox, the Russian Orthodox and the Egyptian Coptic. All of these are branches of the same tree, filled with damnable doctrines that take people to perdition: Mariolatry, transubstantiation, an elevated priesthood, praying to 'saints', a works based salvation of legalism, formalism, ritualism, allegorism, a distorted representation of Jesus and a host of other false doctrines characterize this beast. Whenever it manages to assume political power, it has historically persecuted not only true believers, but anyone who attempts to resist its totalitarianism, and they do this believing they are doing God service and sometimes they even do it in the name of Jesus. By the way, this author understands that there are true believers in Christ that work within the structures erected by this beast to turn the hearts of those caught up in the influence of this particular religious spirit to the love and power and truth of God. May the Lord bless their efforts and strengthen them to build His Kingdom in the hearts of those they find themselves among.

The four heads of the leopard represent the four primary denominations mentioned above and their multiple offspring. The four wings denote its ability to rapidly spread around the world. The spots of the leopard represent its ability to camouflage itself as genuine Christianity. Many Christians simply fail to discern this beast and come under the effects of this religious principality and power. Most probably they don't lose their salvation, but they certainly suffer from a form of Christianity that lacks the power of the Holy Spirit. Historically, every outpouring of the Spirit that has brought revival has eventually been squashed by this evil principality which continually influences: toward a turning of the grace of God into licentiousness and lewdness (Jude 1:4); toward self-effort and legalism that effectively denies the grace of God altogether (Galatians 3:3); or a return to the philosophies of this world as with the acceptance in some denominations of a form of universalism. These three forms of unbelief are warned of in Colossians 2:1-3:11.

The multitude of spots on the leopard could also represent the countless sects and cults this beast is clothed with. Interestingly, this particular beast was singled out to receive dominion in verse 6 and it is quite apparent that wherever it goes it establishes an authoritarian hierarchy or oligarchy within its structure and historically has found the ability to rise into political power. This is in direct conflict with Jesus' statement that His Kingdom was not of this world. It is also in contradiction of Jesus' command to His disciples to not exercise authority nor act like lords as the rulers of the Gentiles do (Matthew 20:25-28; 23:1-12): "It shall not be so among you . . . he who would be great among you, let him be the servant of all."

The ability to camouflage itself is part of the natural state of this beast which is also one of the main characteristics of the false teachers that the apostles warned the church of in various passages:

Jude 1:4 NKJV
For certain men have crept in unnoticed, who long ago were marked out for this condemnation, ungodly men, who turn the grace of our God into lewdness and deny the only Lord God and our Lord Jesus Christ.

2 Peter 2:1 NKJV
But there were also false prophets among the people, even as there will be false teachers among you, who will secretly bring in destructive heresies, even denying the Lord who bought them, *and* bring on themselves swift destruction.

2 Corinthians 11:13-15 NKJV
For such *are* false apostles, deceitful workers, transforming themselves into apostles of Christ. 14 And no wonder! For Satan himself transforms himself into an angel of light. 15 Therefore it is no great thing if his ministers also transform themselves into ministers of righteousness, whose end will be according to their works.

WOW. They creep in unnoticed; they secretly bring in heresies; they transform themselves into ministers of righteousness; they come as wolves in sheep's clothing. There are many more Scriptures describing the people that Jesus said would come in His Name to deceive. Don't think for a minute that these have not been active in our days and in our midst.

Basically, this beast is always working to reduce Christianity to a religion rather than a relationship with God through Christ. It appears Christian but it is not. Some call this beast Christendom, others call it Churchianity or Institutionalism and still others have coined the term Pagan Christianity. Many have adopted the term Mystery Babylon, exhorting believers to come out of it. Estimated adherents to the multitude of sects and cults could be as many as two billion worldwide. Who knows?

The Fourth Beast: The Ten Horned Beast

Daniel 7:7 NKJV
"After this I saw in the night visions, and behold, a fourth beast, dreadful and terrible, exceedingly strong. It had huge iron teeth; it was devouring, breaking in pieces, and trampling the residue with its feet. It *was* different from all the beasts that *were* before it, and it had ten horns.

The Fourth Beast: Antichrist.

Antichrist is also monotheistic. And whilst the Bible says that there are many antichrists, it also makes clear that there is The Antichrist. A number of sects and cults have been defined as antichrist because they present a false Christ to the world: Jehovah's Witnesses, Christadelphians, Mormons, etc. By Biblical definition they are actually Pseudo Christian and as such are included in the previous beast. True Antichrist is described in the Word of God as one who denies the Father and the Son.

1 John 2:22-23 NKJV
Who is a liar but he who denies that Jesus is the Christ? He is antichrist who denies the Father and the Son. 23 Whoever denies the Son does not have the Father either; he who acknowledges the Son has the Father also.

Whilst the Catholics and the aforementioned cults deny the Father and the Son in subtle ways by distorting the meaning of the term 'Son of God', they don't actually come out and say, "God has no Son". The only world-wide religion that explicitly denies the Father and the Son in direct statements from their so called holy book is Islam. The Koran (or Quran) of Islam directly attacks the revelation that we have of Jesus coming as God manifested in the flesh, dying on the cross and being bodily resurrected from the dead to ascend into Heaven. The Koran says, "God has no son." The Koran says, "It is blasphemy to say God has a son." (Here's a list of some Koran quotes on this subject for those interested: 2:116; 5:116; 6:101; 9:30; 10:68; 19:35; 19:88; 23:91; 39:4; 43:82; 72:3; 112:1-4)

Islam is pure Antichrist and it is on the rise. A study of Islam and its 'theology' reveals that it is indeed a ready-made cloak for the Antichrist, a tailor made religion for the 'man of sin'. Islamic theology has a character called the Mahdi; their version of Messiah. How that will evolve I don't really know. We shall just have to wait and see. My guess is that the magnitude of the lying signs and wonders that this man of sin will demonstrate will be sufficient to take the hearts of the unbelieving and the unrepentant in that day.

Daniel 7:23-25
Thus he said, The fourth beast shall be the fourth kingdom upon earth, which shall be diverse from all kingdoms, and shall devour the whole earth, and shall tread it down, and break it in pieces. 24 And the ten horns out of this kingdom are ten kings that shall arise: and another shall rise after them; and he shall be diverse from the first, and he shall subdue three kings. 25 And he shall speak great words against the most High, and shall wear out the saints of the most High, and think to change times and laws: and they shall be given into his hand until a time and times and the dividing of time.

2 Thessalonians 2:3-4 NKJV
Let no one deceive you by any means; for *that Day will not come* unless the falling away comes first, and the man of sin is revealed, the son of perdition, 4 who opposes and exalts himself above all that is called God or that is worshiped, so that he sits as God in the temple of God, showing himself that he is God.

How long it will take this kingdom to subdue the whole world and bring forth its ten kings I don't know. That it is here today on the world scene is quite clear. I would not be surprised, though considerably dismayed, to see Europe become Eurabia in my lifetime. I hope not. In the process of its takeover, it seems that Atheism, Polytheism and Monotheism will all be utterly oppressed but not completely eliminated when the Antichrist kingdom rules the world before the Return of Christ.

Another look at Daniel's description of the manifestation of this beast prior to the coming culmination of the Kingdom of God gives us some notable 'signs of the times'.

Daniel 7:24-25

". . . out of this kingdom are ten kings that shall arise"

". . . another shall rise after them;"

"he . . . . shall subdue three kings."

"he shall speak great words against the most High"

". . . shall wear out the saints of the most High, and think to change times and laws: and they shall be given into his hand until a time and times and the dividing of time.

Most translators render "wear out" as "persecute". So then: ten kings, followed by an eleventh who subdues three of the ten and is the one that speaks against the Most High God and exalts himself. Pretty easy to recognise when the time comes. These signs would probably be before the sun gets darkened and the moon loses its light as mentioned by Jesus. Someday, perhaps not in our time, but sometime we shall surely see.

Now, this last phrase needs a closer look:

Daniel 7:25
. . . a time and times and the dividing of time.

However, it is subject on its own and is best viewed as a separate article. See A Time, Times and Half a Time in the Appendix.

I need to point out that I am not the first to suggest a spiritual reality to the beast kingdoms of Daniel 7. Adolph Ernst Knoch, who brought forth the Concordant Literal New Testament, wrote along these lines in the early 1900s. His version of the Bible was an attempt to overcome the vagaries of translation but ended up being too difficult to read and thus never became popular. Good for a reference only.

My theory differs a little from his as Islam was not on the radar with regard to Bible prophecy back then. Bible prophecy scholarship tended to be more Eurocentric, which it still mostly is. With the resurgence of modern day Islam, awareness of the Muslim Empire as the fifth kingdom of Daniel Chapter 2 is growing and has stirred prophecy pundits to re-evaluate their eschatological prognostics to a more Middle Eastern centred paradigm.

Wherever Islam goes and becomes dominant, it crushes all other religions under its feet with ruthless force. It is infiltrating western civilisation at an astounding pace at the time of this writing (2017AD). Europe seems to be committing cultural suicide, it's just not rational. From a spiritual point of view, however, it is completely understandable.

2 Thessalonians 2:9-12 NKJV
The coming of the *lawless one* is according to the working of Satan, with all power, signs, and lying wonders, 10 and with all unrighteous deception among those who perish, because they

did not receive the love of the truth, that they might be saved. 11 And for this reason God will send them strong delusion, that they should believe the lie, 12 that they all may be condemned who did not believe the truth but had pleasure in unrighteousness.

Yep, it's entirely spiritual. Because they do not receive the "love of the truth", God will deliver them to "the lie", He will send them "strong delusion". The God of love will not put up with evil forever. It's simply not the loving thing to do.

Concerning the manifestation of this beast, these three things are for sure:

1. The fourth beast with its ten horns in Daniel 7 corresponds to the 'iron and clay ten toed kingdom' of Daniel 2.
2. The 'feet and toes kingdom' that comes after the 'legs of iron kingdom' is not the Roman Empire, it is Islam.
3. This final earthly kingdom is destroyed at the culmination of the Kingdom of God at the end of the age.

The kingdom that destroyed the dominion of Rome is different from all other kingdoms that have gone before it. As a geopolitical power it is also totally theocratic and it is EVIL AS. It begins to trample all other religions once it establishes itself within a host nation and it denies the Father and the Son. Interestingly, Islamists rarely completely wipe out the religions they conquer. Whilst they execute many, they often prefer to oppress them and make them second class citizens (*dhimmis*) with practically no rights, subjecting them to random acts of violence (in contrast to random acts of kindness) and forcing them to pay a special tax called *jizra*, otherwise known as extortion money. Thus the description of this kingdom allowing the other kingdoms to live but have no dominion seems to fit. Nevertheless, it is pure Antichrist and it is on the rise today.

There may possibly be something that I cannot see, some other interpretation of Daniel's vision that fits, but just MAYBE I could be seeing something that explains this particular passage in a way that doesn't contradict the unfolding of history or Scripture. In some ways it could be regarded as a moot point. The last kingdom will arrive and the rest will simply be history. Remember, it is but my opinion, but to me it is intellectually satisfying. If I'm correct, all credit must go to Him who opens up the understanding. Amen. If there is something else that God has in mind in this passage, we shall surely see it in good time.

By way of reminder, here is the Scripture quoted above from the prophet Hosea.

Hosea 13:7-10 NKJV
"So I will be to them like a lion;
Like a leopard by the road I will lurk;
8 I will meet them like a bear deprived of her cubs;
I will tear open their rib cage,
And there I will devour them like a lion.

The wild beast shall tear them.
9 "O Israel, you are destroyed,
But your help is from Me.
10 I will be your King.

In summary: The destiny of Israel includes their encounter with these four symbolic beasts: a lion, a bear, a leopard, and finally a wild beast. The spiritual reality of that which is represented in this passage will afflict and attack not only Judah and Israel, but also God's Church which is commonly recognised as 'Spiritual Israel', the Kingdom of God in this age. The promise however is that though Israel be declared 'destroyed', their help is from the Lord and He shall be their King. Hallelujah!

Chapter Six

Introducing Daniel's Synoptic Prophecies

This small chapter is a necessary slight diversion in preparation for the three chapters which follow.

When the Kingdom of Judah was taken into captivity by the Babylonians, it propelled them on a completely separate path from the Kingdom of Israel. That path was plotted in three prophecies written by Daniel, one of which is known by some scholars as the longest and most detailed prophecy in the whole Bible, and another is known as the most important prophecy ever fulfilled. All three of these prophecies cover the period of time from the dominion of the Medes and Persians who conquered Babylon, through the reign of the Greek empires, right up to the time of the Romans and the Abomination of Desolation. Jesus especially referred to the "abomination of desolation spoken of by Daniel the prophet" with the exhortation, "let the reader understand". He was speaking to His disciples and giving them information that was particularly important to them. Let us therefore also understand what Daniel had to say. Later we will see how very relevant Jesus' comments were.

To correctly understand these three prophecies which are found in Daniel Chapters 8-12, it is important to approach them synoptically, not as stand-alone proclamations. (Likewise with the Gospels of Matthew, Mark and Luke) As mentioned above, they all cover the same period of time. Incidentally, Daniel now reverts to writing these passages in Hebrew and the content of the prophecies is centred on the Kingdom of Judah even though much is said of the Gentile nations that afflict them.

In these passages we will find mention of the terms: latter days; appointed time; and time of the end. There are over 400 instances where the phrase 'the end' is used in Scripture and only on rare occasions does it refer to the end of the age. Therefore we must be careful to allow the context to declare just what 'the end' is actually the end of. Many times it is obvious: the end of all flesh; the end of forty days; etc. When it is not so clear however, we must put aside the presumption that it always means the end of the age and allow for the context to reveal the intended meaning. What follows are examples of when the end is not the end but just an end.

Amos 8:2-3
And he said, Amos, what seest thou? And I said, A basket of summer fruit. Then said the Lord unto me, The end is come upon my people of Israel; I will not again pass by them any more. 3 And the songs of the temple shall be howlings in that day, saith the Lord God: there shall be many dead bodies in every place; they shall cast them forth with silence.

The context of the above is found at the beginning of the Book of Amos.

Amos 1:1
The words of Amos, who was among the herdmen of Tekoa, which he saw concerning Israel in the days of Uzziah king of Judah, and in the days of Jeroboam the son of Joash king of Israel, two years before the earthquake.

The situation is during the time when there were two kingdoms in the Promised Land: the Kingdom of Judah and the Kingdom of Israel. Amos was prophesying concerning the imminent invasion by the Assyrians who would conquer and take captive the whole of the Northern Kingdom of Israel. The term 'the end' used by Amos has nothing to do with the end of the age but everything to do with the end of Israel's presence in the Land. Here is another example:

Ezekiel 7:1-9
Moreover the word of the Lord came unto me, saying, 2 Also, thou son of man, thus saith the Lord God unto the land of Israel; An end, the end is come upon the four corners of the land. 3 Now is the end come upon thee, and I will send mine anger upon thee, and will judge thee according to thy ways, and will recompense upon thee all thine abominations. 4 And mine eye shall not spare thee, neither will I have pity: but I will recompense thy ways upon thee, and thine abominations shall be in the midst of thee: and ye shall know that I am the Lord. 5 Thus saith the Lord God; An evil, an only evil, behold, is come. 6 An end is come, the end is come: it watcheth for thee; behold, it is come. 7 The morning is come unto thee, O thou that dwellest in the land: the time is come, the day of trouble is near, and not the sounding again of the mountains. 8 Now will I shortly pour out my fury upon thee, and accomplish mine anger upon thee: and I will judge thee according to thy ways, and will recompense thee for all thine abominations. 9 And mine eye shall not spare, neither will I have pity: I will recompense thee according to thy ways and thine abominations that are in the midst of thee; and ye shall know that I am the Lord that smiteth.

Ezekiel is prophesying to the Kingdom of Judah prior to the final destruction by the Babylonians, the end of Solomon's Temple and the first desolation of Jerusalem that was to last seventy years.

Having examined these examples from the Word, let us proceed with our study of Daniel's Synoptic Prophesies, keeping in mind that the end mentioned is not the end of the age.

Chapter Seven

Vision of a Ram and a Goat

As always, we need to take particular attention to the details in our approach to God's Word in order to avoid stumbling into the error of accepting an interpretation instead of coming to the solid rock of understanding. Daniel sees a vision which is followed by the interpretation given through an angel who is referred to as a 'saint', literally a 'holy one' from the Lord.

Daniel 8:1-27

In the third year of the reign of king Belshazzar a vision appeared unto me, even unto me Daniel, after that which appeared unto me at the first. 2 And I saw in a vision; and it came to pass, when I saw, that I was at Shushan in the palace, which is in the province of Elam; and I saw in a vision, and I was by the river of Ulai. 3 Then I lifted up mine eyes, and saw, and, behold, there stood before the river a ram which had two horns: and the two horns were high; but one was higher than the other, and the higher came up last. 4 I saw the ram pushing westward, and northward, and southward; so that no beasts might stand before him, neither was there any that could deliver out of his hand; but he did according to his will, and became great.

5 And as I was considering, behold, an he goat came from the west on the face of the whole earth, and touched not the ground: and the goat had a notable horn between his eyes. 6 And he came to the ram that had two horns, which I had seen standing before the river, and ran unto him in the fury of his power. 7 And I saw him come close unto the ram, and he was moved with choler against him, and smote the ram, and brake his two horns: and there was no power in the ram to stand before him, but he cast him down to the ground, and stamped upon him: and there was none that could deliver the ram out of his hand.

8 Therefore the he goat waxed very great: and when he was strong, the great horn was broken; and for it came up four notable ones toward the four winds of heaven.

9 And out of one of them came forth a little horn, which waxed exceeding great, toward the south, and toward the east, and toward the pleasant land. 10 And it waxed great, even to the host of heaven; and it cast down some of the host and of the stars to the ground, and stamped upon them. 11 Yea, he magnified himself even to the prince of the host, and by him the daily sacrifice was taken away, and the place of the sanctuary was cast down. 12 And an host was given him against the daily sacrifice by reason of transgression, and it cast down the truth to the ground; and it practised, and prospered.

13 Then I heard one saint speaking, and another saint said unto that certain saint which spake, How long shall be the vision concerning the daily sacrifice, and the transgression of desolation, to give both the sanctuary and the host to be trodden under foot? 14 And he said unto me, Unto two thousand and three hundred days; then shall the sanctuary be cleansed.

15 And it came to pass, when I, even I Daniel, had seen the vision, and sought for the meaning, then, behold, there stood before me as the appearance of a man. 16 And I heard a man's voice between the banks of Ulai, which called, and said, Gabriel, make this man to understand the vision. 17 So he came near where I stood: and when he came, I was afraid, and fell upon my face: but he said unto me, Understand, O son of man: for at the time of the end shall be the vision.

18 Now as he was speaking with me, I was in a deep sleep on my face toward the ground: but he touched me, and set me upright. 19 And he said, Behold, I will make thee know what shall be in the last end of the indignation: for at the time appointed the end shall be. 20 The ram which thou sawest having two horns are the kings of Media and Persia. 21 And the rough goat is the king of Grecia: and the great horn that is between his eyes is the first king. 22 Now that being broken, whereas four stood up for it, four kingdoms shall stand up out of the nation, but not in his power.

23 And in the latter time of their kingdom, when the transgressors are come to the full, a king of fierce countenance, and understanding dark sentences, shall stand up.

24 And his power shall be mighty, but not by his own power: and he shall destroy wonderfully, and shall prosper, and practise, and shall destroy the mighty and the holy people. 25 And through his policy also he shall cause craft to prosper in his hand; and he shall magnify himself in his heart, and by peace shall destroy many: he shall also stand up against the Prince of princes; but he shall be broken without hand. 26 And the vision of the evening and the morning which was told is true: wherefore shut thou up the vision; for it shall be for many days. 27 And I Daniel fainted, and was sick certain days; afterward I rose up, and did the king's business; and I was astonished at the vision, but none understood it.

Daniel has this vision during the reign of King Nebuchadnezzar's son Belshazzar, who was the last king of the Babylonian Empire. In verses 1-14 we have the description of the vision and the rest of the chapter is concerned primarily with the interpretation. In the vision we find a ram that is described as "great" (Daniel 8:4), which is later interpreted as being the kingdom of the Medes and Persians (Daniel 8:20). The goat with one horn is described as "very great" (Daniel 8:8) and it is interpreted as being the kingdom of Greece (Daniel 8:21) which is then divided into four (Daniel 8:22).

Then there is "a little horn" that is then described as growing "exceedingly great" (Daniel 8:9) in the latter time of the Greek Empire (Daniel 8:23), which was long after it had been divided into four. This particular kingdom I have termed the Little Big Horn. This kingdom grew toward the south and toward the east and toward the Pleasant Land (Daniel 8:9) which is a term referring to the Promised Land of Israel.

In the ancient Hebrew language there is no such expression as 'southeast' or 'northwest' when it comes to compass headings. They say, "The north and the west" to indicate northwest. "Toward the south and toward the east" means a south-easterly direction.

This passage perfectly describes the history of the rise of Rome which came to power in the north western portion of the Greek Empire in its latter days. Rome had conquered Corinth in response to Macedonian aggression and had no initial interest in expanding further. It was a "little horn". But a few decades later the new power began to extend its dominion into the Greek territories and we find that the prophecy exactly details the initial direction of the expansion that was to finally dispatch the Greek Empire to the dustbin of history. This passage also perfectly describes the history of the rise of the procession of empires with regards to their size. As mentioned above: The Medes and the Persians were a great empire; The Greeks were a very great empire; The Romans were an exceedingly great empire.

Many scholars have stumbled over the identification of the Little Big Horn, somehow ascribing it as part of the Greek Empire. However, the timing of its appearance as described in the vision places it in the latter part of the reign of the Greeks (Daniel 8:9-12 and 23-25). Latter part means: toward the end of. In giving the interpretation, Daniel gives some details of a king that arises that enables us to define the historical time accurately. The New King James may better describe this character:

Daniel 8:23-25 NKJV
"And in the latter time of their kingdom, When the transgressors have reached their fullness, A king shall arise, Having fierce features, Who understands sinister schemes. 24 His power shall be mighty, but not by his own power; He shall destroy fearfully, And shall prosper and thrive; He shall destroy the mighty, and *also* the holy people. 25 "Through his cunning He shall cause deceit to prosper under his rule; And he shall exalt *himself* in his heart. He shall destroy many in *their* prosperity. He shall even rise against the Prince of princes; But he shall be broken without *human* means.

From the above passage we see that the king of the Little Big Horn is described as having fierce features, sinister, a mighty one who shall "destroy the mighty and the holy people". It was to be during a time when the transgressors had reached their fullness. Note also this phrase:

Daniel 8:11
Yea, he magnified himself even to the prince of the host, and by him the daily sacrifice was taken away, and the place of the sanctuary was cast down.

". . . and the place of the sanctuary was cast down". This mention of the sanctuary enables us to discern that the time period refers to the destruction of the Temple, which was accomplished by the Romans, not the desecration that happened under the rule of the Greeks. Whilst the Greeks were responsible for an abomination of desolation, they did not cast the sanctuary down; they only desecrated and defiled the temple, then they left it desolate, but it was still standing. For more on this subject see The Abomination of Desolation in the Appendix.

Daniel 8:14
And he said unto me, Unto two thousand and three hundred days; then shall the sanctuary be cleansed.

The 2300 days of Daniel 8:14 is a period of time hard to discern. However, history tells us the Roman war with the Jews was not over when Jerusalem was defeated in 70AD. Rebellious Jews continued their resistance and it wasn't until 73AD that the stronghold of Masada was overtaken and the trampling of the host was complete. It was then that the war was finally finished. Whilst no one can measure the 2300 days, the entire war is approximately that period of time.

The meaning of the phrase: "then the sanctuary shall be cleansed" in Daniel 8:14 has generally been regarded as a mystery. The Hebrew word that is normally translated 'cleansed' in English is *taheer* and is used consistently with regard to ritual cleansing. However, the word 'cleansed' in this verse comes from the Hebrew word *tsa-daq* which is normally translated 'justify', 'just', 'justified', 'justice' or 'righteous'. The context declares that *tsa-daq* would be accomplished when both the temple and the host were trampled. In the light of what Jesus said was going to happen to the Temple and the reason He gave for what was coming upon the unbelieving and wicked generation, it makes sense to consider the fate of the Sanctuary and the host being trampled as a 'just' or 'righteous' event, rather than the sanctuary being cleansed or restored. The fact of the matter is that it was neither cleansed nor restored.

The rise against the Prince of the Host (Jesus), the trampling of the host (the Jews), the Abomination of Desolation and the taking away of the daily sacrifices were all accomplished together under the rule of Rome. All of these prophesied events are reiterated in the words of Jesus in the Gospels (covered in a later chapter), and as we shall see, in the following two chapters where we cover Daniel Chapter 9 and Daniel Chapters 11-12 wherein we shall also find more about this king. And remember, be sure to view these three prophecies synoptically.

Chapter Eight

The Seventy Sevens Prophecy

Often called the Seventy Weeks Prophecy, the Seventy Sevens Prophecy of Daniel has got to be the greatest prophecy ever fulfilled. Although aspects of this prophecy are found elsewhere in Scripture, like in Isaiah 53 and Psalm 22, no other Old Testament prophecy presents such a fullness of the Gospel in such a concise manner as is found here in Daniel. In this short passage we find the great work of our Lord Jesus Christ in bringing the grace and mercy of God to His people by His substitutionary work on the cross. And it also sets forth the judgment of God against the sins of the Jewish nation in rejecting and crucifying the Lord of glory. Thus we find both the goodness and the severity of our God.

Of considerable interest, this passage records the precise timing of the coming of Messiah. As such these few verses ought to be presented to the Jews as evidence of the coming of Christ and for that reason the enemy of God has sown untold controversy regarding the meaning of Gabriel's message to Daniel.

Whereas Chapter 8 and Chapters 11-12 deal mainly with the actions of the Gentile nations and their effect upon the Jews, the Seventy Sevens Prophecy speaks mostly of the Messiah and what God was going to accomplish through Him for and on behalf of His people. We will pick up the passage with Daniel interceding for his nation.

Daniel 9:20-23
And whiles I was speaking, and praying, and confessing my sin and the sin of my people Israel, and presenting my supplication before the Lord my God for the holy mountain of my God; 21 Yea, whiles I was- speaking in prayer, even the man Gabriel, whom I had seen in the vision at the beginning, being caused to fly swiftly, touched me about the time of the evening oblation. 22 And he informed me, and talked with me, and said, O Daniel, I am now come forth to give thee skill and understanding. 23 At the beginning of thy supplications the commandment came forth, and I am come to shew thee; for thou art greatly beloved: therefore understand the matter, and consider the vision.

The following prophecy is a direct answer to Daniel's prayer. This portion may be a little easier from the New King James:

Daniel 9:24-27 NKJV
"Seventy weeks are determined
For your people and for your holy city,
To finish the transgression,
To make an end of sins,
To make reconciliation for iniquity,
To bring in everlasting righteousness,
To seal up vision and prophecy,
And to anoint the Most Holy.
25
"Know therefore and understand,
That from the going forth of the command
To restore and build Jerusalem
Until Messiah the Prince,
There shall be seven weeks and sixty-two weeks;
The street shall be built again, and the wall,
Even in troublesome times.
26
"And after the sixty-two weeks
Messiah shall be cut off, but not for Himself;
And the people of the prince who is to come
Shall destroy the city and the sanctuary.
The end of it *shall be* with a flood,
And till the end of the war desolations are determined.
27
Then he shall confirm a covenant with many for one week;
But in the middle of the week
He shall bring an end to sacrifice and offering.
And on the wing of abominations shall be one who makes desolate,
Even until the consummation, which is determined,
Is poured out on the desolate."

Let us now look carefully at the above passages. Daniel is confessing his sin and the sin of Israel when he sees the angel Gabriel. Note that Daniel hasn't seen another vision, he has seen the angel who was in the vision previously mentioned in Chapter 8 (Daniel 9:21), who has come to give him understanding of the vision (Daniel 9:23). Even though Gabriel had previously explained to him what the vision was about, Daniel still did not understand, he was utterly astonished by it and confessed that no-one understood it, presumably not even himself (Daniel 8:27), thus Gabriel has arrived to give him "skill to understand" (Daniel 9:22).

Be aware that the prophesied "seventy weeks" is covering the same time period covered by the vision of Daniel Chapter 8 which described what the actions of the prevailing Gentile kingdoms were going to be. However, there were aspects of that vision that Daniel simply could not comprehend. So in Daniel Chapter 9, Gabriel comes and complements the previous interpretation of the vision by revealing the plan that God was going to accomplish for and on behalf of the Jews while they endured the coming period of continued Gentile domination.

Daniel 9:24 NKJV
"Seventy weeks are determined
For your people and for your holy city,
To finish the transgression,
To make an end of sins,
To make reconciliation for iniquity,
To bring in everlasting righteousness,
To seal up vision and prophecy,
And to anoint the Most Holy.

Seventy weeks are "determined". Many translations use the word "decreed", and the literal from the Hebrew is "cut", as in a something being clearly defined. It can also mean "appointed" as in the phrase "appointed time".

Although almost every English translation has chosen to render the Hebrew word *shabua* as 'weeks', it is literally 'sevens'. Mostly used of days to make a week, but in this case it is used of years.

Seventy sevens are: decreed; determined; defined; appointed, for your people and for your holy city. Now the prophecy defines what is going to be accomplished during the seventy sevens and we find six things mentioned. To cover these things fully would require a thorough exegesis on the revelation of the Gospel given to Paul in the New Testament which is beyond the scope of this study. However, these few passages of Scripture below should suffice.

1: To finish the transgression:

To finish: to add the final touch, to complete a project with a last addition. Some people think it means to stop sinning, but in reality it is talking about capping off the transgression with the supreme sin as we shall see as we continue. Look how Daniel spoke of it in the previous chapter:

Daniel 8:23 NKJV
And in the latter time of their kingdom, when the transgressors have reached their fullness . . .

And look at how Jesus spoke about it:

Matthew 23:32-35 NKJV
Fill up, then, the measure of your fathers' *guilt.* 33 Serpents, brood of vipers! How can you escape the condemnation of hell? 34 Therefore, indeed, I send you prophets, wise men, and scribes:

some of them you will kill and crucify, and *some* of them you will scourge in your synagogues and persecute from city to city, 35 that on you may come all the righteous blood shed on the earth, from the blood of righteous Abel to the blood of Zechariah, son of Berechiah, whom you murdered between the temple and the altar.

The word *'guilt'* in the NKJV is in italics because it was added to the text by the editors for what they thought might clarify the meaning. The vast majority of translations simply say, "Fill up the measure of your fathers." But a few add the word 'sin'. The word sin would actually make it clearer than the word guilt, for no greater crime has ever been committed on this planet than the crime against the Holy Son of God. The embodiment of love and truth and mercy and kindness and patience and goodness and gentleness was first rejected and then cruelly beaten and finally nailed to a cross to die. They nailed the source of all LOVE to a cross. They indeed 'filled up' and 'finished' the transgression; they capped off their wickedness with the ultimate sin.

2: To make an end of sins:

Romans 8:3 NKJV
For what the law could not do in that it was weak through the flesh, God *did* by sending His own Son in the likeness of sinful flesh, on account of sin: He condemned sin in the flesh,

Hebrews 9:25-26 NKJV
. . . not that He should offer Himself often, as the high priest enters the Most Holy Place every year with blood of another— 26 He then would have had to suffer often since the foundation of the world; but now, once at the end of the ages, He has appeared to put away sin by the sacrifice of Himself.

John 1:29 NKJV
The next day John saw Jesus coming toward him, and said, "Behold! The Lamb of God who takes away the sin of the world!"

Through Christ, sin is brought to an end.

3: To make reconciliation for iniquity:

2 Corinthians 5:19
. . . that God was in Christ, reconciling the world unto himself, not imputing their trespasses unto them; and hath committed unto us the word of reconciliation.

Praise the Lord, through Christ we find reconciliation with God.

4: To bring in everlasting righteousness:

Romans 3:21-22
But now the righteousness of God without the law is manifested, being witnessed by the law and the prophets; 22 Even the righteousness of God which is by faith of Jesus Christ unto all and upon all them that believe: for there is no difference:

Through Christ we have been made the righteousness of God.

5: To seal up the vision and prophecy:

Daniel 12:8-10
And I heard, but I understood not: then said I, O my Lord, what shall be the end of these things? 9 And he said, Go thy way, Daniel: for the words are closed up and sealed till the time of the end. 10 Many shall be purified, and made white, and tried; but the wicked shall do wickedly: and none of the wicked shall understand; but the wise shall understand.

Daniel heard but did not understand. Gabriel told him the words were sealed. At the time of the end, referred to above in Romans 9:26 as the end of the ages which is the end time of this prophecy, the wise will understand but the wicked shall not understand. The vision would remain sealed to the wicked.

Matthew 13:14-17
And in them is fulfilled the prophecy of Esaias, which saith, By hearing ye shall hear, and shall not understand; and seeing ye shall see, and shall not perceive: 15 For this people's heart is waxed gross, and their ears are dull of hearing, and their eyes they have closed; lest at any time they should see with their eyes and hear with their ears, and should understand with their heart, and should be converted, and I should heal them. 16 But blessed are your eyes, for they see: and your ears, for they hear. 17 For verily I say unto you, That many prophets and righteous men have desired to see those things which ye see, and have not seen them; and to hear those things which ye hear, and have not heard them.

The words were sealed to the wicked, so that they heard but did not understand, the vision was sealed so that they saw but did not perceive.

6: To anoint the Most Holy:

Acts 10:38
How God anointed Jesus of Nazareth with the Holy Ghost and with power: who went about doing good, and healing all that were oppressed of the devil; for God was with him.

At the baptism of John, Jesus, the Most Holy Son of God was anointed with the Holy Spirit and so we find in this passage that Daniel is preaching the Gospel of Christ, the Messiah, the

Anointed One. All of the six defining things that the prophecy says were to be accomplished were all fulfilled in the ministry of our Lord and Saviour Jesus Christ: in His life, His Baptism, His death and His Resurrection.

Daniel 9:25 NKJV
Know therefore and understand,
That from the going forth of the command
To restore and build Jerusalem
Until Messiah the Prince,
There shall be seven weeks and sixty-two weeks;
The street shall be built again, and the wall,
Even in troublesome times.

Seventy sevens equals four hundred and ninety and based on the day for a year principle that God has used in the Scriptures, this equals 490 years. The above verse divides this period into seven sevens plus sixty-two sevens which equals sixty-nine sevens. The seven sevens covers the troublesome times of the rebuilding of Jerusalem, which spanned 49 years and is recorded in the book of Nehemiah. This was followed by the sixty-two sevens representing 434 years, when added to the 49 years spans a total of 483 years from the going forth of the command to rebuild Jerusalem until the baptism of Jesus where He was anointed as Messiah by John the Baptist.

Daniel 9:26 NKJV
"And after the sixty-two weeks
Messiah shall be cut off, but not for Himself;

So then, after the seven weeks we have the sixty-two weeks, which means that sixty-nine weeks have been completed when Messiah is anointed. After the sixty-two weeks, after not during, Messiah shall be cut off. Therefore, following very ordinary and logical norms of comprehension and logic, and in accordance with the simplest laws of mathematics, we can safely with simplicity of mind assume that seventy actually does follow sixty-nine, and that it takes no stretch of the imagination to come to the conclusion that Messiah was cut off in the middle of the seventieth week, the week that followed the sixty-ninth week. I have laboured the point here because of so called scholars that insert a two thousand year gap between the 69th and 70th weeks, who are simply giving their minds over to the convoluted fantasy of leapfrog mathematics and a wild theory about some supposed future peace treaty that is supposed to be broken after three and a half years. How people read such a thing into the above verses is beyond me. In so doing, they take a Scripture speaking of the coming of Messiah and try to turn it into a future Antichrist. What spirit is behind that?! Mind you, there's plenty of money to be made selling books predicting when the 70th week is supposed to happen so perhaps they are smarter than I think. Excuse my rant.

The use of Hebrew parallelism in this next portion of the passage causes some confusion to western thinking, but it is a common literary feature in the Old Testament (and even on occasion in the New) in which the words of two or more phrases of text are directly related in some way, usually repeating a statement in another form. This Hebraism can be found in many poetic passages, and sometimes even in the narrative, although it is more commonly found in the Psalms and Proverbs.

Recognizing Hebraic parallelism as a literary feature can aid in understanding a passage. Specific words or phrases that may be ambiguous or used in unusual ways can be clarified or more narrowly defined by seeing them in the context of a parallel structure. In fact, if you take a linear approach to a Hebrew parallelism you will simply be confused and you will end up with a 'private interpretation'. It should be kept in mind that Old Testament writers were very creative, and a great number of variations and combinations of these basic types of parallelism occur in the biblical text.

Here are a couple of examples to illustrate:

Psalm 19:1-2 NKJV

The heavens declare the glory of God;
And the firmament shows His handiwork.

Day unto day utters speech,
And night unto night reveals knowledge.

In the first verse "the heavens declare the glory of God" parallels with the "firmament shows His handiwork." The second verse has "day unto day utters speech" in parallel with "night unto night reveals knowledge." Also in these two verses the general theme of God's handiwork is paralleled. Clever poetry.

See if you can see the parallelism in this next example:

Psalm 24:1-2

The earth is the Lord's, and the fulness thereof;
the world, and they that dwell therein.

For he hath founded it upon the seas,
and established it upon the floods.

Psalm 24:3-4

Who shall ascend into the hill of the Lord?
or who shall stand in his holy place?

He that hath clean hands,
and a pure heart;

who hath not lifted up his soul unto vanity,
nor sworn deceitfully.

Note: Verse 1. "The earth and the fullness thereof" parallels with "the world and they that dwell therein." And in verse 2. "Upon the seas" parallels with "upon the floods." In verses 3-4 we have a triple parallel.

These are rather simple examples, but I hope you see the principle even though the parallelisms used here in Daniel are a little more complex. Okay, back to the prophecy:

"And after the sixty-two weeks . . . . .

26
Messiah shall be cut off, but not for Himself;
And the people of the prince who is to come
Shall destroy the city and the sanctuary.
The end of it *shall be* with a flood,
And till the end of the war desolations are determined.

The next verse has the same message repeated in parallel form:

27
Then He shall confirm a covenant with many for one week;
But in the middle of the week He shall bring an end to sacrifice and offering.
And on the wing of abominations shall be one who makes desolate,
Even until the consummation, which is determined,
Is poured out on the desolate."

To help some of you 'get it', here is a repeat of the above parallelism, but this time phrase by phrase with the addition of the revelation from the New Testament:

26
Messiah shall be cut off

Paralleled with . . .

27
Then He shall confirm a covenant with many for one week

Luke 22:20 NKJV
Likewise He also *took* the cup after supper, saying, "This cup *is* the new covenant in My blood, which is shed for you.

1 Corinthians 11:25 NKJV
In the same manner *He* also *took* the cup after supper, saying, "This cup is the new covenant in My blood. This do, as often as you drink *it,* in remembrance of Me."

Messiah being cut off parallels with Him confirming a covenant. We continue:

26
but not for Himself

27
But in the middle of the week He shall bring an end to sacrifice and offering.

Jesus dying "not for Himself" parallels with "He shall bring an end to sacrifice and offering."

So now we can see the entire message more clearly. I shall paraphrase it for you. After three and a half years of anointed ministry (thus making it the "middle of the week" or more literally the middle of the seven), Jesus confirms a covenant with many in His own Blood, bringing to an end the need to make sacrifice and offering for sin when He was cut off, not for Himself, but for us.

The remainder of the "seventieth seven" is not given much attention in the passage. We only have the phrase, "He shall confirm a covenant with many for one week" (Dan 9:27). Later we will find mention of the three and a half years in Daniel 12 and from the New Testament we can gather the following: For three and a half years after the resurrection of our Lord, (the remainder of 'the week') the Gospel went to the Jews first and many entered into the New Covenant. Then the Gospel door was opened to the Gentiles. See also A Time, Times and Half a Time in the Appendix.

Truly this prophecy was fulfilled in every way. The precise event marking the end of the seventieth week is difficult to ascertain. Some consider it to be the martyrdom of Stephen in Acts Chapter 7 after which the Church was scattered under great persecution and they went everywhere preaching the Word. Others think it may have been the conversion of the household of Cornelius in Acts Chapter 10. Whilst not dogmatic as both suggestions have merit, I favour the latter as it was with this event that the Apostles recognised that, "God has also granted to the Gentiles repentance unto life" (Acts 11:18), so that the preaching was no longer to be exclusively for the Jews. Perhaps it was the Ethiopian eunuch, or the conversion and commissioning of Saul who later became Paul, the Apostle to the Gentiles. Whichever it was, there can be no doubt that many came into the Covenant in those first three and a half years. On the day of Pentecost there were three thousand converts in one day. James and all the elders declared to Paul before he was arrested in Jerusalem, "You see, brother, how many myriads of Jews there are who have believed" (Acts 21:20). The Greek word translated 'myriads' is literally 'tens of thousands'.

What follows is the final warning about what would happen soon after. Again we have Daniel presenting it in a parallelism:

Daniel 9:26b
And the people of the prince who is to come shall destroy the city and the sanctuary. The end of it shall be with a flood, and till the end of the war desolations are determined.

Daniel 9:27b
And on the wing of abominations shall be one who makes desolate, Even until the consummation, which is determined, is poured out on the desolate.

The awful prediction of "the prince who is to come shall destroy" parallels with "one who makes desolate." Followed by "the end of the war" brings desolation like "a flood" is paralleled with "the consummation . . . is poured out on the desolate." Truly the rest of the prophecy declared the awful consequences that were to follow. For those who would not believe, there was the destruction of the city and the sanctuary and the utter trampling of the host of Jews. This destruction is also mentioned in the interpretation of the vision in Chapter 8 and, as we shall see, in Daniel 12.

Daniel 8:11-13
Yea, he magnified himself even to the prince of the host, and by him the daily sacrifice was taken away, and the place of the sanctuary was cast down. 12 And an host was given him against the daily sacrifice by reason of transgression, and it cast down the truth to the ground; and it practised, and prospered. 13 Then I heard one saint speaking, and another saint said unto that certain saint which spake, How long shall be the vision concerning the daily sacrifice, and the transgression of desolation, to give both the sanctuary and the host to be trodden under foot?

Daniel 12:1
And at that time shall Michael stand up, the great prince which standeth for the children of thy people: and there shall be a time of trouble, such as never was since there was a nation even to that same time:

Daniel 12:6-12
And one said to the man clothed in linen, which was upon the waters of the river, How long shall it be to the end of these wonders? 7 And I heard the man clothed in linen, which was upon the waters of the river, when he held up his right hand and his left hand unto heaven, and sware by him that liveth for ever that it shall be for a time, times, and an half; and when he shall have accomplished to scatter the power of the holy people, all these things shall be finished. 8 And I heard, but I understood not: then said I, O my Lord, what shall be the end of these things? 9

And he said, Go thy way, Daniel: for the words are closed up and sealed till the time of the end. 10 Many shall be purified, and made white, and tried; but the wicked shall do wickedly: and none of the wicked shall understand; but the wise shall understand. 11 And from the time that the daily sacrifice shall be taken away, and the abomination that maketh desolate set up, there shall be a thousand two hundred and ninety days. 12 Blessed is he that waiteth, and cometh to the thousand three hundred and five and thirty days.

These things Jesus reiterated in His discourse recorded synoptically in Matthew, Mark and Luke:

Matthew 23:37-39
O Jerusalem, Jerusalem, thou that killest the prophets, and stonest them which are sent unto thee, how often would I have gathered thy children together, even as a hen gathereth her chickens under her wings, and ye would not! 38 Behold, your house is left unto you desolate. 39 For I say unto you, Ye shall not see me henceforth, till ye shall say, Blessed is he that cometh in the name of the Lord.

Matthew 24:1-2
And Jesus went out, and departed from the temple: and his disciples came to him for to shew him the buildings of the temple. 2 And Jesus said unto them, See ye not all these things? verily I say unto you, There shall not be left here one stone upon another, that shall not be thrown down.

Mark 13:1-2
And as he went out of the temple, one of his disciples saith unto him, Master, see what manner of stones and what buildings are here! 2 And Jesus answering said unto him, Seest thou these great buildings? there shall not be left one stone upon another, that shall not be thrown down.

Luke 21:5-6
And as some spake of the temple, how it was adorned with goodly stones and gifts, he said, 6 As for these things which ye behold, the days will come, in the which there shall not be left one stone upon another, that shall not be thrown down.

Daniel 8:13
". . . both the sanctuary and the host to be trodden under foot?

Luke 21:21-22
Then let them which are in Judaea flee to the mountains; and let them which are in the midst of it depart out; and let not them that are in the countries enter thereinto. 22 For these be the days of vengeance, that all things which are written may be fulfilled.

It is Jesus that said the destruction that was about to happen were the days of vengeance and that it was **the fulfilment of all the things that were written.** All the things written in Daniel 8, 9 and 12, concerning Messiah making a Covenant with many, the following Abomination of Desolation, and the trampling of the host of Jews was fulfilled in graphic detail. These passages in Daniel are clearly what Jesus was referring to as there are no other references to the Abomination of Desolation anywhere else in the Word of God.

A fuller account of the destruction wrought by the "people of the prince that was to come" can be found in the writings of Josephus, the Jewish historian whose historical record confirms the Gospel accounts (Josephus: *The Wars of the Jews*). "Let the reader understand."

Chapter Nine

The King of the North and
The King of the South

Judah's trail through history (from the time of King Cyrus to the Abomination of Desolation) was recorded in advance with an incredible amount of detail in this prophecy found in Daniel Chapters 11 and 12. Secular and liberal scholars consider these proclamations of Daniel to have been written after the fact and that Daniel was in effect but an historian and not a prophet. They believe that the accuracy of the events in these writings could not have come about by prior knowledge. But we know that he was a true prophet of God and the historical fulfilment of these prophecies testify to the reality that Daniel was truly inspired by the Holy Spirit. As surely as the prophecy concerning the writing on the wall was fulfilled the very night after Daniel spoke the Word of the Lord to King Belshazzar, and the prophecy concerning Nebuchadnezzar's humiliation and restoration was fulfilled in his life time, the other prophecies of Daniel will either have been fulfilled in history or will yet be fulfilled in due course.

In this study we will be examining one of the longest and certainly the most detailed prophecy in the whole Bible. To assist in understanding, the historical events that fulfilled each prediction are given verse by verse in an abbreviated form so as to keep the reader from being overwhelmed with information overload. John Calvin wrote over forty pages of historical references in his treatment of Daniel Chapter 11 which one is welcome to pursue if they are interested. (Commentary on Daniel Volume Two can be viewed at biblestudyguide.org/ebooks/comment/calcom25.pdf) The reality of the historical fulfilment of this prophecy is greatly contested so although I have not gone to the lengths that John Calvin did in his treatment of this passage, I have found it necessary to present more than I have for other parts of Scripture. Other sources substantiating the historical record can be found in the writings of Josephus and the Books of the Maccabees.

In Daniel Chapter Ten, the angel Gabriel again appears to the prophet and tells him he has a message for his people.

Daniel 10:14
Now I am come to make thee understand what shall befall thy people in the latter days: for yet the vision is for many days.

The prophecy begins in Chapter Eleven:

Daniel 11:1
Also I in the first year of Darius the Mede, even I, stood to confirm and to strengthen him.

Gabriel declares that he had strengthened Darius the Mede when he had come with the message about the coming of the Messiah in Daniel Chapter 9:1

Daniel 11:2
And now will I shew thee the truth. Behold, there shall stand up yet three kings in Persia; and the fourth shall be far richer than they all: and by his strength through his riches he shall stir up all against the realm of Grecia.

This prophecy was given in the third year of Cyrus, king of Persia 535BC. After Cyrus came his son, Cambyses II 530-522BC; then Gaumata the Magian, aka Smerdis 522BC; then Darius the Great 522-486BC (not Darius the Mede of Daniel 9:1). The fourth was Xerxes 486-465BC who shortly after becoming king began extensive preparations to attack Greece. He made alliances with many smaller states and gathered a huge fleet and a massive army that some have numbered around two million. Around 480BC he set out from Sardis and was at first successful but despite outnumbering the Greeks, the elements were against him and his fleet of over 1200 ships was defeated by the Greek fleet of less than four hundred. This was the beginning of the end of the Persian Empire.

Daniel 11:3
And a mighty king shall stand up, that shall rule with great dominion, and do according to his will.

This refers to Alexander the Great who established an empire that stretched from Southern Europe to North Africa to central Asia.

Daniel 11:4
And when he shall stand up, his kingdom shall be broken, and shall be divided toward the four winds of heaven; and not to his posterity, nor according to his dominion which he ruled: for his kingdom shall be plucked up, even for others beside those.

After Alexander died, his family and his generals fought for control of his empire. In the process the family members were killed and these four generals prevailed: Cassander ruled over Macedonia; Lysimachus ruled in Asia Minor; Seleucus I ruled over Syria, Babylon and Persia; and Ptolemy I ruled over the Holy Land and Egypt.

Daniel 11:5-6
And the king of the south shall be strong, and one of his princes; and he shall be strong above him, and have dominion; his dominion shall be a great dominion. 6 And in the end of years they shall join themselves together; for the king's daughter of the south shall come to the king of

the north to make an agreement: but she shall not retain the power of the arm; neither shall he stand, nor his arm: but she shall be given up, and they that brought her, and he that begat her, and he that strengthened her in these times.

Twenty years later in 281BC, when Seleucus I killed Lysimachus in battle, the main dynasties that remained were the Seleucid kings in the North and the Ptolemaic kings in the South and a much reduced smaller kingdom in Macedonia. In 249BC, Ptolemy II, King of the South, sought to make peace and unite with the King of the North, Antiochus II.

His plan was to unite the two kingdoms through marrying off his daughter Berenice. Antiochus II divorced his wife Laodice and married Berenice, figuring through peace he could regain what his father had lost to the king of the South. When Ptolemy II died in 246BC, Antiochus II decided to renounce his marriage to Berenice and return to Laodice. Laodice didn't trust him and soon murdered Antiochus II with poison and persuaded her son to kill both Berenice and her son, thus fulfilling the prophecy. Ptolemy II King of the South, Berenice, and Antiochus II King of the North all became losers in their power struggle.

Daniel 11:7
But out of a branch of her roots shall one stand up in his estate, which shall come with an army, and shall enter into the fortress of the king of the north, and shall deal against them, and shall prevail:

Ptolemy III, brother of Berenice, decided to avenge the murder of his sister. He immediately invaded the Seleucid Empire and defeated the forces of Seleucus II, son of Antiochus II. Laodice he captured and put to death.

Daniel 11:8
And he shall also carry their gods captive to Egypt, with their princes and their precious articles of silver and gold; and he shall continue more years than the king of the North.

Ptolemy III recovered many of the 'sacred' statues that had previously been taken from Egypt some three hundred years earlier. Ptolemy III also acquired much gold and silver from his campaign in Seleucia, receiving 1,500 talents of silver annually as tribute. He outlived Seleucus II 222BC, by four or five years.

Daniel 11:9
So the king of the south shall come into his kingdom, and shall return into his own land.

Note: This verse could be a summation of verses 7 and 8. The NKJV has the king of the North coming into the realm of the king of the South. Scholars and historians agree that during this period of time there were ongoing wars between the two kingdoms and thus the meaning of this verse could go either way and this disagreement is reflected in the different versions of this verse in English translations.

Daniel 11:10
But his sons shall be stirred up, and shall assemble a multitude of great forces: and one shall certainly come, and overflow, and pass through: then shall he return, and be stirred up, even to his fortress.

The sons of Seleucus II were Seleucus III Ceraunos (Thunder) and Antiochus III (the Great). Seleucus III, was unsuccessful in his attacks against Egypt and was killed by members of his own army in 223BC. Antiochus III who took the throne after his brother's death, went victoriously through Judea, and near the borders of Egypt.

Daniel 11:11
And the king of the south shall be moved with choler, and shall come forth and fight with him, even with the king of the north: and he shall set forth a great multitude; but the multitude shall be given into his hand.

Antiochus III met Ptolemy IV at the Battle of Gaza in 217BC, with 62,000 infantry, 6,000 cavalry, and over a hundred war elephants. But Ptolemy IV, King of the South, was nevertheless victorious and Antiochus III was forced to withdraw.

Daniel 11:12
And when he hath taken away the multitude, his heart shall be lifted up; and he shall cast down many ten thousands: but he shall not be strengthened by it.

After his victory, Ptolemy IV was hasty in settling affairs in Judea, returning quickly to his luxurious and decadent lifestyle in Egypt. After his victory at Gaza, the Egyptian troops who had fought the Seleucids began a successful guerrilla campaign against his rule and gained total independence in the southern part of Egypt.

Daniel 11:13
For the king of the north shall return, and shall set forth a multitude greater than the former, and shall certainly come after certain years with a great army and with much riches.

After the death of Ptolemy IV in 204BC, Antiochus III rallied his forces once again to attack the King of the South 202-195BC, taking Judea. But when he withdrew for the winter, the Egyptian commander Scopas reconquered the lost territory, including Judea and Jerusalem.

Daniel 11:14
And in those times there shall many stand up against the king of the south: also the robbers of thy people shall exalt themselves to establish the vision; but they shall fall.

Antiochus III made an alliance with King Philip V of Macedonia to take over the Ptolemaic Empire, and soon gained a significant victory against Scopas about 199BC at Paneas, north of Galilee. From the writings of Josephus:

Yet was it not long afterward when Antiochus overcame Scopas, in a battle fought at the fountains of Jordan, and destroyed a great part of his army. But afterward, when Antiochus subdued those cities of Celesyria which Scopas had gotten into his possession, and Samaria with them, the Jews, of their own accord, went over to him, and received him into the city [Jerusalem], and gave plentiful provision to all his army, and to his elephants, and readily assisted him when he besieged the garrison which was in the citadel of Jerusalem. (Ant. 12.3.3).

Daniel 11:15
So the king of the north shall come, and cast up a mount, and take the most fenced cities: and the arms of the south shall not withstand, neither his chosen people, neither shall there be any strength to withstand.

Scopas sought refuge in the fortified city of Sidon. Antiochus III besieged it and Scopas surrendered in 199BC in exchange for safe passage back to Egypt. They were allowed to leave the city naked and disarmed.

Daniel 11:16
But he that cometh against him shall do according to his own will, and none shall stand before him: and he shall stand in the glorious land, which by his hand shall be consumed.

With this victory over Scopas, Antiochus III then took the Holy Land from Egypt and so Judea and Jerusalem came under the dominion of the King of the North.

Daniel 11:17
He shall also set his face to enter with the strength of his whole kingdom, and upright ones with him; thus shall he do: and he shall give him the daughter of women, corrupting her: but she shall not stand on his side, neither be for him.

Young Ptolemy V made a treaty with Antiochus III. Ptolemy V surrendered Asia to the King of the North and married Antiochus III's daughter, Cleopatra I, in 194BC. Antiochus III sought access to Egypt through his daughter. But Cleopatra I was a true wife to Ptolemy V, standing by him and was beloved by the Egyptian people for her loyalty.

Daniel 11:18
After this shall he turn his face unto the isles, and shall take many: but a prince for his own behalf shall cause the reproach offered by him to cease; without his own reproach he shall cause it to turn upon him.

In 192BC, the ambitious Antiochus III crossed into Greece. To cover himself he sent ambassadors to Rome asking for friendship. Not accepting their conditions, Antiochus went to war against Rome. Defeated at the Battle of Magnesia, the Roman general Publius Scipio set a high cost on Antiochus III for peace. He demanded twenty hostages (including his son, Antiochus IV, who he later managed to exchange for his nephew Demetrius) and 15,000 talents over the next twelve years. Antiochus' all-consuming ambition eventually brought him to defeat.

Daniel 11:19
Then he shall turn his face toward the fort of his own land: but he shall stumble and fall, and not be found.

After the Roman victory over Antiochus III, the Seleucid Empire began to shrink. The kingdom was reduced to Syria, Mesopotamia, and western Iran and Antiochus III was in dire need of funds with which to pay Rome for the cost of the war. In 187BC, Antiochus III was killed while plundering a pagan temple in Babylon.

Daniel 11:20
Then shall stand up in his estate a raiser of taxes in the glory of the kingdom: but within few days he shall be destroyed, neither in anger, nor in battle.

Seleucus IV Philopater, took over after his father. Due to the heavy debt burden imposed by Rome, he began an ambitious taxation policy on his shrunken empire which included the people of Israel. Seleucus IV was poisoned by his minister Heliodorus.

Daniel 11:21
And in his estate shall stand up a vile person, to whom they shall not give the honour of the kingdom: but he shall come in peaceably, and obtain the kingdom by flatteries.

Antiochus IV, who later called himself Epiphanes (meaning 'manifest god') having been released from being a hostage, then arrived in Seleucia and thwarted Heliodorus' designs on the throne. He became co-regent and protector of Seleucus IV's infant son (also named Antiochus). In 170BC, the younger Antiochus was murdered while Antiochus IV was conveniently absent, paving the way for him to take sole possession of the throne.

Daniel 11:22
And with the arms of a flood shall they be overflown from before him, and shall be broken; yea, also the prince of the covenant.

Antiochus IV Epiphanes overcame all threats to his throne and became King of the North. The prince of the covenant here refers to the Jewish high priest Onias III who was the high priest when Antiochus IV came to the throne. The high priests were also the political rulers during this time when the Kingdom of Judah had no king, thus the term prince of the covenant. Antiochus IV forced Onias out and installed his brother Jason as high priest in Jerusalem in 174BC after receiving promises of a large bribe from Jason. Two years later, Jason was himself deposed by another contender named Menelaus by yet another bribe to Antiochus. Judah was at this time still a vassal state to the King of the North and was ruled by the priesthood.

Daniel 11:23

And after the league made with him he shall work deceitfully: for he shall come up, and shall become strong with a small people.

Antiochus IV sought to take advantage of the perceived weakness in the Ptolemaic kingdom. He moved through Syria and Judea into Egypt with a small army, hiding his true motive to take over Egypt, pretending he was coming to provide support for his young nephew, Ptolemy VI.

Daniel 11:24

He shall enter peaceably even upon the fattest places of the province; and he shall do that which his fathers have not done, nor his fathers' fathers; he shall scatter among them the prey, and spoil, and riches: yea, and he shall forecast his devices against the strong holds, even for a time.

Antiochus IV devised a clever plan for taking over the Ptolemaic kingdom. He began to give away the spoils of war to win the favour of the public. The historical book of I Maccabees mentions this particular method of gaining the loyalty of the citizens (I Maccabee 3:30). He also covertly visited the Egyptian strongholds to find out their strengths and weaknesses.

Daniel 11:25-26

And he shall stir up his power and his courage against the king of the south with a great army; and the king of the south shall be stirred up to battle with a very great and mighty army; but he shall not stand: for they shall forecast devices against him. 26 Yea, they that feed of the portion of his meat shall destroy him, and his army shall overflow: and many shall fall down slain.

In 170BC, in what came to be known as the Sixth Syrian War, Antiochus IV began to take Egypt by force. He had by this time corrupted many of the generals and high officials of the Egyptian army who considered the young king as being weak. The King of the South was betrayed and although his army was greater in numbers he was defeated at both Pelusium and Memphis though he still held on to his capitol in Alexandria.

Daniel 11:27

And both of these kings' hearts shall be to do mischief, and they shall speak lies at one table; but it shall not prosper: for yet the end shall be at the time appointed.

After Pelusium and Memphis, Antiochus IV made plans to take Alexandria, but whilst the high officials were disenchanted with Ptolemy VI, they had made his younger brother king; Ptolemy Euergetes. Antiochus IV turned to diplomacy, professing friendship and concern for his nephew, but his true plan was to further weaken Egypt by setting the brothers against one another. Meanwhile Ptolemy VI sought peace with his brother Ptolemy Euergetes so they could join forces against their conniving uncle. (Kind of confusing with all these descendants constantly called by the same name)

Daniel 11:28
Then shall he return into his land with great riches; and his heart shall be against the holy covenant; and he shall do exploits, and return to his own land.

While Antiochus IV was in Egypt, a false report arose in Judea that he had been killed. The scheming and deposed high priest Jason took the opportunity to raise an army of 1,000 men and attack Jerusalem, forcing Menelaus to take refuge in the fortress in Jerusalem. When Antiochus IV received the news, he took it that Judea was in revolt, so he left Egypt and marched against Jerusalem, commanding his soldiers to kill everyone they encountered; men, women, and children. Within three days, his forces had killed somewhere between 40,000 and 80,000 people. Many were captured and sold into slavery. Not satisfied with the slaughter, Antiochus IV entered the Temple and took everything of value that he and his soldiers could lay their hands on.

Daniel 11:29
At the time appointed he shall return, and come toward the south; but it shall not be as the former, or as the latter.

Meanwhile, the Egyptian brothers had reconciled and agreed to share power, asserting themselves against Antiochus IV. In 168BC, he again sought to go to war against Egypt. However, things were not the same.

Daniel 11:30
For the ships of Chittim shall come against him: therefore he shall be grieved, and return, and have indignation against the holy covenant: so shall he do; he shall even return, and have intelligence with them that forsake the holy covenant.

The Ptolemy brothers had appealed to Rome for help and the Romans agreed to provide assistance. The "ships of Chittim" here refer to the ships which brought the Roman legions to Egypt. Chittim is the ancient name for Cyprus. When Antiochus IV marched toward Alexandria, he was confronted by a delegation of three Roman senators. The Roman ambassador Popillius delivered to Antiochus IV the Senate's demand that he withdraw from Egypt. Realizing he had been outwitted and was now outnumbered, he returned to Syria. On the way back he decided to take his frustration out on the Jews yet again, encircling and attacking Jerusalem and giving favour to those Jews who were pro-hellenistic and had allied themselves with him.

Daniel 11:31
And arms shall stand on his part, and they shall pollute the sanctuary of strength, and shall take away the daily sacrifice, and they shall place the abomination that maketh desolate.

Antiochus IV's army defiled the Temple and stopped the daily sacrifices. They turned the altar of burnt offering into a pagan altar, erected an image of Zeus and offered pigs to their god. They then placed a garrison to prohibit the Jews from using the Temple and it was left desolate for over three years. It is understandable to confuse this mention of an abomination of desolation with that which appears at the end of Chapters 8 & 9 because at first mention it seems like the same event. But careful attention to detail does not allow us to come to the conclusion that they are speaking of the same incident, as this abomination of desolation did not result in the total destruction of the temple and merely left it defiled and desecrated. As we come toward the end of Chapter 12, near the conclusion of this present prophecy, we will find another abomination of desolation which did result in the temple being utterly cast down and which does conform with that revealed in Daniel's previous prophecies. For more on this subject see The Abomination of Desolation in the Appendix.

Daniel 11:32-35
And such as do wickedly against the covenant shall he corrupt by flatteries: but the people that do know their God shall be strong, and do exploits. 33 And they that understand among the people shall instruct many: yet they shall fall by the sword, and by flame, by captivity, and by spoil, many days. 34 Now when they shall fall, they shall be holpen with a little help: but many shall cleave to them with flatteries. 35 And some of them of understanding shall fall, to try them, and to purge, and to make them white, even to the time of the end: because it is yet for a time appointed.

Antiochus began a program of aggressive Hellenization, commanding all to forsake their laws and customs. Using flattery, he corrupted many of the Jews to profane their feasts and Sabbaths. Those who were caught teaching the law or possessing a copy of the Torah were put to death along with any families who circumcised their children. Many chose to be martyred rather than break the holy covenant.

These atrocities eventually led to the rebellion by "the people who know their God". This was started by the priest Mattathias and his five sons, the most prominent being Judas Maccabee. Recorded in the Books of the Maccabees and also in Josephus' writings, the Maccabean revolt eventually resulted in the Jews throwing off the yoke of the Greeks and rededicating the temple. The Jews celebrate this event to this day with the Feast of Dedication which was inaugurated in 164BC. This was one of the feasts of the Jews recorded in the New Testament that Jesus visited the temple on (John 10:22). This feast is also known as the Feast of Lights or Hanukah. Incidentally, in that same year (164BC) Antiochus IV fell sick, became bedridden and died.

After the Judean victory over the Seleucids, the surrounding Gentile nations (mostly still under Greek dominion) began a severe persecution of those Jews who lived among them. Judas Maccabee and his brother Simon went to war against those nations and defeated them. Judas was killed in battle in 161BC, but persecution continued upon the Jews. Many wicked Jews who had been Hellenized took opportunity after his death to kill righteous Jews. However, the Jews, led by the Hasmoneans (named after Mattathias' grandfather, Asmoneus) continued to prevail and their rule lasted from 168BC until about 37BC, during which time the Kingdom of Judah regained boundaries not far short of Solomon's realm.

At the same time the Greek Seleucid Empire entered into its final stages. Having been weakened by the successes of the Jews, the rising Parthian Empire of the Persians captured Seleucia in 141BC. Later the Armenians expanded their borders into Syria throughout the early first century and finally the Roman Empire under general Pompey put an end to the Greeks being identified as the 'King of the North' in 64BC.

Daniel 11:36

And the king shall do according to his will; and he shall exalt himself, and magnify himself above every god, and shall speak marvellous things against the God of gods, and shall prosper till the indignation be accomplished: for that that is determined shall be done.

In this verse, the king being spoken of again changes as it has throughout the passage. But this time "the king" is not referenced as the King of the North or the King of the South as the rest of prophecy does, but simply introduces him as "the king". From verse 21, Antiochus IV Epiphanes was the referenced King of the South, and in verses 32 through 35 we find the prophecy of the Maccabees/Hasmoneans which resulted in the rule of their dynasty. Therefore, the remaining verses in this chapter cannot apply to Antiochus IV as many assert, for as noted above, history declares that he was already long dead.

Most Christian scholars insert a huge chronological gap in the prophecy here in their efforts to make the rest of the prophecy apply to an end-time Antichrist (as they do with Daniel Chapter 9), despite the fact that there is absolutely nothing in the text to warrant such an illogical leap. (Not saying there isn't an end-time Antichrist, just that this passage of Scripture is not concerned with that subject.) Therefore, at this point this author departs from the consensus of the majority in order to follow recorded history, both secular and biblical.

Secular history AND the New Testament record the acts of a king who appeared on the scene in Israel at the end of the Hasmonean period. By way of reminder we will repeat Daniel 8:23-25 which also describes this king and gives us the necessary details that will enable us to identify this character.

Daniel 8:23-25 NKJV

And in the latter time of their kingdom,
When the transgressors have reached their fullness,
A king shall arise,
Having fierce features,
Who understands sinister schemes.
24 His power shall be mighty, but not by his own power;
He shall destroy fearfully,
And shall prosper and thrive;
He shall destroy the mighty, and *also* the holy people.
25 Through his cunning
He shall cause deceit to prosper under his rule;

And he shall exalt *himself* in his heart.
He shall destroy many in *their* prosperity.
He shall even rise against the Prince of princes;
But he shall be broken without *human* means.

In particular note the following phrases from the above passage:

Verse 24 "His power shall be mighty, but not by his own power"

There was a vassal king appointed by Rome.

Verse 25b "He shall even rise against the Prince of princes"

The Prince of princes is most certainly a reference to Jesus and there was a king who attempted to kill Jesus when he was a child.

Verse 25b "But he shall be broken without *human* means."

There was a king at this time in history who died of sickness and disease. Despite his many enemies, Herod's death was not by the hand of any man.

These verses from Daniel 8 speak of the same period of time as these verses here in Daniel 11. There was a king who fulfilled every prophetic description given in verses 36 through 39 and that king was Herod the Great who came to power in Judea around 37BC.

In verse 36, as we noted above, the one spoken of is not identified as either the King of the North or the King of the South, but simply as "the king." Herod was seated as king on the throne of Israel when Jesus was born. He is simply called "the king" in the Gospels (Matt. 2:1, 3, 9; Luke 1:5). Let's look at the specific points in the prophecy and see how Herod fulfilled them.

Daniel 11:36
And the king shall do according to his will; and he shall exalt himself, and magnify himself above every god, and shall speak marvellous things against the God of gods, and shall prosper till the indignation be accomplished: for that that is determined shall be done.

". . . the king shall do according to his will"

This phrase is used previously during this prophecy. In Daniel 11:3, it refers to Alexander the Great that he would "do according to his will" and in Daniel 11:16 it is Antiochus the Great who "shall do according to his own will". This means more than simply being a strong-willed ruler. Alexander and Antiochus III had great success achieving their own goals and maintaining power.

Through bribery, polygamous marriage arrangements, ingratiating himself with clever diplomacy, scheming and even murder; doing according to his own will suitably describes the behaviour of Herod the Great.

"... he shall exalt himself, and magnify himself above every god"

The word "god" here is the Hebrew word *el*, the primary meanings being: 'god', as in a pagan or false god; 'God' as in the true God of Israel; and less frequently, 'the mighty', referring to men or angels. Herod exalted and magnified himself above all, whether priests or rulers or gods. He appointed whomever he chose to the sacred office of high priest; in his lust for absolute power he murdered even close family members. Herod truthfully could be said to have exalted and magnified himself above all other gods including the God of Israel. (More on this below)

"(he) shall speak marvellous things against the God of gods"

The Hebrew word *niphla'ot* that is rendered "marvellous" in the KJV is rendered "blasphemies" in the NKJV, but it actually means 'marvellous' if it used in a positive sense or 'astonishing' if it is used in a negative sense, so the KJV is partially correct along with many other translations. The Merriam-Webster Dictionary lists astonishing, staggering and stunning as synonyms of marvellous. This charge against Herod primarily refers to his command to slaughter the male babies of Bethlehem, which is astonishing in its absolute ruthless disregard for the lives of countless children. His express purpose was to destroy the coming Messiah (Matthew 2:4), the one God had promised to send to be King over His people Israel. Herod's astonishing command was a direct blasphemous attack against the will of God.

Daniel 11:37
Neither shall he regard the God of his fathers, nor the desire of women, nor regard any god: for he shall magnify himself above all.

"Neither shall he regard the God of his fathers . . . nor regard any god"

Herod was an Idumean, which is Greek for Edomite (a descendant of Esau), whose family had converted to Judaism in the 2nd century BC. Yet, contrary to his fathers, Herod promoted Greek and Roman gods. He built a huge temple dedicated to the worship of Caesar Augustus, the Roman emperor/god. He also supported the restoration of the temple of Pythian Apollo on the Greek island of Rhodes and participated in the building of temples in Tyre and Sidon. Herod extensively remodelled the Temple in Jerusalem and placed a huge golden Roman eagle at the main entrance. When some devout Jews destroyed this emblem of idolatry, Herod had them burned alive. Herod's religious activities were totally of expedience as he exalted himself above all gods.

"... nor the desire of women"

In biblical times, children were indeed "the desire of women". It was considered a reproach to be childless and the Scriptures provide us with many examples of this desire being expressed in various ways: The women in Isaiah 4:1; Hannah in 1 Samuel 1:1-20; Rachel in Genesis 30:23; Lot's daughters in Genesis 19:30-36; and Elizabeth in Luke 1:25. (How unlike many women of our present generation who use contraception and kill their children in the womb.) Herod's attempt to murder the infant Messiah by having countless babies killed shows that he had no regard for the maternal nature of women. Every one of the little children was the desire of his own mother.

Daniel 11:38
But in his estate shall he honour the god of forces: and a god whom his fathers knew not shall he honour with gold, and silver, and with precious stones, and pleasant things.

Herod's actions in securing and holding on to power provide an impressive fulfilment of this verse. The phrase "god of forces," or "fortresses" as it is rendered in the NKJV, is uncommon enough that it provides us a ready means of identification. The Roman emperors exalted themselves as "gods," and it was by their military "forces" or "fortresses" that they enlarged and sustained their power and their empire.

Herod was constantly honouring the Roman emperors who proclaimed themselves to be gods. He rebuilt the ancient Phoenician coastal fortress and renamed it Caesarea in honour of Caesar Augustus; he rebuilt Samaria, and renamed it Sebaste (*sebastos* was the Greek word for reverend and is equivalent to the Latin *augustus*). He also built many other fortified cities and named them in honour of Caesar and often sent delegations to Rome with gifts of silver and gold.

Daniel 11:39
Thus shall he do in the most strong holds with a strange god, whom he shall acknowledge and increase with glory: and he shall cause them to rule over many, and shall divide the land for gain.

By promoting the glory of the Romans, Herod secured their support and backing to overcome all of his enemies. Herod also gave land and authority in order to secure the allegiance of those who supported him.

Daniel 11:40
And at the time of the end shall the king of the south push at him: and the king of the north shall come against him like a whirlwind, with chariots, and with horsemen, and with many ships; and he shall enter into the countries, and shall overflow and pass over.

During the time of Herod's rise to power in Judea, the internal politics of the Roman Empire resulted in the assassination of Julius Caesar in 44BC and a resultant civil war. After the assassin's forces were defeated, a further civil war broke out, but this time it included the realm of the King of the South as the Roman Mark Antony had married Cleopatra VII, the Ptolemaic

Greek Queen of Egypt, and sought with her aid to take over the entire Roman Empire in 31BC. Thus the King of the South here is Mark Antony with his wife and ally Cleopatra VII; the King of the North is Octavius, the official representative of Rome and ruler of the former Seleucid Empire.

The Roman historian Plutarch wrote that the first move in the war was made by Antony at the insistence of Cleopatra. Thus we see that the King of the South indeed first attacked the King of the North. The Roman Senate quickly pronounced Antony an outlaw and declared war on Cleopatra.

The prophecy's mention of "chariots, horsemen, and with many ships" was accurately fulfilled. Despite the fact that each side had large infantry forces, Plutarch records that these infantry were not used at all in the short war which was fought mainly with hundreds of ships off the coast of Actium, Greece in 31BC. Antony and Cleopatra's naval fleet was completely routed and thus their infantry deserted and never saw battle.

Daniel 11:41
He shall enter also into the glorious land, and many countries shall be overthrown: but these shall escape out of his hand, even Edom, and Moab, and the chief of the children of Ammon.

Octavius pursued Antony and Cleopatra through Syria, Judea (the glorious land) and Egypt, and although a failed attempt was made some years later against the lands of Edom, Moab, and Ammon (about 25BC), it was not successful and eventually they were left alone.

Daniel 11:42
He shall stretch forth his hand also upon the countries: and the land of Egypt shall not escape.

Antony's efforts to regroup his forces in Alexandria failed as most of his soldiers deserted to join Octavius. Rather than suffer being captured, both Antony and Cleopatra ended up committing suicide.

Daniel 11:43
But he shall have power over the treasures of gold and of silver, and over all the precious things of Egypt: and the Libyans and the Ethiopians shall be at his steps.

The days of Egypt's power and wealth came to an end as Octavius utterly plundered the immense wealth that had been accumulated during the Ptolemaic rule. Octavius celebrated his triumph in Rome in 29BC, leaving his general, Cornelius Balbus to take Libya and Ethiopia for the Empire. The events of verses 40-43 show how Rome's domination over Judea was fully established and also shows the end of the King of the South.

Daniel 11:44-45
But tidings out of the east and out of the north shall trouble him: therefore he shall go forth with great fury to destroy, and utterly to make away many. 45 And he shall plant the tabernacles of his palace between the seas in the glorious holy mountain; yet he shall come to his end, and none shall help him.

The accuracy of this entire prophecy is astounding. As mentioned before, secular critics want to make Daniel a historian and not a prophet. However, when it comes to this part of the passage, it seems that many Christian scholars have difficulty identifying who the "he" is in these final verses of Chapter 11, and that is fully understandable considering some of the vagaries of Hebrew grammar and its lack of punctuation, and also the cryptic metaphoric reference to historical characters as horns, King of the South etc.

History does not allow us to attribute the events contained in these two verses to the King of the North, UNLESS we see Herod as being the northern king's proxy. Indeed, that is what he had become. During the Roman civil war, Herod initially sided with Mark Antony and Cleopatra, but when he saw the turn of events, he shrewdly went to Octavius declaring that just as he had been loyal to Antony he would now be loyal to Octavius. Octavius accepted his pleadings and thus Herod continued to rule Judea as a vassal king of the King of the North.

The vision in Chapter 8 with its interpretation supports this view as noted above in Daniel 8:23-25 where we have a clear description of Herod as being "mighty but not by his own power". Yet that very 'horn' rises from the north west of the Greek empire which is definitely historically Rome (Daniel 8:9-13). There is a consistency in this all through the prophecy where the actual person doing the deeds changes in history, yet is still called King of the North or King of the South in the narrative.

The correctness of this view is confirmed by the accuracy of the predictions being fulfilled in the life of Herod as recorded in both secular history and the New Testament.

Matthew 2:1-3
Now when Jesus was born in Bethlehem of Judaea in the days of Herod the king, behold, there came wise men from the east to Jerusalem, 2 Saying, Where is he that is born King of the Jews? for we have seen his star in the east, and are come to worship him.

3 When Herod the king had heard these things, he was troubled, and all Jerusalem with him.

What could be a more literal fulfilment of the words "But tidings out of the east and out of the north shall trouble him" than this account in Matthew's Gospel, ". . . there came wise men from the east . . . When Herod the king had heard these things, he was troubled". Here is the rest of verse 44 from the NKJV which is a little easier to understand: "therefore he shall go out with great fury to destroy and annihilate many." These words are clearly fulfilled in the following account of Herod's furious anger:

Matthew 2:16
Then Herod, when he saw that he was mocked of the wise men, was exceeding wroth, and sent forth, and slew all the children that were in Bethlehem, and in all the coasts thereof, from two years old and under, according to the time which he had diligently inquired of the wise men.

Daniel 11:45
And he shall plant the tabernacles of his palace between the seas in the glorious holy mountain; yet he shall come to his end, and none shall help him.

The final words of Daniel 11 are: "Yet he shall come to his end, and none shall help him." Here's an account of Herod's death: James Farquharson *Daniel's Last Vision And Prophecy* Pages 148-149.

"This part of the prediction obviously implies that, in his last hours, the king would apply for deliverance or remedy, from some affliction or disease, but would receive none. And how literally was this fulfilled in the end of Herod the Great! History has preserved to us few such circumstantial accounts of the last days of remarkable men, as that which Josephus has transmitted to us of his; but we deem it too long for insertion here. It exhibits the most fearful picture to be found anywhere of the end of an impenitent sinner, who, having cast out of his heart all fear of God and all feeling of responsibility to Him, had equally lost all sense of duty to man; and after committing innumerable crimes and cruelties-in which he spared not those connected with him by the dearest and tenderest ties, any more than others-was at last seized in his old age with a painful and loathsome disease; and suffering alike from that, and from the pangs of guilty fear, yet continued in a course of extreme wickedness to his last hour, seeking no remedy for his evil passions, but exhausting all the resources of the physician's skill to mitigate his bodily distemper and lengthen out his wretched life. We refer to Josephus for an account of the remedies and expedients to which he had recourse by the advice of his physicians; all of which failed to relieve or arrest the disease which cut him off while he was meditating new crimes of matchless cruelty."

Thus he came to his end, and none helped him. He died a prey to horrible diseases, and to horrible remorse, just five days after he had ordered the execution of his oldest son. Herod the king was 70 years old at the time of his death. After Herod's death, Joseph and Mary returned from Egypt after being instructed yet again by an angel in a dream. Truly those who knew the Scriptures should have been well able to recognize the signs of the times with these clear references in the Book of Daniel to enlighten their eyes. No wonder Jesus rebuked the Scribes and the Pharisees for their failure to recognize the times they were in. This wicked King Herod who had arisen, whose deeds and manner of death were there in the prophecies with which they were familiar, yet they missed it. However, many today still miss the obvious correlation of prophecy and history in these passages from Daniel and Matthew. As a consequence, they have to invent all manner of confusing scenarios. Let us continue and carefully examine precisely what is being said as we continue into Daniel Chapter Twelve.

Let us be aware that the angel Gabriel is still giving Daniel the understanding of the vision. Just as Gabriel had instructed Daniel in chapters 8 and 9 concerning the culmination of the vision being the destruction associated with the Abomination of Desolation, he is explaining the same scenario here. By way of reminder, in the prelude to this long prophecy, Gabriel revealed that the message Daniel was to understand is directly concerned with Daniel's people, the Jews.

Daniel 10:14
Now I am come to make thee understand what shall befall **thy people** in the latter days: for yet the vision is for many days . . . (Emphasis mine)

Daniel 12:1
"And at that time shall Michael stand up, the great prince which standeth for the children of **thy people**: and there shall be a time of trouble, such as never was since there was a nation even to that same time: and at that time **thy people** shall be delivered, every one that shall be found written in the book. (Emphasis mine)

The time of trouble is all to do with Judah. This is not a prophecy concerning the fate of the Gentiles. The Gentile kings of the North and the South are mentioned for they are the kingdoms that afflicted Judah through this long period of time. Gabriel made it clear in these two verses that the prophecy concerns "thy people" or if you prefer: "your people" as we say these days. In so doing he set the parameters by which we are to understand what he was saying.

And just as there is no gap between 69 and 70 in mathematics, nor in the seventy week prophecy, there is no two thousand year gap in time between the last verse in chapter 11 and the first verse of chapter 12. As we are all aware, the original writing had no chapter divisions and so we will continue with the narrative given by the angel.

Daniel 12:1
". . . there shall be a time of trouble, such as never was since there was a nation even to that same time"

Precisely at the time of history foretold in this prophecy, there was a time of great trouble without precedent. The Romans declared war against the Jews in order to quell their rebellion, which culminated with the destruction of the city of Jerusalem and the second temple in 70AD.

Over a million people were slaughtered by the Roman soldiers, many died from starvation during the siege, there was a civil war going on inside the city as three different factions of the Jews fought among themselves for dominance. It was absolute mayhem, a time of unprecedented turmoil and trouble.

Truly we can see the fulfilment of these words in the writings in the Gospels.

Matthew 24:19
For then shall be great tribulation, such as was not since the beginning of the world to this time, no, nor ever shall be.

Mark 13:19
For in those days shall be affliction, such as was not from the beginning of the creation which God created unto this time, neither shall be.

Luke 19:41-44
And when he was come near, he beheld the city, and wept over it, 42 Saying, If thou hadst known, even thou, at least in this thy day, the things which belong unto thy peace! but now they are hid from thine eyes. 43 For the days shall come upon thee, that thine enemies shall cast a trench about thee, and compass thee round, and keep thee in on every side, 44 And shall lay thee even with the ground, and thy children within thee; and they shall not leave in thee one stone upon another; because thou knewest not the time of thy visitation.

Mark 13:14-19
But when ye shall see the abomination of desolation, spoken of by Daniel the prophet, standing where it ought not, (let him that readeth understand,) then let them that be in Judaea flee to the mountains: 15 And let him that is on the housetop not go down into the house, neither enter therein, to take any thing out of his house: 16 And let him that is in the field not turn back again for to take up his garment. 17 But woe to them that are with child, and to them that give suck in those days! 18 And pray ye that your flight be not in the winter. 19 For in those days shall be affliction, such as was not from the beginning of the creation which God created unto this time, neither shall be.

Matthew 24:15-21
When ye therefore shall see the abomination of desolation, spoken of by Daniel the prophet, stand in the holy place, (whoso readeth, let him understand:) 16 Then let them which be in Judaea flee into the mountains: 17 Let him which is on the housetop not come down to take any thing out of his house: 18 Neither let him which is in the field return back to take his clothes. 19 And woe unto them that are with child, and to them that give suck in those days! 20 But pray ye that your flight be not in the winter, neither on the sabbath day: 21 For then shall be great tribulation, such as was not since the beginning of the world to this time, no, nor ever shall be.

Luke 21:20-24
And when ye shall see Jerusalem compassed with armies, then know that the desolation thereof is nigh. 21 Then let them which are in Judaea flee to the mountains; and let them which are in the midst of it depart out; and let not them that are in the countries enter thereinto. 22 For these be the days of vengeance, that all things which are written may be fulfilled. 23 But woe unto them that are with child, and to them that give suck, in those days! for there shall be great distress in the land, and wrath upon this people. 24 And they shall fall by the edge of the sword, and shall be led away captive into all nations: and Jerusalem shall be trodden down of the Gentiles, until the times of the Gentiles be fulfilled.

Paul also writes about that which was to come upon them because of their utter unbelief and sinfulness.

1 Thessalonians 2:14-16

For ye, brethren, became followers of the churches of God which in Judaea are in Christ Jesus: for ye also have suffered like things of your own countrymen, even as they have of the Jews: 15 Who both killed the Lord Jesus, and their own prophets, and have persecuted us; and they please not God, and are contrary to all men: 16 Forbidding us to speak to the Gentiles that they might be saved, to fill up their sins alway: for the wrath is come upon them to the uttermost.

So, we have Daniel saying, ". . . there shall be a time of trouble, such as never was since there was a nation even to that same time." We have Matthew saying "For then shall be great tribulation, such as was not since the beginning of the world to this time, no, nor ever shall be." We have Mark saying, "For in those days shall be affliction, such as was not from the beginning of the creation which God created unto this time, neither shall be." We have Luke saying, ". . . there shall be great distress in the land, and wrath upon this people. And finally we have Paul saying, ". . . wrath is come upon them to the uttermost."

And with particular attention to the context we then find Daniel saying these words:

Daniel 12:1b

"and at that time thy people shall be delivered, every one that shall be found written in the book."

Daniel 12:2

And many of them that sleep in the dust of the earth shall awake, some to everlasting life, and some to shame and everlasting contempt.

Some people think these two verses are speaking of the resurrection because of the mention of the book of life. Having already assumed a two thousand year gap, their conjecture is understandable. But let us look closely at what is written for it will reveal that the ones who were delivered and the ones sleeping in the dust of the earth are not to be equated with those who rise from the dead in the resurrection at the end of the age which Jesus says is on the last day (John 6:39,40,44,54). More on that later.

As mentioned above, Daniel is told that it is "your people" that shall be delivered. During the introduction to the prophecy in verse 10:14, Gabriel limited the scope of the prophecy to "your people". This has nothing to do with the Gentiles, but everything to do with the Jews.

A study of the use of the word "delivered" reveals that in over two hundred instances it speaks of deliverance from one's enemies. The first ten are listed here to give you some idea how this word is normally used.

Genesis 14:20
And blessed be the most high God, which hath delivered thine enemies into thy hand.

Genesis 32:16
And he delivered them into the hand of his servants, every drove by themselves; and said unto his servants, Pass over before me, and put a space betwixt drove and drove.

Genesis 37:21
And Reuben heard it, and he delivered him out of their hands; and said, Let us not kill him.

Exodus 2:19
And they said, An Egyptian delivered us out of the hand of the shepherds, and also drew water enough for us, and watered the flock.

Exodus 5:23
For since I came to Pharaoh to speak in thy name, he hath done evil to this people; neither hast thou delivered thy people at all.

Exodus 12:27
That ye shall say, It is the sacrifice of the Lord's passover, who passed over the houses of the children of Israel in Egypt, when he smote the Egyptians, and delivered our houses. And the people bowed the head and worshipped.

Exodus 18:4
And the name of the other was Eliezer; for the God of my father, said he, was mine help, and delivered me from the sword of Pharaoh:

Exodus 18:8
And Moses told his father in law all that the Lord had done unto Pharaoh and to the Egyptians for Israel's sake, and all the travail that had come upon them by the way, and how the Lord delivered them.

Exodus 18:9
And Jethro rejoiced for all the goodness which the Lord had done to Israel, whom he had delivered out of the hand of the Egyptians.

Exodus 18:10
And Jethro said, Blessed be the Lord, who hath delivered you out of the hand of the Egyptians, and out of the hand of Pharaoh, who hath delivered the people from under the hand of the Egyptians.

Apart from the droves of sheep Jacob delivered into the care of his servants, all of these refer to being delivered from their enemies who would destroy them. It is never used as a reference to the resurrection.

Writings from the early church record a great deliverance that happened during that period of time. In Eusebius' Book III, 5:4 we find recorded the following:

"The members of the Jerusalem church by means of an oracle, given by revelation to acceptable persons there, were ordered to leave the city before the war began and settle in a town in Peraea called Pella".

All the believing Jews, i.e. everyone whose name was written in the Book of Life, were delivered from that terrible time of trouble. The whole of the Jewish church in the land escaped into the mountain villages east of the Jordan and Lake Galilee, the bulk of the Jerusalem church entering a city called Pella. For those in Jerusalem, Josephus records at least two opportunities for this deliverance to have been accomplished besides the opportunities before the beginning of the war.

In 66AD, the Roman military commanded by Cestius Gallus, came to Jerusalem to put down the Jewish rebellion. After surrounding the city they began their siege. Then, for no apparent reason, Cestius withdrew his troops and left the area. The Jews pursued the Romans, slaughtering many and capturing their abandoned war machinery. This fact of history has been recorded for us by Josephus, in his work entitled, *The Wars of the Jews*, Book 2, Chapter 19, Paragraph 7.

Referring to them as Jews (which the believers were), Josephus also verifies their departure from Jerusalem when he wrote, *"after this calamity had befallen Cestius, many of the most eminent of the Jews swam [left, departed] away from the city, as from a ship when it was going to sink."* Josephus, The Wars of the Jews, Book 2, Chapter 20, Paragraph 1.

Deliverance is exactly what was accomplished for the people of God who knew the instructions of the Lord to flee when the armies were surrounding Jerusalem. They were delivered; all of them. And their names are written in the Book of Life. And so is mine. Hallelujah! And so is yours, if your faith is in the one true God and in His Son, Jesus Christ. May you be delivered from all that Satan would send against you. Amen.

In 67AD, Vespasian, a veteran general was then sent to Jerusalem to crush the Jewish uprising and to avenge Rome's humiliation and the damage to its ruling prestige by the Cestius incident. Vespasian advanced into Galilee, a region north of Jerusalem. He conquered its major cities and subdued the land of that area. After his Galilean campaign in the north, he marched south and encamped around Jerusalem. But when word came of Nero's death back in Rome. Vespasian then delayed his plan for taking Jerusalem, withdrew his troops, and returned to Rome to become emperor. Once again, the Jews believed they had prevailed and the church was given additional time to leave the city, if they had not already left.

In 70AD, shortly before Passover, Titus, the son of Vespasian, arrived with his legions at the northern outskirts of Jerusalem to finally put an end to the Jewish revolt and to crush the insurrection. He marched south through Galilee and set up three camps overlooking the city. During the final siege, those who sought to flee were either prevented from doing so; killed by the Jewish factions inside who treated them as cowards; or captured, tortured, and crucified by the Romans near the city wall so that all could see. By this time it was too late to flee; Titus and the Roman legions trapped all those inside the city walls.

Josephus details how the Romans encircled and built an embankment or rampart to breach the city walls, just as Jesus had foretold in Luke 19:43-44. Josephus further notes: *that five hundred or more were captured daily and that soldiers out of rage and hatred amused themselves by nailing their prisoners in different postures; so great was their number that space could not be found for the crosses nor crosses for their bodies (The Wars of the Jews,* book five, chapter 11). Josephus goes on to say that 1.1 million Jews were killed in the city and 97,000 were taken into captivity after the destruction of Jerusalem.

In obedience to Jesus' command to flee when they saw the armies, everyone whose name was written in the Book of Life fled to the mountain villages of the Decapolis, east and south-east of Galilee. Other early church writers make mention of this great escape, but let us continue with the prophecy and take another look at this verse:

Daniel 12:2
And many of them that sleep in the dust of the earth shall awake, some to everlasting life, and some to shame and everlasting contempt.

The historical context shows this is not a portrait of the resurrection, but is similar to Ezekiel's prophecy of the dry bones which draws on resurrection imagery. Here is how the Lord interprets the "dry bones".

Ezekiel 37:11-14
Then he said unto me, Son of man, these bones are the whole house of Israel: behold, they say, Our bones are dried, and our hope is lost: we are cut off for our parts. 12 Therefore prophesy and say unto them, Thus saith the Lord God; Behold, O my people, I will open your graves, and cause you to come up out of your graves, and bring you into the land of Israel. 13 And ye shall know that I am the Lord, when I have opened your graves, O my people, and brought you up out of your graves, 14 And shall put my spirit in you, and ye shall live, and I shall place you in your own land: then shall ye know that I the Lord have spoken it, and performed it, saith the Lord.

Ezekiel saw a valley of bones but the Lord calls them the house of Israel. The whole dry bones prophecy is symbolic of their state of being. They were dead in trespasses and sin, they were 'cut off' and without hope and the Lord was promising a time when they would be filled with His Spirit and back in the Land. It is not a portrait of the resurrection, it's a portrait of REVIVAL. Likewise here in Daniel.

Now let us consider how the New Testament speaks on this matter.

Ephesians 5:14
Wherefore he saith, Awake thou that sleepest, and arise from the dead, and Christ shall give thee light.

Ephesians 2:1-7
And you hath he quickened, who were dead in trespasses and sins; 2 Wherein in time past ye walked according to the course of this world, according to the prince of the power of the air, the spirit that now worketh in the children of disobedience: 3 Among whom also we all had our conversation in times past in the lusts of our flesh, fulfilling the desires of the flesh and of the mind; and were by nature the children of wrath, even as others. 4 But God, who is rich in mercy, for his great love wherewith he loved us,

5 Even when we were dead in sins, hath quickened us together with Christ, (by grace ye are saved;)

6 And hath raised us up together, and made us sit together in heavenly places in Christ Jesus: 7 That in the ages to come he might shew the exceeding riches of his grace in his kindness toward us through Christ Jesus.

John 5:24
Verily, verily, I say unto you, He that heareth my word, and believeth on him that sent me, hath everlasting life, and shall not come into condemnation; but is passed from death unto life.

Matthew 4:16
The people which sat in darkness saw great light; and to them which sat in the region and shadow of death light is sprung up.

Luke 1:79
To give light to them that sit in darkness and in the shadow of death, to guide our feet into the way of peace.

John 3:18
He that believeth on him is not condemned: but he that believeth not is condemned already, because he hath not believed in the name of the only begotten Son of God.

How beautifully these words of Daniel were fulfilled:

Daniel 12:2b
"some to everlasting life, and some to shame and everlasting contempt.

Notice also that John says that he that refuses to believe is already condemned. This completely conforms with Daniel's statement that they rise to everlasting contempt. Neither of these verses is speaking of the resurrection and the following sentence with its reference to turning "many to righteousness" confirms that it is in this life.

Daniel 12:3
And they that be wise shall shine as the brightness of the firmament; and they that turn many to righteousness as the stars for ever and ever.

There was a new class of people coming, who would be born again, filled with the Spirit and the knowledge of God. The apostles, prophets, evangelists, and pastor/teachers of our Lord Jesus Christ fulfil this verse. These men, who had passed from death into life, were gifted with wisdom to teach the people knowledge. They turned men to God. They turned many to righteousness; their enemies admitted they turned the world upside down! Jesus commanded them to let their light shine.

Daniel 12:4
But thou, O Daniel, shut up the words, and seal the book, even to the time of the end: many shall run to and fro, and knowledge shall be increased.

Gabriel tells Daniel to close up the vision until the time of the end when many would be bringing knowledge. An example of typical Hebrew parallelism: the increase of knowledge is brought about by those who turned many to righteousness. In the midst of it Daniel is told that the understanding of the words of the book would be sealed until that time of the end.

Daniel then sees another vision:

Daniel 12:5-13
Then I Daniel looked, and, behold, there stood other two, the one on this side of the bank of the river, and the other on that side of the bank of the river. 6 And one said to the man clothed in linen, which was upon the waters of the river, How long shall it be to the end of these wonders? 7 And I heard the man clothed in linen, which was upon the waters of the river, when he held up his right hand and his left hand unto heaven, and sware by him that liveth for ever that it shall be for a time, times, and an half; and when he shall have accomplished to scatter the power of the holy people, all these things shall be finished.

Verse 7 mentions "a time, times and an half" and "scatter the power of the holy people". As you will see in the continuation of the passage below, Daniel didn't understand these words as at that time the words were sealed. To fully explain these phrases which have since been revealed in the New Testament has required nearly five pages so I've put it in an article in the Appendix titled: A Time, Times and Half a Time.

8 And I heard, but I understood not: then said I, O my Lord, what shall be the end of these things? 9 And he said, Go thy way, Daniel: for the words are closed up and sealed till the time of the end. 10 Many shall be purified, and made white, and tried; but the wicked shall do wickedly: and none of the wicked shall understand; but the wise shall understand.

Again we must carefully note the context with regard to the word "end". Gabriel says in verse 7 that when the power of the holy people is "scattered" (NKJV), all these things shall be finished. In verse 8 Gabriel links the word "end" to "these things" he had been speaking of. So we see it is speaking of the end of the days mentioned in the prophecy and not the end of the world.

11 And from the time that the daily sacrifice shall be taken away, and the abomination that maketh desolate set up, there shall be a thousand two hundred and ninety days. 12 Blessed is he that waiteth, and cometh to the thousand three hundred and five and thirty days.

Here in verse 11 is where we have the Abomination of Desolation spoken of by Daniel the prophet. It is the same act of desolation mentioned in Daniel 8:13 and Daniel 9:27. It is the Abomination of Desolation mentioned by Jesus to His disciples saying, "Let the reader understand." It happens at the end of the historical period contained in this most detailed and lengthy prophecy, as Daniel put it, ". . . the end of these things" (Daniel 12:8). It was the time of the end of many things: The end of Jewish dominion over the city of Jerusalem till the time of the Gentiles is fulfilled; The end of Sheol's captivity of the dead saints; The end of the Temple; The end of the priesthood; The end of the works of the law; The end of the nation's sovereignty and the beginning of their long exile; The end for many who had filled up the measure of their sin.

We also note in verse 11 the mention of the daily sacrifices being taken away. In the writings of Josephus, we find in Book 5 of the War of the Jews that seditious factions were fighting within the city and had taken over the Temple, killing most of the priests and murdering those who came to sacrifice. The final words of Chapter 1, Paragraph 2 reads, ". . . *the temple was defiled everywhere with murders.*" These events happened shortly before, or perhaps simultaneously with the beginning of the siege by Titus. No doubt about it, the Word of God accurately predicted these occurrences hundreds of years before hand.

After the New Covenant was made through the death and resurrection of our Lord Jesus Christ, the believers were not to expect a victory for the Jews in the coming siege of Jerusalem, rather, the Abomination of Desolation served as the harbinger for the destruction that was to come upon the unbelieving, and a signal for the Christians to escape to the mountain villages south east of Galilee across the Jordan.

With regards to the 1290 days and the 1335 days mentioned in Daniel 12:11-12, there is nothing definitive from recorded history that can explicitly explain what these days relate to. I believe they would have been known by those to whom it was meant for at that period of time. They could count them, we cannot. My opinion is that it referred to the optimum time for the church to make their escape. No way of proving that assumption, but the timing is at least approximate.

13 But go thou thy way till the end be: for thou shalt rest, and stand in thy lot at the end of the days.

Daniel is promised that he would rest until the end of those days. I believe he would have been among the saints that came out of their graves and that appeared in Jerusalem mentioned in Matthew 27:51-53. Many modern English translations listed in biblegateway.com render the last phrase of Daniel 12:13 "stand in your lot at the end of the days" as "rise to your inheritance" or "rise from the dead" and other like phrases which would give credence to that idea. For more on this subject see First Fruits Resurrection in the Appendix.

In summary: Daniel is not a false prophet and neither are these words a fraud written after the fact. Daniel saw it all in a vision that even with the interpretation he could not at first understand the meaning of in Daniel 8. He was then given the time frame of seventy weeks and what it was that God was going to accomplish on behalf of his people in Daniel 9. Then in the subsequent revelation of Daniel 11-12, he gets to hear the untold details that should have prepared the Jews for what was going to happen with sufficient signs of the times.

Jesus rebuked the religious leaders for not knowing their time and season and I am sure he might rebuke a few in our time for not being able to see the correlation between these prophecies and the historical fulfilment. The Abomination of Desolation is 'done and dusted'. To proclaim it as something in the future promotes all manner of confusion and subjects oneself to a spirit that twists the Scriptures and conceals the truth.

A Messianic Jewish neighbour of mine from some time ago was writing a book on the prophecy in Daniel Chapter 9 because he realized it was positive proof to his people that the Messiah had come and that it could be historically verified. He shared a dream he had with me, that described himself wrestling with Daniel for the scroll that was sealed. Interesting . . .

Chapter Ten

The Kingdom of God

Although the Kingdom of Judah was expecting their Messiah sooner or later, the arrival of the Kingdom of God was not what they were looking for, even though the prophecies of Daniel, in particular the Seventy Sevens Prophecy of Daniel Chapter 9, ought to have given the Jews both an indication of when He would arrive and what He would accomplish.

The Promised Messiah comes

And takes them by surprise

They thought He'd be a Lion

But as a Lamb . . . He dies

Rising from the grave

He conquers everything

Ascends through clouds to Heaven

Becomes our reigning King

There are about forty Scriptures that speak fairly explicitly about various aspects of His appearance among men and about four hundred more that allude to Him in some form or another. Many scholars have documented these prophecies and much has been written on the Scriptures that foretold the coming of our Lord Jesus Christ. It is the presumption of this author that those reading what is presented in this book are already Christians. Therefore, although the prophecies concerning Messiah's appearance is certainly a worthy and interesting subject, it has been well covered by many authors already and I am not inclined to reinvent the wheel. Besides, it is slightly off topic as this study is more directly concerned with the prophetic destinies of Judah, Israel and the Kingdom of God.

In this chapter the focus will be on the details of the Kingdom of God that will help us identify the fundamental nature of this Kingdom whereby we will be thoroughly equipped to recognise any false ideas about its manifestation and destiny in this age and in this world. What follows will also serve to give clarity regarding the future destiny of the Kingdom of Judah and the Kingdom of Israel.

When Messiah came, He fulfilled the function of three interrelated roles: As Prophet He demonstrated and defined the Kingdom of God. His word still stands and He watches over everything that He has uttered to ensure that it will come to pass. As King He came to take up the Throne of David. He will return to judge the earth and to subdue all authorities under His rule before delivering the entire Kingdom to His Father. As Great High Priest He came to offer the sacrifice that would atone for our sin and to intercede on our behalf before God. The sacrifice He made was His own life, His own body. Because death was the punishment for sin, He became sin for us that we might become the righteousness of God in Christ. Rising from the dead, He conquered the grave and He lives forever more, making intercession for us before the Father. Let us now examine the Kingdom of God which Jesus defined in His preaching as He functioned as Prophet:

Mark 1:1-3
The beginning of the gospel of Jesus Christ, the Son of God; 2 As it is written in the prophets, Behold, I send my messenger before thy face, which shall prepare thy way before thee. 3 The voice of one crying in the wilderness, Prepare ye the way of the Lord, make his paths straight.

Luke 16:16
The law and the prophets were until John: since that time the kingdom of God is preached . . .

Matthew 11:13
For all the prophets and the law prophesied until John.

Matthew 3:1-2
In those days came John the Baptist, preaching in the wilderness of Judaea, 2 And saying, Repent ye: for the kingdom of heaven is at hand.

Mark 1:14-15
Now after that John was put in prison, Jesus came into Galilee, preaching the gospel of the kingdom of God, 15 And saying, The time is fulfilled, and the kingdom of God is at hand: repent ye, and believe the gospel.

Matthew 4:17
From that time Jesus began to preach and to say, "Repent, for the kingdom of heaven is at hand."

Matthew 10:7
And as ye go, preach, saying, The kingdom of heaven is at hand.

I think we get it: the Kingdom of God was declared to be "at hand" by both John the Baptist and Jesus. Readily available would perhaps be a way to say what these words imply. Note also that the terms Kingdom of Heaven and Kingdom of God are synonymous. However, calling it the Kingdom of Heaven is not without significance. Also note that the primary message of the prophet is to preach repentance.

Luke 17:20-21

And when he was demanded of the Pharisees, when the kingdom of God should come, he answered them and said, The kingdom of God cometh not with observation: 21 Neither shall they say, Lo here! or, lo there! for, behold, the kingdom of God is within you.

Basically this is saying you won't be able to see the Kingdom of God with your eyes. Jesus' answer to this question of the Pharisees is an indication that the prophesied restoration of the Kingdom of Judah with the Kingdom of Israel and the manifestation of the Kingdom of God are not to be equated, even though they are inter-related. This teaching was new to the understanding of the Jews, though it had been in the heart of God from before the foundation of the world. The Jews were anticipating the restoration of their sovereignty, interpreting that to be the manifestation of the Kingdom of God. But Jesus came preaching the Kingdom of God which was concerned with restoring the sovereignty of God in their hearts and the restoration of their earthly sovereignty was a separate issue that would be fulfilled in its own time (Acts 1:6-7).

John 3:3-8

Jesus answered and said unto him, Verily, verily, I say unto thee, Except a man be born again, he cannot see the kingdom of God. 4 Nicodemus saith unto him, How can a man be born when he is old? can he enter the second time into his mother's womb, and be born? 5 Jesus answered, Verily, verily, I say unto thee, Except a man be born of water and of the Spirit, he cannot enter into the kingdom of God. 6 That which is born of the flesh is flesh; and that which is born of the Spirit is spirit. 7 Marvel not that I said unto thee, Ye must be born again. 8 The wind bloweth where it listeth, and thou hearest the sound thereof, but canst not tell whence it cometh, and whither it goeth: so is every one that is born of the Spirit.

Sometimes I wonder if King James had a lisp . . . The Kingdom of God that began with the preaching of Jesus and John the Baptist is a spiritual kingdom that cannot be seen with the natural eye, but when one is 'born again' of the Spirit, it can be seen with the understanding because it is something that is apprehended from within.

John 3:9-10

Nicodemus answered and said unto him, How can these things be? 10 Jesus answered and said unto him, Art thou a master of Israel, and knowest not these things?

Here Jesus is gently rebuking Nicodemus for being a teacher in Israel and not knowing these things about the Kingdom of God. Things that were there in the Word of God for him to apprehend.

Elihu Ben Ephraim

Jeremiah 31:33
But this shall be the covenant that I will make with the house of Israel; After those days, saith the Lord, I will put my law in their inward parts, and write it in their hearts; and will be their God, and they shall be my people.

Ezekiel 11:19
And I will give them one heart, and I will put a new spirit within you; and I will take the stony heart out of their flesh, and will give them an heart of flesh:

Ezekiel 36:26
A new heart also will I give you, and a new spirit will I put within you: and I will take away the stony heart out of your flesh, and I will give you an heart of flesh.

The indwelling Spirit of God and a change of heart so that the law of God is within was promised by the prophets. However, Jesus also made clear that although the Kingdom of God was to be an inward reality, it had some signs that were outward.

Matthew 12:28
But if I cast out devils by the Spirit of God, then the kingdom of God is come unto you.

Luke 11:20
But if I with the finger of God cast out devils, no doubt the kingdom of God is come upon you.

Matthew 10:7-8
And as ye go, preach, saying, The kingdom of heaven is at hand. 8 Heal the sick, cleanse the lepers, raise the dead, cast out devils: freely ye have received, freely give.

Luke 10:8-11
And into whatsoever city ye enter, and they receive you, eat such things as are set before you: 9 And heal the sick that are therein, and say unto them, The kingdom of God is come nigh unto you. 10 But into whatsoever city ye enter, and they receive you not, go your ways out into the streets of the same, and say, 11 Even the very dust of your city, which cleaveth on us, we do wipe off against you: notwithstanding be ye sure of this, that the kingdom of God is come nigh unto you.

Matthew 11:4-5
Jesus answered and said unto them, Go and shew John again those things which ye do hear and see: 5 The blind receive their sight, and the lame walk, the lepers are cleansed, and the deaf hear, the dead are raised up, and the poor have the gospel preached to them.

1 Corinthians 2:4-5
And my speech and my preaching was not with enticing words of man's wisdom, but in demonstration of the Spirit and of power: 5 That your faith should not stand in the wisdom of men, but in the power of God.

The Kingdom of God itself may not be seen with the eye but the effect of its presence certainly can be seen, just as one cannot see the wind but can see the clouds move.

Before His crucifixion, Jesus mentioned a couple of other interesting details about the Kingdom of God.

Luke 22:14-19
And when the hour was come, he sat down, and the twelve apostles with him. 15 And he said unto them, With desire I have desired to eat this Passover with you before I suffer: 16 For I say unto you, I will not any more eat thereof, until it be fulfilled in the kingdom of God. 17 And he took the cup, and gave thanks, and said, Take this, and divide it among yourselves: 18 For I say unto you, I will not drink of the fruit of the vine, until the kingdom of God shall come. 19 And he took bread, and gave thanks, and brake it, and gave unto them, saying, This is my body which is given for you: this do in remembrance of me.

Matthew 26:27-29
And he took the cup, and gave thanks, and gave it to them, saying, Drink ye all of it; 28 For this is my blood of the new testament, which is shed for many for the remission of sins. 29 But I say unto you, I will not drink henceforth of this fruit of the vine, until that day when I drink it new with you in my Father's kingdom.

Luke reports that Jesus said, "I will not drink of the fruit of the vine, until the Kingdom of God shall come", implying that the Kingdom was yet to arrive. This seems contrary to His previous statements about the Kingdom beginning with John the Baptist which was declared to be "at hand". Matthew speaking of this event has Jesus saying, "I will not drink henceforth of this fruit of the vine, until that day when I drink it new with you in my Father's Kingdom."

So whilst we have the Kingdom of God at hand, Jesus is saying His Father's Kingdom is yet to come. In the writings of Paul we find the necessary light regarding the "Father's Kingdom" that helps us understand what appears to be a contradiction.

1 Corinthians 15:20-28 NKJV
But now Christ is risen from the dead, *and* has become the firstfruits of those who have fallen asleep. 21 For since by man *came* death, by Man also *came* the resurrection of the dead. 22 For as in Adam all die, even so in Christ all shall be made alive. 23 But each one in his own order: Christ the firstfruits, afterward those *who are* Christ's at His coming.

24 Then *comes* the end, when He delivers the kingdom to God the Father, when He puts an end to all rule and all authority and power.

25 For He must reign till He has put all enemies under His feet. 26 The last enemy *that* will be destroyed *is* death. 27 For "He has put all things under His feet." But when He says "all things are put under *Him,*" *it is* evident that He who put all things under Him is excepted. 28 Now when

all things are made subject to Him, then the Son Himself will also be subject to Him who put all things under Him, that God may be all in all.

Oh, those long sentences of Paul. Sometimes it takes a bit to wrap your head around what he means. Never mind, the main point we want to take from this passage is found in verse 24, "Then comes the end, when He delivers the Kingdom to God the Father". From this we understand that Jesus must reign until death, "the last enemy", is destroyed, and that happens at the resurrection of the dead.

1 Corinthians 15:51-54
Behold, I shew you a mystery; We shall not all sleep, but we shall all be changed, 52 In a moment, in the twinkling of an eye, at the last trump: for the trumpet shall sound, and the dead shall be raised incorruptible, and we shall be changed. 53 For this corruptible must put on incorruption, and this mortal must put on immortality. 54 So when this corruptible shall have put on incorruption, and this mortal shall have put on immortality, then shall be brought to pass the saying that is written, Death is swallowed up in victory.

From that moment on, there will be no more death. All things will be under Jesus feet, He will then deliver all things to the Father. At that point, the Kingdom of the Father begins with a new Heaven and a new Earth. Let us now look again at the Kingdom of God which is presently described as being "at hand".

Colossians 1:13
Who hath delivered us from the power of darkness, and hath translated us into the kingdom of his dear Son:

Ephesians 5:5
For this ye know, that no whoremonger, nor unclean person, nor covetous man, who is an idolater, hath any inheritance in the kingdom of Christ and of God.

We see then that the Kingdom of God in this present age is referred to as the Kingdom of God's Son or the Kingdom of Christ. Scripture reveals that it is not until Jesus hands the Kingdom over that it will become the Kingdom of His Father. Of course, being in the Kingdom of the Son guarantees us an entrance into the Kingdom of the Father for they are both the Kingdom of God.

Jesus revealed yet another facet to the Kingdom of God that defined it and contrasted it to every other kingdom and it was summed up in these words:

John 18:36
Jesus answered, My kingdom is not of this world: if my kingdom were of this world, then would my servants fight, that I should not be delivered to the Jews: but now is my kingdom not from hence.

Along with this passage that follows, Jesus is explaining about being in the world but not of the world.

John 17:9-16
I pray for them: I pray not for the world, but for them which thou hast given me; for they are thine. 10 And all mine are thine, and thine are mine; and I am glorified in them. 11 And now I am no more in the world, but these are in the world, and I come to thee. Holy Father, keep through thine own name those whom thou hast given me, that they may be one, as we are. 12 While I was with them in the world, I kept them in thy name: those that thou gavest me I have kept, and none of them is lost, but the son of perdition; that the scripture might be fulfilled. 13 And now come I to thee; and these things I speak in the world, that they might have my joy fulfilled in themselves. 14 I have given them thy word; and the world hath hated them, because they are not of the world, even as I am not of the world. 15 I pray not that thou shouldest take them out of the world, but that thou shouldest keep them from the evil. 16 They are not of the world, even as I am not of the world.

Being in the Kingdom of God whilst being in the world is spoken of in other expressions in the New Testament as found in the following Scripture:

2 Corinthians 5:17
Therefore if any man be in Christ, he is a new creature: old things are passed away; behold, all things are become new.

May I recommend that if you have not yet done so, go through the letters of Paul and look up all the Scriptures that speak of being in Him, in Christ and other like phrases and let the truth of them penetrate your heart. Christ in us and us in Christ. Hallelujah!

So then, the Kingdom of God that began to be preached by John the Baptist is also known as the Kingdom of God's Son and it continues right through to the resurrection of the dead when we are raised up on what Jesus called the last day (John 6:39, 40, 44, 54). Those who are in the Kingdom of God's Son are presently called by various names: the Church, the Body of Christ, Born Again Believers, and are also referred to as being in Him, that is, in Christ and of course most commonly in our time we are called Christians, though that term has come to be rather loosely defined lately. It is a Kingdom of power in the Holy Spirit and the evidence of its presence is to be found in changed lives where people are converted to righteous living, demons are cast out, the lame and the sick are healed and the gospel is preached to the poor in spirit. It is in the world but not of the world. It is spiritual and not political. You cannot say, "See it is here" or "See it is there", for it is within your heart through faith in our Lord Jesus Christ. Individuals can enter the Kingdom, whole families can enter the Kingdom, whole villages can enter the Kingdom, and whole nations can enter the Kingdom. But that nation, village, family or individual does not define the Kingdom. We will never be able to look at the Kingdom of Judah or the Kingdom of Israel and say, "There is the Kingdom of God" If they repent and believe the Gospel, we will only be able to say that they have entered into the Kingdom of God's Son, also known as the Kingdom of Christ and are guaranteed entrance into the Kingdom of the Father. To be in Christ, to be in Him, is to be in the Kingdom of God. In this manner the Kingdom of God defined.

The Messiah came as Prophet and He also came as King in order that He might take up what the Scriptures called the Throne of David. When the angel Gabriel came to Mary, in the midst of his message he declared:

Luke 1:32
He shall be great, and shall be called the Son of the Highest: and the Lord God shall give unto him the throne of his father David:

Wise men came from the East inquiring:

Matthew 2:2
Where is he that is born King of the Jews? for we have seen his star in the east, and are come to worship him.

Nathanael exclaimed:

John 1:49
Nathanael answered and saith unto him, Rabbi, thou art the Son of God; thou art the King of Israel.

Jesus was born King of the Jews and King of Israel to take up the Throne of David. What the Jews did not understand, nor any of the disciples, is that the path to the Throne was via the cross. Jesus said all along that His Kingdom was not of this world. That is why the Kingdom of God is also called the Kingdom of Heaven; it is not of this world. Prior to Jesus, it was unthinkable to consider the Throne of David as anything other than a restoration of the Kingdom of Judah and of Israel. However, if we go back to when this throne was first established we find something interesting and revealing. Let us now look at when the Children of Israel first asked for a king:

1 Samuel 8:6-7
But the thing displeased Samuel, when they said, Give us a king to judge us. And Samuel prayed unto the Lord. 7 And the Lord said unto Samuel, Hearken unto the voice of the people in all that they say unto thee: for they have not rejected thee, but they have rejected me, that I should not reign over them.

1 Samuel 12:12-13
And when ye saw that Nahash the king of the children of Ammon came against you, ye said unto me, Nay; but a king shall reign over us: when the Lord your God was your king. 13 Now

therefore behold the king whom ye have chosen, and whom ye have desired! and, behold, the Lord hath set a king over you.

The LORD was already their King, but He gave them what they desired. However, unlike the kings of the heathen, the king of Israel did not have absolute authority. They were to be subject to the Law and they were not to interfere with the priesthood. They were also to be subject to the prophets.

1 Samuel 9:16
To morrow about this time I will send thee a man out of the land of Benjamin, and thou shalt anoint him to be captain over my people . . .

1 Samuel 10:1
Then Samuel took a vial of oil, and poured it upon his head, and kissed him, and said, Is it not because the Lord hath anointed thee to be captain over his inheritance?

The word "captain" in the above verses is from the Hebrew term *nagiyd* and is otherwise translated: governor, prince, commander. It could also be rendered in English as viceroy, governor-general or a vassal king. The Scriptures reveal that Israel's King Solomon "sat on the throne of the LORD".

1 Chronicles 29:23
Then Solomon sat on the throne of the Lord as king instead of David his father, and prospered; and all Israel obeyed him.

2 Chronicles 9:8
Blessed be the Lord thy God, which delighted in thee to set thee on his throne, to be king for the Lord thy God: because thy God loved Israel, to establish them for ever, therefore made he thee king over them, to do judgment and justice.

So the Throne of David is actually the Throne of the LORD. Placing a man on the Throne of the LORD was symbolic of Christ coming as a Man to take up His Throne. And like every other symbolic institution that God directed for the Children of Israel, through the law or through the prophets, they never understood its import until after the resurrection. Unfortunately, many fail to see it even to this day, even in the Church of God.

The Lord made certain promises to David and to Solomon concerning this throne that they would be seated on:

2 Samuel 7:12-16
And when thy days be fulfilled, and thou shalt sleep with thy fathers, I will set up thy seed after thee, which shall proceed out of thy bowels, and I will establish his kingdom. 13 He shall build an

house for my name, and I will stablish the throne of his kingdom for ever. 14 I will be his father, and he shall be my son. If he commit iniquity, I will chasten him with the rod of men, and with the stripes of the children of men: 15 But my mercy shall not depart away from him, as I took it from Saul, whom I put away before thee. 16 And thine house and thy kingdom shall be established for ever before thee: thy throne shall be established for ever.

1 Kings 9:1-9

And it came to pass, when Solomon had finished the building of the house of the Lord, and the king's house, and all Solomon's desire which he was pleased to do, That the Lord appeared to Solomon the second time, as he had appeared unto him at Gibeon. 3 And the Lord said unto him, I have heard thy prayer and thy supplication, that thou hast made before me: I have hallowed this house, which thou hast built, to put my name there for ever; and mine eyes and mine heart shall be there perpetually.

4 And if thou wilt walk before me, as David thy father walked, in integrity of heart, and in uprightness, to do according to all that I have commanded thee, and wilt keep my statutes and my judgments:

5 Then I will establish the throne of thy kingdom upon Israel for ever, as I promised to David thy father, saying, There shall not fail thee a man upon the throne of Israel. 6 But if ye shall at all turn from following me, ye or your children, and will not keep my commandments and my statutes which I have set before you, but go and serve other gods, and worship them: 7 Then will I cut off Israel out of the land which I have given them; and this house, which I have hallowed for my name, will I cast out of my sight; and Israel shall be a proverb and a byword among all people: 8 And at this house, which is high, every one that passeth by it shall be astonished, and shall hiss; and they shall say, Why hath the Lord done thus unto this land, and to this house? 9 And they shall answer, Because they forsook the Lord their God, who brought forth their fathers out of the land of Egypt, and have taken hold upon other gods, and have worshipped them, and served them: therefore hath the Lord brought upon them all this evil.

Jeremiah 33:17

For thus saith the Lord; David shall never want a man to sit upon the throne of the house of Israel;

Did you notice in 1 Kings 9:4 that big little word "if"? There were some conditions laid upon the descendants of David being enabled to sit on that throne. At this point in time I would like to bring to the fore the tremendous amount of debate there is within the Body of Christ on this subject of the Throne of David. Some say the above mentioned verses show that the succession of kings would never cease, that there would always be someone on the Throne of David until Jesus returns and they claim to trace the continuation of the Sceptre via one of Zedekiah's daughters and that when He returns, the Throne will be delivered to Him and He will reign from Jerusalem. Without a doubt, there are descendants of David alive and well today, however, there is one obvious problem with this theory and it is that although Zedekiah was a descendant of David, he was only an appointed king set up by the pagan King

Nebuchadnezzar, for Jeconiah, the actual king, was still alive in captivity and actually outlived him and thus the inheritance was never passed onto Zedekiah. Zedekiah was Jeconiah's uncle and could only have inherited the throne of David if all the other heirs were dead.

Others say that Jesus came and did not take up His Throne because the Jews rejected Him, but when He returns they will accept Him and then He will take up His Throne in Jerusalem and reign for a thousand years. In the meantime it is simply on hold. Well, about a third of them did receive Him as King and the majority of the rest were slaughtered, and maybe a tenth of them were brought as slaves to Rome. Jesus could easily have taken up His throne in this world at that time, BUT, His Kingdom was not of this world.

Yet another viewpoint is that the Throne of David was always the Throne of the LORD. The conditions that gave the ability to sit on that Throne were ultimately something that only Christ Himself could fulfil. The privilege of sitting on it was symbolic, and that privilege was taken from the descendants of David due to their rebellion when the Tribe of Judah was taken captive to Babylon, but the kingly line continued until Messiah came. They say that even if there are descendants of David from the line of Zedekiah (or any other line for that matter) ruling over some portion of Israel to this day, it has nothing to do with the actual Throne of David, because the genealogy which contained the right of inheritance to the Throne followed the two blood lines which culminated with Joseph and Mary the mother of Jesus. This author favours this latter view. For more on that topic see The Two Genealogies in the Appendix.

The truth of this subject becomes clear when we understand that Jesus came not only as Prophet and King, but also to fulfil His role as Great High Priest. Let us now look at a couple of prophecies about this aspect of His coming:

Psalm 110:1-4
The Lord said unto my Lord, Sit thou at my right hand, until I make thine enemies thy footstool. 2 The Lord shall send the rod of thy strength out of Zion: rule thou in the midst of thine enemies. 3 Thy people shall be willing in the day of thy power, in the beauties of holiness from the womb of the morning: thou hast the dew of thy youth. 4 The Lord hath sworn, and will not repent, Thou art a priest for ever after the order of Melchizedek.

Zechariah 6:12-13
And speak unto him, saying, Thus speaketh the Lord of hosts, saying, Behold the man whose name is The Branch; and he shall grow up out of his place, and he shall build the temple of the Lord: 13 Even he shall build the temple of the Lord; and he shall bear the glory, and shall sit and rule upon his throne; and he shall be a priest upon his throne . . .

Zechariah makes it clear that the promise to be fulfilled is that of a Royal Priesthood. One Man fulfilling both roles; "He shall be a priest upon His Throne." In the Book of Hebrews we find much about Jesus coming as priest according to the order of Melchizedek. At this point you would do well to read the first ten chapters of Hebrews as it's a bit much to quote the entire passage here. It will help you understand the connection and unity of the Kingship and the Priesthood. What follows are the pertinent verses for this study:

Hebrews 7:1-3 NKJV
For this Melchizedek, king of Salem, priest of the Most High God, who met Abraham returning from the slaughter of the kings and blessed him, 2 to whom also Abraham gave a tenth part of all, first being translated "king of righteousness," and then also king of Salem, meaning "king of peace," 3 without father, without mother, without genealogy, having neither beginning of days nor end of life, but made like the Son of God, remains a priest continually.

As mentioned above, the order of Melchizedek combines the functions of both king and priest.

Hebrews 10:11-13 NKJV
And every priest stands ministering daily and offering repeatedly the same sacrifices, which can never take away sins. 12 But this Man, after He had offered one sacrifice for sins forever, sat down at the right hand of God, 13 from that time waiting till His enemies are made His footstool.

1 Corinthians 15:25-26
For he must reign, till he hath put all enemies under his feet. 26 The last enemy that shall be destroyed is death.

Romans 15:12
There shall be a root of Jesse; And He who shall rise to reign over the Gentiles, In Him the Gentiles shall hope.

Acts 2:30-31
Therefore being a prophet, and knowing that God had sworn with an oath to him, that of the fruit of his loins, according to the flesh, he would raise up Christ to sit on his throne; 31 He seeing this before spake of the resurrection of Christ, that his soul was not left in hell, neither his flesh did see corruption.

Let us grasp the import of the above verses. Jesus as Priest is sitting at the right hand till His enemies are all under His feet (Hebrews 10:11). Zechariah's prophecy says He will be a Priest upon His Throne (Zechariah 6:13). He must reign till all enemies are under His feet (1 Corinthians 15:25); He shall rise to reign (Romans 15:12); His being raised up to sit on His Throne speaks of His resurrection (Acts 2:30-31). Because He was both King and Priest, when He sat down at the Right Hand, He sat down as both King and Priest. If we say that Christ is not reigning presently as King, we would also have to say He is not our Great High Priest presently interceding for us. But thank God He is always interceding for us for He is already upon His Throne as Priest and King.

1 Timothy 6:13-15 NKJV
I urge you in the sight of God who gives life to all things, and *before* Christ Jesus who witnessed the good confession before Pontius Pilate, 14 that you keep *this* commandment without spot,

blameless until our Lord Jesus Christ's appearing, 15 which He will manifest in His own time, *He who is* the blessed and only Potentate, the King of kings and Lord of lords.

There are many more Scriptures that testify to the fact that Jesus is already reigning as King of kings and Lord of lords and that He has complete authority. Thus He can say:

Matthew 28:18-20
All authority has been given to Me in heaven and on earth. 19 Go therefore and make disciples of all the nations, baptizing them in the name of the Father and of the Son and of the Holy Spirit, 20 teaching them to observe all things that I have commanded you; and lo, I am with you always, *even* to the end of the age. Amen.

As Prophet, Priest and King, Jesus has taken up His Throne, the Throne of David, which has already been identified as the Throne of the LORD. He would not be able to say that He has "all authority" if He wasn't already on the Throne. If we say He has not taken up His Throne, we are at a loss to explain how it is that He is seated at the right hand of the Father, waiting till He has subdued all authorities and powers in order to submit the Kingdom to the Father. We are not looking forward to Him setting up an earthly kingdom for as we learnt from Daniel 2 and 7, the coming of the Kingdom of God is the end of the age and the end of this world. It is a time when "the court is seated and the books are opened." It's Judgment Day (Daniel 7:10). It is the Antichrist who is the only one in all of Scripture that is prophesied to set up a one world government in this world and in this age, not Jesus.

King David was a type of Christ. King Solomon was a type of Christ. Moses was a type of Christ. Joseph was a type of Christ. Jonah was a type of Christ. The high priesthood and the temple and the entire sacrificial system were all a type of Christ. All the types were of this world. But when Christ came He explicitly declared that His Kingdom was not of this world. Therefore we should never expect the Throne of David to be of this world. Even the temple that He was prophesied to build (Zechariah 6:12-13) is not of this world. It is a temple made of living stones (1 Peter 2:5). Those of us who are in His Kingdom are in the world but not of it and we are exhorted to look forward to the Day of the Lord when Christ shall return and do away with this world and bring us into a new Heaven and a new Earth and fulfil His promise which He made saying that He would go and prepare a place for us (John 14:2). Hallelujah!

2 Peter 3:10
But the day of the Lord will come as a thief in the night; in the which the heavens shall pass away with a great noise, and the elements shall melt with fervent heat, the earth also and the works that are therein shall be burned up.

2 Peter 3:13
Nevertheless we, according to his promise, look for new heavens and a new earth, wherein dwelleth righteousness.

1 Corinthians 15:24-26 NKJV

Then *comes* the end, when He delivers the kingdom to God the Father, when He puts an end to all rule and all authority and power. 25 For He must reign till He has put all enemies under His feet. 26 The last enemy *that* will be destroyed *is* death.

At the end of the age, we who have died in Christ will be resurrected on the last day. This present world and everything in it will be utterly destroyed. The Kingdom of God's Son, the Kingdom of Christ, has one last function before Jesus delivers it to our Father. When all other thrones are cast down, all things will be subject to Him. The Son of Man, the Lord Jesus Christ will be sitting on the Throne of His Glory, otherwise known as the Throne of David, ready to judge the world.

Daniel 7:9-10

I beheld till the thrones were cast down, and the Ancient of days did sit, whose garment was white as snow, and the hair of his head like the pure wool: his throne was like the fiery flame, and his wheels as burning fire. 10 A fiery stream issued and came forth from before him: thousand thousands ministered unto him, and ten thousand times ten thousand stood before him: the judgment was set, and the books were opened.

The above verse is the very first mention in the Word of God about the coming Kingdom of God and we note that the scene that it describes is the Day of Judgment.

Matthew 25:31-33 NKJV

"When the Son of Man comes in His glory, and all the holy angels with Him, then He will sit on the throne of His glory. 32 All the nations will be gathered before Him, and He will separate them one from another, as a shepherd divides *his* sheep from the goats. 33 And He will set the sheep on His right hand, but the goats on the left.

Matthew 13:40-43

Therefore as the tares are gathered and burned in the fire, so it will be at the end of this age. 41 The Son of Man will send out His angels, and they will gather out of His kingdom all things that offend, and those who practice lawlessness, 42 and will cast them into the furnace of fire. There will be wailing and gnashing of teeth. 43 Then the righteous will shine forth as the sun in the kingdom of their Father. He who has ears to hear, let him hear!

Matthew 13:47-50

"Again, the kingdom of heaven is like a dragnet that was cast into the sea and gathered some of every kind, 48 which, when it was full, they drew to shore; and they sat down and gathered the good into vessels, but threw the bad away. 49 So it will be at the end of the age. The angels will come forth, separate the wicked from among the just, 50 and cast them into the furnace of fire. There will be wailing and gnashing of teeth."

These four passages just mentioned, where Jesus is explaining the Kingdom to His disciples, all show us that the judgment is immediately after the resurrection of both the righteous and the wicked at the end of the age. Jesus explains this fact further in the following verses:

Matthew 12:41 NKJV
The men of Nineveh will rise up in the judgment with this generation and condemn it, because they repented at the preaching of Jonah; and indeed a greater than Jonah *is* here.

Matthew 12:42 NKJV
The queen of the South will rise up in the judgment with this generation and condemn it, for she came from the ends of the earth to hear the wisdom of Solomon; and indeed a greater than Solomon *is* here.

Luke 11:31 NKJV
The queen of the South will rise up in the judgment with the men of this generation and condemn them, for she came from the ends of the earth to hear the wisdom of Solomon; and indeed a greater than Solomon *is* here.

Luke 11:32 NKJV
The men of Nineveh will rise up in the judgment with this generation and condemn it, for they repented at the preaching of Jonah; and indeed a greater than Jonah *is* here.

In the resurrection the righteous rise up **with** the wicked and condemn them. This understanding is also expressed by Paul in the Book of Acts.

Acts 24:15 NKJV
I have hope in God, which they themselves also accept, that there will be a resurrection of *the* dead, both of *the* just and *the* unjust.

The wheat and the tares are taken from the field and then they are sorted out. The dragnet brings the fish out of their world to the shore and then they are sorted out. The Lord comes in flaming fire, the elements burn with fervent heat, the sheep and the goats are before His Throne and then they are sorted out. That this Throne is not in Jerusalem should be abundantly clear for the heavens and the earth have passed away. For more on this particular subject, see Judgment Day in the Appendix.

Thus we have Jesus' teaching on the Kingdom of God. Everything will be made subject to Him. The wicked will be condemned to the eternal fire and we who believe will inherit a new Heaven and a new Earth. Then Jesus will hand the Kingdom to His Father having defeated death, first of all in His own resurrection, and finally in The Resurrection. The Kingdom of God referred to by Jesus as the Kingdom of His Father is the Kingdom that will never end.

In the meantime, Jesus is on His Throne now. He's not in some state of limbo waiting to assume His Throne sometime in the future. He is King of kings now, He is Lord of lords now. Hallelujah! With this understanding we can now approach the prophecies of Jesus and the Apostles concerning the destiny of the people who carry the manifestation of the Kingdom of God while it is in the world but not of the world. In the process we will discover more details regarding the latter days and the end of the age.

Chapter Eleven

The Synoptic Gospel Prophecies

As members of His Church, we are built on the foundation laid by the Apostles and the Prophets, with Jesus Christ as the Chief Cornerstone (Ephesians 2:20). Accordingly, we ought to build our prophetic understanding of the destinies of Judah, Israel and the Kingdom of God and how they all intertwine during the latter days on what He said. Whilst there are a few comments elsewhere, the bulk of Jesus' Prophetic Teaching is found in the following chapters: Matthew 13 and 24, Mark 13 and Luke 21 and a particularly definitive repeated statement in John 6.

It is important to take all the gospel accounts into consideration. You probably know of the term 'synoptic' being applied to the Gospels of Matthew, Mark and Luke. Secular critics look at the differences in the Gospel records of certain events or teachings as being contradictions. However, when we look at them carefully, we discover they are actually complimentary and that the differences are simply the individual writers taking note of certain details not mentioned by the others. We can then move from a partial comprehension of the event or teaching to a complete understanding. It is written: "by two or three witnesses the word shall be established" (Deuteronomy 17:6; 19:15; 2 Corinthians 13:1).

By the way, for those of you who are finding it hard going with the King James Bible, here's hoping that you're coping with its antiquity and that it's not too much of a bother for you to read along with your favourite translation. Like I said, if it wasn't for the publishing and copyright considerations I would have used a reader friendly version.

Whereas in the previous chapter we saw that Jesus defined and demonstrated the Kingdom of God in His combined roles of Prophet, Priest and King, in this chapter we will see how His prophecies seamlessly dovetail with the utterances of the prophet Daniel concerning the destiny of the Kingdom of Judah, with particular attention being made to the Abomination of Desolation.

After giving a series of woes to the Scribes and Pharisees, Jesus began to make some prophetic statements. Soon afterwards, the disciples came to Jesus and asked Him about what He had just been declaring concerning Jerusalem and the Temple. To maintain the context we will pick it up beginning at Matthew 23:31:

Matthew 23:31-24:3

Wherefore ye be witnesses unto yourselves, that ye are the children of them which killed the prophets. 32 Fill ye up then the measure of your fathers. 33 Ye serpents, ye generation of vipers, how can ye escape the damnation of hell? 34 Wherefore, behold, I send unto you prophets, and wise men, and scribes: and some of them ye shall kill and crucify; and some of them shall ye scourge in your synagogues, and persecute them from city to city: 35 That upon you may come all the righteous blood shed upon the earth, from the blood of righteous Abel unto the blood of Zacharias son of Barachias, whom ye slew between the temple and the altar. 36 Verily I say unto you, All these things shall come upon this generation.

37 O Jerusalem, Jerusalem, thou that killest the prophets, and stonest them which are sent unto thee, how often would I have gathered thy children together, even as a hen gathereth her chickens under her wings, and ye would not! 38 Behold, your house is left unto you desolate. 39 For I say unto you, Ye shall not see me henceforth, till ye shall say, Blessed is he that cometh in the name of the Lord.

24:1 And Jesus went out, and departed from the temple: and his disciples came to him for to shew him the buildings of the temple. 2 And Jesus said unto them, See ye not all these things? verily I say unto you, There shall not be left here one stone upon another, that shall not be thrown down.

3 And as he sat upon the mount of Olives, the disciples came unto him privately, saying, Tell us, when shall these things be? and what shall be the sign of thy coming, and of the end of the world?

Mark 13:1-4

And as he went out of the temple, one of his disciples saith unto him, Master, see what manner of stones and what buildings are here! 2 And Jesus answering said unto him, Seest thou these great buildings? there shall not be left one stone upon another, that shall not be thrown down. 3 And as he sat upon the mount of Olives over against the temple, Peter and James and John and Andrew asked him privately,

4 Tell us, when shall these things be? and what shall be the sign when all these things shall be fulfilled?

Luke 21:5-7

And as some spake of the temple, how it was adorned with goodly stones and gifts, he said, 6 As for these things which ye behold, the days will come, in the which there shall not be left one stone upon another, that shall not be thrown down.

7 And they asked him, saying, Master, but when shall these things be? and what sign will there be when these things shall come to pass?

Take note: there were four questions that were asked.

The disciples asked Him, "When shall these things be?"

The disciples asked Him, "What sign will there be when these things shall come to pass?"

The disciples asked Him, ". . . what shall be the sign of thy coming?"

The disciples asked Him, "of the end of the world?"

Later translations say, "end of the age". A little note on that variation of rendering: the Greek word translated 'world' is *aion* which indeed is 'age', as in a period of time. However, the KJV people were fully aware of this and translated it 'world' due to the overall context of all that Daniel, Jesus and the Apostles taught that reveals the end of the age Jesus was speaking of is indeed the end of the world.

Let us examine the context wherein the disciples asked these questions. Jesus had just made these statements to the Scribes and the Pharisees:

Matthew 23:35-36,38
That upon you may come all the righteous blood shed upon the earth, from the blood of righteous Abel unto the blood of Zacharias son of Barachias, whom ye slew between the temple and the altar. 36 Verily I say unto you, All these things shall come upon this generation."

38 Behold, your house is left unto you desolate.

Matthew 24:2
There shall not be left here one stone upon another, that shall not be thrown down.

Some people contend that because what is known as The Wailing Wall, also known as The Western Wall in Jerusalem, still has stones one upon another, that this prophecy has not yet been fulfilled. However, Jesus was speaking of the things the disciples brought His attention to, the Temple and the surrounding buildings. The Western Wall is not one of the buildings, nor a part of any building, but is the ancient remains of the retaining wall built to contain the extension of the Temple Mount grounds during the renovations of King Herod. (The upper portions of which have been laid in later times.) Every stone of every building that Jesus and the Disciples were looking at was cast down and that was what the Lord was prophesying about. No wonder the disciples asked about the end of the age. They must have figured if all this was going to go down, it must be all over. But Jesus lets them know that it's not the end.

Matthew 24:4-6
And Jesus answered and said unto them, Take heed that no man deceive you. 5 For many shall come in my name, saying, I am Christ; and shall deceive many. 6 And ye shall hear of wars and rumours of wars: see that ye be not troubled: for all these things must come to pass, but the end is not yet.

Mark 13:5-7
And Jesus answering them began to say, Take heed lest any man deceive you: 6 For many shall come in my name, saying, I am Christ; and shall deceive many. 7 And when ye shall hear of wars and rumours of wars, be ye not troubled: for such things must needs be; but the end shall not be yet.

Luke 21:8-9
And he said, Take heed that ye be not deceived: for many shall come in my name, saying, I am Christ; and the time draweth near: go ye not therefore after them. 9 But when ye shall hear of wars and commotions, be not terrified: for these things must first come to pass; but the end is not by and by.

Jesus says to them, "Take heed that ye be not deceived".

Jesus says to them, "Many shall come in my name . . . and shall deceive many".

Jesus says to them, "And ye shall hear of wars and rumours of wars".

Jesus says to them, "The end is not yet".

Matthew 24:7-14
For nation shall rise against nation, and kingdom against kingdom: and there shall be famines, and pestilences, and earthquakes, in divers places. 8 All these are the beginning of sorrows. 9 Then shall they deliver you up to be afflicted, and shall kill you: and ye shall be hated of all nations for my name's sake. 10 And then shall many be offended, and shall betray one another, and shall hate one another. 11 And many false prophets shall rise, and shall deceive many. 12 And because iniquity shall abound, the love of many shall wax cold. 13 But he that shall endure unto the end, the same shall be saved. 14 And this gospel of the kingdom shall be preached in all the world for a witness unto all nations; and then shall the end come.

Mark 13:8-13
For nation shall rise against nation, and kingdom against kingdom: and there shall be earthquakes in divers places, and there shall be famines and troubles: these are the beginnings of sorrows. 9 But take heed to yourselves: for they shall deliver you up to councils; and in the synagogues ye shall be beaten: and ye shall be brought before rulers and kings for my sake, for a testimony against them. 10 And the gospel must first be published among all nations. 11 But when they shall lead you, and deliver you up, take no thought beforehand what ye shall speak, neither do ye premeditate: but whatsoever shall be given you in that hour, that speak ye: for it is not ye that speak, but the Holy Ghost. 12 Now the brother shall betray the brother to death, and the father the son; and children shall rise up against their parents, and shall cause them to be put to death. 13 And ye shall be hated of all men for my name's sake: but he that shall endure unto the end, the same shall be saved.

Luke 21:10-19

Then said he unto them, Nation shall rise against nation, and kingdom against kingdom: 11 And great earthquakes shall be in divers places, and famines, and pestilences; and fearful sights and great signs shall there be from heaven. 12 But before all these, they shall lay their hands on you, and persecute you, delivering you up to the synagogues, and into prisons, being brought before kings and rulers for my name's sake. 13 And it shall turn to you for a testimony. 14 Settle it therefore in your hearts, not to meditate before what ye shall answer: 15 For I will give you a mouth and wisdom, which all your adversaries shall not be able to gainsay nor resist. 16 And ye shall be betrayed both by parents, and brethren, and kinsfolks, and friends; and some of you shall they cause to be put to death. 17 And ye shall be hated of all men for my name's sake. 18 But there shall not an hair of your head perish. 19 In your patience possess ye your souls.

Jesus says that it's all going to turn to custard, the pawpaw is going to hit the fan, look forward to trials, tribulations and betrayal, but hang in there 'cause you're gonna be alright and by the way, here's your sign for the end of the age: **THIS GOSPEL OF THE KINGDOM WILL BE PREACHED IN ALL THE WORLD AS A WITNESS TO ALL THE NATIONS.**

Matthew 24:15 NKJV **"THEREFORE"**

When you see a 'therefore', you must look for what it's there for. The disciples had asked, "When will these things be?" That is: when will all the stones of the Temple be cast down? When will the 'house' be left desolate? Jesus now answers this question:

Matthew 24:15-16 NKJV

Therefore when you see the 'abomination of desolation,' spoken of by Daniel the prophet, standing in the holy place" (whoever reads, let him understand), 16 "then let those who are in Judea flee to the mountains.

Mark 13:14

But when ye shall see the abomination of desolation, spoken of by Daniel the prophet, standing where it ought not, (let him that readeth understand,) then let them that be in Judaea flee to the mountains:

Luke 21:20-21

And when ye shall see Jerusalem compassed with armies, then know that the desolation thereof is nigh. 21 Then let them which are in Judaea flee to the mountains; and let them which are in the midst of it depart out; and let not them that are in the countries enter thereinto.

Let the reader understand. Let the reader understand.

Hear what Jesus said. The armies are coming, the desolation is near, but the Gospel must be preached; . . . . . THEREFORE FLEE! Head for the hills! Don't hang about expecting Me to turn up. You've got work to do, a Gospel to preach; THEREFORE FLEE! Despite the wars and rumours of wars it is not the end of the age. FLEE. When you see the Abomination of Desolation; when you see the armies; FLEE!

Matthew: When you see . . . flee.

Mark: When you see . . . flee.

Luke: When you see . . . flee.

Matthew 24:17-22
Let him which is on the housetop not come down to take any thing out of his house: 18 Neither let him which is in the field return back to take his clothes. 19 And woe unto them that are with child, and to them that give suck in those days! 20 But pray ye that your flight be not in the winter, neither on the sabbath day: 21 For then shall be great tribulation, such as was not since the beginning of the world to this time, no, nor ever shall be. 22 And except those days should be shortened, there should no flesh be saved: but for the elect's sake those days shall be shortened.

Mark 13:15-20
And let him that is on the housetop not go down into the house, neither enter therein, to take any thing out of his house: 16 And let him that is in the field not turn back again for to take up his garment. 17 But woe to them that are with child, and to them that give suck in those days! 18 And pray ye that your flight be not in the winter. 19 For in those days shall be affliction, such as was not from the beginning of the creation which God created unto this time, neither shall be. 20 And except that the Lord had shortened those days, no flesh should be saved: but for the elect's sake, whom he hath chosen, he hath shortened the days.

Luke 21:21-24
Then let them which are in Judaea flee to the mountains; and let them which are in the midst of it depart out; and let not them that are in the countries enter thereinto. 22 For these be the days of vengeance, that all things which are written may be fulfilled. 23 But woe unto them that are with child, and to them that give suck, in those days! for there shall be great distress in the land, and wrath upon this people. 24 And they shall fall by the edge of the sword, and shall be led away captive into all nations: and Jerusalem shall be trodden down of the Gentiles, until the times of the Gentiles be fulfilled.

Jesus said flee because: "These be the days of vengeance."

Jesus said flee because: "There shall be great distress in the land, and wrath upon this people."

Jesus said flee because: "There will be tribulation."

Jesus said flee because: "For then shall be great tribulation."

Have you noticed that there are at least two tribulations, possibly three? The one in the verses following is the time when all will hate Christians for His Names sake. He says that they will deliver you to tribulation, kill you, hate you and betray you.

Matthew 24:9

Then shall they deliver you up to be afflicted, and shall kill you: and ye shall be hated of all nations for my name's sake.

Mark 13:13

And ye shall be hated of all men for my name's sake: but he that shall endure unto the end, the same shall be saved.

Luke 21:16

And ye shall be betrayed both by parents, and brethren, and kinsfolks, and friends; and some of you shall they cause to be put to death.

In describing the other tribulation, the Scripture does not use the word 'you' at all. The word is 'they': 'they' will fall by the sword; 'they' will be led away; there will be wrath upon 'this' people. And so that it doesn't proceed and effect the elect, the days are cut short. This great tribulation, which came upon Jerusalem, is referred to in Luke as the "days of vengeance". Jesus said it was on account of all the righteous blood shed on the earth. It was a great tribulation upon the Jews to be followed by the trampling of Jerusalem until the time of the Gentiles is fulfilled. It was not something that the nascent Christian Church was to experience, rather they were to be delivered from it as per Daniel 12:1.

Having answered the disciples question about the destruction of the Temple, adding that it is then the time to flee on account of the great tribulation coming upon the city and nation, He moves on to the signs of the times that pertain to the end of the age saying, "THEN"

"Then" means: at that time; or after that time; or the next thing to happen. After the great tribulation upon the unbelieving Jews, Jesus reiterates his warning about the coming of false Christs and false prophets that he made at the beginning of His discourse.

Matthew 24:23-26

Then if any man shall say unto you, Lo, here is Christ, or there; believe it not. 24 For there shall arise false Christs, and false prophets, and shall shew great signs and wonders; insomuch that, if it were possible, they shall deceive the very elect. 25 Behold, I have told you before. 26 Wherefore if they shall say unto you, Behold, he is in the desert; go not forth: behold, he is in the secret chambers; believe it not.

Mark 13:21-23

And then if any man shall say to you, Lo, here is Christ; or, lo, he is there; believe him not: 22 For false Christs and false prophets shall rise, and shall shew signs and wonders, to seduce, if it were possible, even the elect. 23 But take ye heed: behold, I have foretold you all things.

The Jews have had at least fifteen claimants to the title of Messiah over the centuries. The first major figure was Simon Bar Kochba early in the second century, about sixty years after the fall of Jerusalem. Among those who call themselves Christian there have been at least thirty notable characters claiming to be Christ, the vast majority being during the last century till now. In Jerusalem, they have a special team of psychologists who are regularly dealing with people who consider themselves to be the Messiah, or the Christ, or Elijah, or John the Baptist; I think the list goes on. They are labelled as suffering from Messianic Delusional Syndrome, some call it the Jerusalem Syndrome, and others call it the Messianic Complex. I remember once seeing an ad in a magazine saying that the Christ was in London. No doubt we will see more. So when someone tells me He is in a temple in Jerusalem, I'm not going to believe it. The Scripture already warns me about a man of sin who is going to tell the world that he is God as he sits in the Temple of God. But with Jesus, we won't have to go looking for Him for we will be caught up to meet Him in the clouds (1 Thessalonians 4:17). Hallelujah! Until He comes to raise us up at the last day, He reigns in our hearts and is seated at the Right Hand of God.

Luke doesn't bother to reiterate about the deceptions but instead gives us an unspecified time period.

Luke 21:24

And they shall fall by the edge of the sword, and shall be led away captive into all nations: and Jerusalem shall be trodden down of the Gentiles, until the times of the Gentiles be fulfilled.

Some might say that because the Jews are back in Jerusalem that this period of time is finished; over. I heard the Israeli Prime Minister Benjamin Netanyahu mention recently (July 2017) that only about a third of the world's Jews are living in Israel while others estimate about half the Jews are back. Faced with that fact and the continuing presence of Gentiles still dominating the Temple Mount and much of Jerusalem, we have ample reason to reject that idea in favour of something more definite happening in the future. While the Dome of the Rock is still standing, Gentiles who are given to the Islamic faith will continue to trample that area as they do to this day. When Jesus made His statements about this, the context He was speaking of was directly concerning the Temple Mount.

Continuing with His prophecy, Jesus gives us a few more details regarding the end of the age; signs in the sky that will appear after we have done our part preaching the Gospel in ALL the world. Have you preached it in all your part of the world? Time to be about His business.

Matthew 24:29-31
Immediately after the tribulation of those days shall the sun be darkened, and the moon shall not give her light, and the stars shall fall from heaven, and the powers of the heavens shall be shaken: 30 And then shall appear the sign of the Son of man in heaven: and then shall all the tribes of the earth mourn, and they shall see the Son of man coming in the clouds of heaven with power and great glory. 31 And he shall send his angels with a great sound of a trumpet, and they shall gather together his elect from the four winds, from one end of heaven to the other.

Luke 21:24-26
And they shall fall by the edge of the sword, and shall be led away captive into all nations: and Jerusalem shall be trodden down of the Gentiles, until the times of the Gentiles be fulfilled. 25 And there shall be signs in the sun, and in the moon, and in the stars; and upon the earth distress of nations, with perplexity; the sea and the waves roaring; 26 Men's hearts failing them for fear, and for looking after those things which are coming on the earth: for the powers of heaven shall be shaken.

Mark 13:24-27
But in those days, after that tribulation, the sun shall be darkened, and the moon shall not give her light, 25 And the stars of heaven shall fall, and the powers that are in heaven shall be shaken. 26 And then shall they see the Son of man coming in the clouds with great power and glory. 27 And then shall he send his angels, and shall gather together his elect from the four winds, from the uttermost part of the earth to the uttermost part of heaven.

Matthew 24:27
For as the lightning cometh out of the east, and shineth even unto the west; so shall also the coming of the Son of man be.

Yep, looks like a last-days tribulation to be endured with perseverance by the saints before the sun, moon and stars diminish. Jesus refers to this period of time as "the tribulation of those days" when He speaks about the end of the age and He had already mentioned it in Matthew 24:9, Mark 13:13 and Luke 21:17 and also prophesied by Daniel:

Daniel 7:21-22
I beheld, and the same horn made war with the saints, and prevailed against them; 22 Until the Ancient of days came, and judgment was given to the saints of the most High; and the time came that the saints possessed the kingdom.

Jesus explains the resurrection, the Kingdom of Heaven and the end of the age with these parables. We touched on this in the last chapter for the subjects overlap somewhat, however, it's an important matter and worth repeating.

Matthew 13:24-30
Another parable put he forth unto them, saying, The kingdom of heaven is likened unto a man which sowed good seed in his field: 25 But while men slept, his enemy came and sowed tares among the wheat, and went his way. 26 But when the blade was sprung up, and brought forth fruit, then appeared the tares also. 27 So the servants of the householder came and said unto him, Sir, didst not thou sow good seed in thy field? from whence then hath it tares? 28 He said unto them, An enemy hath done this. The servants said unto him, Wilt thou then that we go and gather them up? 29 But he said, Nay; lest while ye gather up the tares, ye root up also the wheat with them. 30 Let both grow together until the harvest: and in the time of harvest I will say to the reapers, Gather ye together first the tares, and bind them in bundles to burn them: but gather the wheat into my barn.

Not leaving us to interpret the parable for ourselves, Jesus gives the explanation:

Matthew 13:36-43
Then Jesus sent the multitude away, and went into the house: and his disciples came unto him, saying, Declare unto us the parable of the tares of the field. 37 He answered and said unto them, He that soweth the good seed is the Son of man; 38 The field is the world; the good seed are the children of the kingdom; but the tares are the children of the wicked one; 39 The enemy that sowed them is the devil; the harvest is the end of the world; and the reapers are the angels. 40 As therefore the tares are gathered and burned in the fire; so shall it be in the end of this world. 41 The Son of man shall send forth his angels, and they shall gather out of his kingdom all things that offend, and them which do iniquity; 42 And shall cast them into a furnace of fire: there shall be wailing and gnashing of teeth. 43 Then shall the righteous shine forth as the sun in the kingdom of their Father. Who hath ears to hear, let him hear.

Matthew 13:47-50
Again, the kingdom of heaven is like unto a net, that was cast into the sea, and gathered of every kind: 48 Which, when it was full, they drew to shore, and sat down, and gathered the good into vessels, but cast the bad away. 49 So shall it be at the end of the world: the angels shall come forth, and sever the wicked from among the just, 50 And shall cast them into the furnace of fire: there shall be wailing and gnashing of teeth.

In the explanation of both these parables we see that the end of the age immediately becomes the Day of Judgment. The wheat and the tares are brought off the field which represents the world and are sorted out; the fish are brought up out of their world and are sorted out. Jesus used another metaphoric expression, that of sheep and goats in Matthew 25, which also has some details of the Day of Judgment.

Matthew 25:31:46 NKJV
"When the Son of Man comes in His glory, and all the holy angels with Him, then He will sit on the throne of His glory. 32 All the nations will be gathered before Him, and He will separate them one from another, as a shepherd divides *his* sheep from the goats. 33 And He will set the sheep

on His right hand, but the goats on the left. 34 Then the King will say to those on His right hand, 'Come, you blessed of My Father, inherit the kingdom prepared for you from the foundation of the world: 35 for I was hungry and you gave Me food; I was thirsty and you gave Me drink; I was a stranger and you took Me in; 36 I *was* naked and you clothed Me; I was sick and you visited Me; I was in prison and you came to Me.' 37 "Then the righteous will answer Him, saying, 'Lord, when did we see You hungry and feed *You,* or thirsty and give *You* drink? 38 When did we see You a stranger and take *You* in, or naked and clothe *You?* 39 Or when did we see You sick, or in prison, and come to You?' 40 And the King will answer and say to them, 'Assuredly, I say to you, inasmuch as you did *it* to one of the least of these My brethren, you did *it* to Me.'

41 "Then He will also say to those on the left hand, 'Depart from Me, you cursed, into the everlasting fire prepared for the devil and his angels: 42 for I was hungry and you gave Me no food; I was thirsty and you gave Me no drink; 43 I was a stranger and you did not take Me in, naked and you did not clothe Me, sick and in prison and you did not visit Me.' 44 "Then they also will answer Him, saying, 'Lord, when did we see You hungry or thirsty or a stranger or naked or sick or in prison, and did not minister to You?' 45 Then He will answer them, saying, 'Assuredly, I say to you, inasmuch as you did not do *it* to one of the least of these, you did not do *it* to Me.' 46 And these will go away into everlasting punishment, but the righteous into eternal life."

The Gospel of John has little to say of the last day but what it does say is definitive:

John 6:39
And this is the Father's will which hath sent me, that of all which he hath given me I should lose nothing, but should raise it up again at the last day.

John 6:40
And this is the will of him that sent me, that every one which seeth the Son, and believeth on him, may have everlasting life: and I will raise him up at the last day.

John 6:44
No man can come to me, except the Father which hath sent me draw him: and I will raise him up at the last day.

John 6:54
Whoso eateth my flesh, and drinketh my blood, hath eternal life; and I will raise him up at the last day.

Jesus said, "I will raise him up at the last day."

Jesus said, "I will raise him up at the last day."

Jesus said, "I will raise him up at the last day."

Jesus said, "I will raise him up at the last day."

Jesus said, ". . . the harvest is the end of the age, and the reapers are the angels." By way of reminder, here are the passages from Matthew again with Jesus describing the end of the age, or as the King James has it: "the end of this world."

Matthew 13:40-43
As therefore the tares are gathered and burned in the fire; so shall it be in the end of this world. 41 The Son of man shall send forth his angels, and they shall gather out of his kingdom all things that offend, and them which do iniquity; 42 And shall cast them into a furnace of fire: there shall be wailing and gnashing of teeth. 43 Then shall the righteous shine forth as the sun in the kingdom of their Father. Who hath ears to hear, let him hear.

Matthew 13:49-50
So shall it be at the end of the world: the angels shall come forth, and sever the wicked from among the just, 50 And shall cast them into the furnace of fire: there shall be wailing and gnashing of teeth.

In summary, Jesus answered these four questions given Him by the Apostles:

1. When will these things be?
2. What will be the sign that these things will come to be?
3. What is the sign of the end of the age?
4. What is the sign of your coming?

He began by answering concerning the end of the age as the proclamations concerning Jerusalem and the Temple had clearly provoked the disciples concerning this particular event. He assures them that despite tribulation, betrayal and wars, the end is not yet and that it will not come immediately. He then tells them that the Gospel will be preached in all the world first, and then the end shall come. Question 3 answered first. (Matthew 24:4-14: Mark 13:5-13)

Because they had the great commission to fulfil, He then warned them not to stay in Jerusalem to be destroyed with the wicked, but when they see the Abomination of Desolation, the armies surrounding the city, they were to flee to the mountains. Question 1 and Question 2 answered. (Matthew 24:15-22; Mark 13:14-20; Luke 21:8-19)

He told them that a great tribulation was coming upon the nation and that these would be the days of vengeance for all the righteous blood that had been shed since Abel. He told them that the surviving Jews would be led away captive into the nations and that Jerusalem and the Temple Mount would be trampled by Gentiles until the time of the Gentiles was fulfilled. (Luke 21:24)

During that period of time before His return, which includes the time of the Gentiles, there would be many false Christs and false prophets with lying signs and wonders. He told them His coming would be "after the tribulation of those days", a time when the final earthly kingdom will make war against the saints (Daniel 7:21; Matthew 24:23:28; Mark 13:21-23; Luke 21:20-24).

Then the sun loses its light and the moon becomes blood red and the stars of the heavens fall. Luke includes "distress of nations", "men's hearts failing them for fear" and the "powers of the heavens" being shaken. Question 4 partially answered. (Matthew 24:29; Mark 13:24-25; Luke 21:25-26)

Then the sign of the Son of Man would appear (Question 4: answer completed) and His angels would be sent to gather His elect from Heaven and Earth. The gathering of all the saints from Heaven would of course be the dead in Christ who rise first and then those who remain are caught up to meet them in the air in what is commonly referred to as the Rapture. (Matthew24:30-31; Mark 13:26-27; Luke 21:27)

Contrary to a popular contemporary teaching, the Rapture, or to use the biblical expression, the Resurrection, happens on the last day. Jesus said that the harvest is the end of the age and as noted in the above Scriptures, it is when the wicked are cast into the fire and the righteous go on to shine forth in the Kingdom of their Father. He said again and again that He will raise up those who believe on the last day (John 6:39, 40, 44, 54).

With this understanding given to us from the Lord Himself, we have every reason to believe that the Abomination of Desolation is not a future event for us in this present age. It was the harbinger of destruction and an early warning to the disciples that they were to flee from Judea and Jerusalem before the Jews experienced the great tribulation that was to come upon the city. The wrath of God was abiding upon the unbelieving nation that had filled its cup of sin to the brim and the vengeance of God for all the righteous blood was about to be poured out upon the nation.

The prophetic teaching of Jesus accurately describes the events that unfolded upon the unbelieving Jews. A graphic description of the details of the fall of Jerusalem accomplished by the Romans is to be found in the writings of the first century Jewish historian Josephus whom I've mentioned a few times now. I encourage you to read the Josephus account. It's a real eye opener to the extent of the calamity that came upon the unbelieving Jews.

There are secular confirmations of the occurrence of this event which include written records of the Roman's celebration of their victory and evidence of large memorials built and minted commemorative coins which remain to this day. As already mentioned, early Christian writers speak of the escape of the Church who had heeded the warnings in the Gospels and went into the mountainous area of the Decapolis, east and south east of Lake Galilee where most of them from Jerusalem found safety in a city called Pella. Apparently this area was Roman friendly and did not suffer the destruction of the Jewish villages as the Legions made their way down through Samaria and Judea to Jerusalem.

The Jews to this day remember the event of the destruction of their Second Temple. The amazing 'coincidence' is that it occurred on the exact same day on their calendar as the destruction of the First Temple by the Babylonians. They call their day of remembrance *'Tisha B'Av.'*

The Kingdom of Judah and the Kingdom of Israel are now both in exile. And a new Kingdom has arisen. A Kingdom not of this world that exists and grows whilst the kingdoms of this world continue to come and go until the end of the age. But what of the promises regarding the restoration of Israel? The disciples asked the same question.

Acts 1:6-8
When they therefore were come together, they asked of him, saying, Lord, wilt thou at this time restore again the kingdom to Israel? 7 And he said unto them, It is not for you to know the times or the seasons, which the Father hath put in his own power. 8 But ye shall receive power, after that the Holy Ghost is come upon you: and ye shall be witnesses unto me both in Jerusalem, and in all Judaea, and in Samaria, and unto the uttermost part of the earth.

Jesus did not tell them it wasn't going to be or that they had misinterpreted the prophecies of old. He simply told them the time and the season for the restoration of Israel's kingdom to come to pass was none of their business and directed them to the work of preaching the Gospel as His witnesses. And the promised restoration? Probably not accomplished until after the time of the Gentiles is fulfilled. We will look at the Scriptures on that subject in a following chapter and see what we shall see.

Chapter Twelve

The Apostolic Prophecies

The Lion brought forth a Lamb and the Lamb brought forth a Kingdom.

Acts 2:1-18
And when the day of Pentecost was fully come, they were all with one accord in one place. 2 And suddenly there came a sound from heaven as of a rushing mighty wind, and it filled all the house where they were sitting. 3 And there appeared unto them cloven tongues like as of fire, and it sat upon each of them. 4 And they were all filled with the Holy Ghost, and began to speak with other tongues, as the Spirit gave them utterance.

5 And there were dwelling at Jerusalem Jews, devout men, out of every nation under heaven. 6 Now when this was noised abroad, the multitude came together, and were confounded, because that every man heard them speak in his own language. 7 And they were all amazed and marvelled, saying one to another, Behold, are not all these which speak Galilaeans? 8 And how hear we every man in our own tongue, wherein we were born? 9 Parthians, and Medes, and Elamites, and the dwellers in Mesopotamia, and in Judaea, and Cappadocia, in Pontus, and Asia, 10 Phrygia, and Pamphylia, in Egypt, and in the parts of Libya about Cyrene, and strangers of Rome, Jews and proselytes, 11 Cretes and Arabians, we do hear them speak in our tongues the wonderful works of God. 12 And they were all amazed, and were in doubt, saying one to another, What meaneth this? 13 Others mocking said, These men are full of new wine.

14 But Peter, standing up with the eleven, lifted up his voice, and said unto them, Ye men of Judaea, and all ye that dwell at Jerusalem, be this known unto you, and hearken to my words: 15 For these are not drunken, as ye suppose, seeing it is but the third hour of the day. 16 But this is that which was spoken by the prophet Joel; 17 And it shall come to pass in the last days, saith God, I will pour out of my Spirit upon all flesh: and your sons and your daughters shall prophesy, and your young men shall see visions, and your old men shall dream dreams: 18 And on my servants and on my handmaidens I will pour out in those days of my Spirit; and they shall prophesy:

The Kingdom of God burst forth from Heaven with a demonstration of the Spirit that inwardly transformed the disciples and was accompanied by some notable outward signs so that three thousand people were immediately converted. WOW. With the Lord now reigning in their hearts by the Holy Spirit, His sheep were sent forth into the midst of savage wolves to establish the Kingdom of the Lamb in the hearts of men, women and children from every other kingdom on earth.

Jesus had forewarned them that they would be faced with all manner of deceptions, persecutions, trials and tribulations that would continue till the end of the age, but with His Spirit dwelling within, the Body of Christ would go forth into this world: with His power, His strength, His joy, His love, His healing, His message of forgiveness, the free gift of His Righteousness and the promise of Eternal Life to all who would believe. Hallelujah!

Following on the heels of what Jesus proclaimed, the Apostles reinforced and added a few more details on what to expect in this world and we discover that almost all the Apostolic Prophecies can be gathered together under the following subjects: the Deception, the Apostasy, the Persecution, the Antichrist and the Resurrection. In this chapter we will also get a glimpse of some early church doctrine and practices which reveal that the fulfilment of some of these prophecies began immediately after the departure of the Apostles.

And what of Judah? And what about the restoration of the kingdom to Israel? Do the Apostles not speak of it at all? Admittedly, they speak next to nothing. However, they already had the Holy Scriptures. They already had the Lord say to them that the Scriptures cannot be broken; saying again and again that they must all be fulfilled. They already had the sure word of prophecy. Nevertheless, we do have a little squeak, and that is in this verse from Paul in Romans.

Romans 11:25-29
For I would not, brethren, that ye should be ignorant of this mystery, lest ye should be wise in your own conceits; that blindness in part is happened to Israel, until the fulness of the Gentiles be come in. 26 And so all Israel shall be saved: as it is written, There shall come out of Sion the Deliverer, and shall turn away ungodliness from Jacob: 27 For this is my covenant unto them, when I shall take away their sins. 28 As concerning the gospel, they are enemies for your sakes: but as touching the election, they are beloved for the father's sakes. 29 For the gifts and calling of God are without repentance.

The gifts and the calling of God are without repentance; that is God doesn't change His mind about what He has planned for them. All Israel shall be saved, and we in His church will have a part to play in that. In the meantime, we've got work to do and the letters of the Apostles are to equip us and prepare us for the things to come. Right from the start, in the time of their writing, we find that deceptions had already begun.

Jude 1:3-4
Beloved, when I gave all diligence to write unto you of the common salvation, it was needful for me to write unto you, and exhort you that ye should earnestly contend for the faith which was once delivered unto the saints. 4 For there are certain men crept in unawares, who were before of old ordained to this condemnation, ungodly men, turning the grace of our God into lasciviousness, and denying the only Lord God, and our Lord Jesus Christ.

The word lasciviousness is also translated licentiousness which colloquially rendered in our modern day means: 'a licence to sin'.

1 Timothy 6:9-11
But they that will be rich fall into temptation and a snare, and into many foolish and hurtful lusts, which drown men in destruction and perdition. 10 For the love of money is the root of all evil: which while some coveted after, they have erred from the faith, and pierced themselves through with many sorrows. 11 But thou, O man of God, flee these things; and follow after righteousness, godliness, faith, love, patience, meekness.

As we can all appreciate, the entirety of the letters have corrections of one sort or another that bear witness to the reality of deception in the midst of the churches.

One of the often addressed problems the nascent church faced was with regard to leadership within the Body of Christ. The servant leadership that Jesus demonstrated and taught was filled with authority, but it was not authoritarian. He called for submission, but not subjugation. He came to serve, not to be served. In the Book of Acts we have Paul speaking to the Ephesian elders:

Acts 20:28-31
Take heed therefore unto yourselves, and to all the flock, over the which the Holy Ghost hath made you overseers, to feed the church of God, which he hath purchased with his own blood. 29 For I know this, that after my departing shall grievous wolves enter in among you, not sparing the flock. 30 Also of your own selves shall men arise, speaking perverse things, to draw away disciples after them. 31 Therefore watch, and remember, that by the space of three years I ceased not to warn every one night and day with tears.

3 John 9-10
I wrote unto the church: but Diotrephes, who loveth to have the preeminence among them, receiveth us not. 10 Wherefore, if I come, I will remember his deeds which he doeth, prating against us with malicious words: and not content therewith, neither doth he himself receive the brethren, and forbiddeth them that would, and casteth them out of the church.

2 Peter 2:1-3 NKJV
But there were also false prophets among the people, even as there will be false teachers among you, who will secretly bring in destructive heresies, even denying the Lord who bought them, *and* bring on themselves swift destruction. 2 And many will follow their destructive ways, because of whom the way of truth will be blasphemed. 3 By covetousness they will exploit you with deceptive words; for a long time their judgment has not been idle, and their destruction does not slumber.

I saw a paraphrase of these verses from 2 Peter some time ago, can't remember where, that went something like this: "Watch out for smooth talking, money hungry Bible teachers with large followings that will attempt to exploit you with their deceptions and will give Christianity a bad name by their deeds." From the very beginning the true believers would have encounters with false teachers, false prophets and those who draw people to themselves. It says that they have "crept in unnoticed", that they "secretly bring in destructive heresies". Paul writes extensively in 2 Corinthians to equip the church to recognise false apostles. No wonder we are exhorted to test all things:

1 Thessalonians 5:21 NKJV
Test all things; hold fast what is good.

The historical fulfilment of the predicted massive deception has been recorded for us by the early 'church fathers'. In their writings they were from time to time refuting various heresies that arose and we must give them credit where credit is due. Unfortunately, at the same time as they were refuting the heresies of others, they themselves fell into grievous error. Even though some perished as martyrs, from their own pens flowed forth the seeds of corruption and deception that culminated with the tyranny of the Catholic Church and that period of history known as the dark ages.

They instituted and held fast to an ecclesiastical hierarchical system that was totally antithetical to the teachings of Jesus and the Apostles. They assumed authority over God's people by making themselves preeminent and exercising an illegitimate authority that conformed to the ways of the Gentiles. It was this rebellion to the words of Jesus that opened the door to the incremental inclusion of numerous other false doctrines. Here are the commands of Jesus, reinforced by Peter, that were being totally ignored:

Matthew 20:25-28 NKJV
But Jesus called them to *Himself* and said, "You know that the rulers of the Gentiles lord it over them, and those who are great exercise authority over them. 26 Yet it shall not be so among you; but whoever desires to become great among you, let him be your servant. 27 And whoever desires to be first among you, let him be your slave— 28 just as the Son of Man did not come to be served, but to serve, and to give His life a ransom for many."

Matthew 23:8-11 NKJV
But you, do not be called 'Rabbi'; for One is your Teacher, the Christ, and you are all brethren. 9 Do not call anyone on earth your father; for One is your Father, He who is in heaven. 10 And do not be called teachers; for One is your Teacher, the Christ. 11 But he who is greatest among you shall be your servant.

If it was today that these words were spoken, I imagine the contemporary titles assumed and given in today's churches would be included in the above short list. Do not be called Reverent, Bishop, Pastor, etc., for we are all brethren. Nor call anyone your: Mother, Father, Teacher, Pastor, etc. This ongoing rebellion to the words of Jesus is a serious matter in need of repentance.

1 Peter 5:1-4

The elders which are among you I exhort, who am also an elder, and a witness of the sufferings of Christ, and also a partaker of the glory that shall be revealed: 2 Feed the flock of God which is among you, taking the oversight thereof, not by constraint, but willingly; not for filthy lucre, but of a ready mind; 3 Neither as being lords over God's heritage, but being examples to the flock. 4 And when the chief Shepherd shall appear, ye shall receive a crown of glory that fadeth not away.

Jesus said that you can't serve God and mammon. Nothing wrong with money itself, but it is the love of money which is a root to all manner of evil (1 Timothy 6:10). Clearly what Paul was addressing was the motive of the heart and was exhorting them to truly serve out of love for God and man and not for the love of money. An early church writing declared that those who asked for money were false prophets (Didache 11b), except if they were asking to supply a need other than their own. If that rule were applied today it would soon sort out who were truly trusting in the Lord. Perhaps we would see the end of begging bags and offering plates prompting people to give. Giving could then be secret and motivated by the Spirit of the Lord. We would then discover who are really walking by faith.

Notice how Peter does not exalt himself over the elders he is writing to. The sort of leadership that the believers were to submit to was completely servant oriented, without titles, devoid of the lordship model of this world. Watching over the flock as an overseer is entirely different to being a lord. The sort of overseers that exemplify the heart of God are those who really care for a person's soul. Their primary concern is to see that those that are entrusted to them receive the maximum reward from the Father. Therefore they correct and teach for the sake of others, not for position and recognition and not for 'filthy lucre'.

As we now look at some of the early church writings, it will show that they were actually fathers of the monstrosity we now call the Catholic Church. What follows is a few of the notable characters from among the 'church fathers' who were responsible for the progressively downward trend in the doctrines of the post apostolic age with their corresponding heresies.

Ignatius (50-110AD)

Although he suffered martyrdom, before his death Ignatius was one of the first on record to introduce authoritarianism in the church. The very thing Paul warned the Ephesians of in Acts 20 was beginning to happen. What follows is an example of his teaching:

Ignatius to the Smyrnaeans
Chapter VIII. Let Nothing Be Done Without the Bishop.
See that ye all follow the bishop, even as Jesus Christ does the Father, and the presbytery as ye would the apostles; and reverence the deacons, as being the institution of God. Let no man do anything connected with the Church without the bishop. Let that be deemed a proper Eucharist, which is [administered] either by the bishop, or by one to whom he has entrusted it. Wherever the bishop shall appear, there let the multitude [of the people] also be; even as, wherever Jesus

Christ is, there is the Catholic Church. It is not lawful without the bishop either to baptize or to celebrate a love-feast; but whatsoever he shall approve of, that is also pleasing to God, so that everything that is done may be secure and valid.

Chapter IX.-Honour the Bishop.
*Moreover, it is in accordance with reason that we should return to soberness [of conduct], and, while yet we have opportunity, exercise repentance towards God. It is well to reverence both God and the bishop. He who honours the bishop has been honoured by God; **he who does anything without the knowledge of the bishop, does [in reality] serve the devil.** Let all things, then, abound to you through grace, for ye are worthy. Ye have refreshed me in all things, and Jesus Christ [shall refresh] you. Ye have loved me when absent as well as when present. May God recompense you, for whose sake, while ye endure all things, ye shall attain unto Him.* (Emphasis mine)

The cult like obedience this teaching espouses results in all manner of spiritual abuse and is found among people suitably described as control freaks. The above quotation became the very seed that grew up to become the institution of the Papacy and it is totally contrary to the Body of Christ being under the Headship of Jesus Christ. His writings also contained elements of the Catholic transubstantiation heresy that has people believing that the bread and wine we take in remembrance literally becomes the body and blood of Jesus.

Irenaeus (125-202AD)

Irenaeus wrote a polemic titled *Against Heresies* in about 170-185AD that was primarily refuting the doctrine of the Gnostics, yet he himself held heretical ideas. In one of his teachings he claimed that Jesus was fifty years old at His death, a statement which He claimed was attested to by at least one apostle. *Against Heresies, Book 2, Chapter 22:5.* It was not his only claim to apostolic authority for his erroneous teaching. More on this aspect of Irenaeus later.

He supported the authority of a 'bishop' as a ruler over many churches AND promoted the idea of the authority of church traditions. *Against Heresies, Book 3, Chapters 3-5.*

He sowed the seeds of Mariolatry, claiming that Mary came as the second Eve. *Against Heresies, Book 3, Chapter 22:4 "Eve's disobedience was loosed by the obedience of Mary. For what the virgin Eve had bound fast through unbelief, this did the virgin Mary set free through faith."*

He also taught the Catholic heresy that declares the Eucharist becomes the real presence of the body and blood of Christ. *Against Heresies, Book 5, Chapter 2.* What an incredible departure from sharing wine and bread at a meal and remembering Him.

Clement of Alexandria (150-230AD)

He mixed the philosophy of Plato with Christianity in his attempt to synthesise the 'wisdom' of the Greeks with the Word of God, he thus promoted the allegorising of the Scriptures. *Clement of Alexandria: The Stromata Book 5 Chapter 1.* As a consequence He developed the doctrine of purgatory and introduced universal salvation.

Tertullian (155-255AD)

For his defence of a move of the Holy Spirit and support for the flow of God's spiritual gifts through the believers, Tertullian is to be commended. He also truthfully argued against Gnosticism, however he had a number of false ideas that later were incorporated into the institution of the Catholic Church.

He taught that the church's authority comes through apostolic succession. *The Prescription Against Heretics: Chapter 32.* He taught against widows remarrying, calling it fornication. *Tertullian: Exhortation to Chastity 1-13.* He taught baptism as a requirement for the forgiveness of sins. *Tertullian Book 1, Chapter 28.* He lays the blame for sin on Eve rather than Adam and from his aberrant theology believed that woman are to carry the guilt of it to this day. This teaching was used as support for the false doctrine that Mary atoned for Eve's sin.

Tertullian: De Cultu Feminarum, Book 1, Chapter 1.
And do you not know that you are (each) an Eve? The sentence of God on this sex of yours lives in this age: the guilt must of necessity live too. You are the devil's gateway: you are the unsealer of that (forbidden) tree: you are the first deserter of the divine law: you are she who persuaded him whom the devil was not valiant enough to attack. You destroyed so easily God's image, man. On account of your desert, that is, death, even the Son of God had to die.

Totally misogynistic and totally wrong. The Bible makes it clear: it was Adam's sin that brought in sin and death. Eve may have eaten the fruit first, but Adam was right there saying nothing and was responsible (Genesis 3:6). Christ came as the Second Adam; He alone atoned for all sin. The Scriptures make no mention of Mary being anything other than a blessed mother who had the privilege of bearing the only sinless child this world has ever seen. I guess she discovered a bit when she had her other children.

Origen (185-254AD)

Though he endured persecution and torture for the cause of Christ under Emperor Decius in 250AD, Origen was loaded with false teachings.

He believed in a form of purgatory and universalism, denying the literal fire of hell and believing that even Satan would be saved eventually. *Origen: On First Principles, Book 1, Chapter 6:3*

He believed the Holy Spirit was a created being of some sort. *Origen. Commentary on John: Book 2:6. "How the Word is the maker of all things, and even the Holy Spirit was made through Him."*

He believed that men's souls are pre-existent and that stars and planets could possibly have souls. *"In regard to the sun, however, and the moon and the stars, as to whether they are living beings or are without life, there is not clear tradition"* (Origen, cited by W.A. Jurgens, *The Faith of the Early Fathers*).

Nothing but a wild speculation and not at all inspired. He also believed that Jesus was a created being and not eternal. *"He held an aberrant view on the nature of Christ, which gave rise to the later Arian heresy"* (*Encyclopedia of Christian Apologetics*, Origen).

He denied the bodily resurrection, claiming that the resurrection body is spherical, non-material, and does not have members. *"He denied the tangible, physical nature of the resurrection body in clear contrast to the teaching of Scripture"* (*Encyclopedia of Christian Apologetics*, Origen). He was condemned by the Council of Constantinople on this count.

Origen allegorized the Bible saying, *"The Scriptures have little use to those who understand them literally."* The unfortunate result of this extreme allegorical teaching is to deny the actual literal meaning of the Scriptures. A balanced approach is to see the types and symbols of historical events without losing the original plain meaning. Much of the Church is still suffering from this man's influence.

Eusebius of Caesarea (270-340AD)

Eusebius collected the writings of Origen and promoted his erroneous teachings. *"Whatever proof exists that Origen and his school deteriorated the correctness of the text, it is to the same extent clear that Eusebius accepted and perpetuated that injury"* (*Discussions of Robert Lewis Dabney*, I, p. 387).

Constantine the Great, who had joined church and state in the Roman Empire and had thereby opened the door for the establishment of the Roman Catholic Church, hired Eusebius to produce some Greek New Testaments. Frederick Nolan and other authorities have charged Eusebius with making many changes in the text of Scripture. (Nolan, *Inquiry into the Integrity of the Greek Vulgate*, p. 35).

Many of the noted omissions in the modern versions can be traced to this period, including Mark 16:9-20 and John 8:1-11. After intensive investigation, Frederick Nolan concluded that Eusebius *"suppressed those passages in his edition"* (Nolan, p. 240). In fact, many textual authorities have identified Vaticanus and Sinaiticus, the manuscripts so revered by modern textual critics, as two of the copies of the Greek New Testament made by Eusebius. These manuscripts also contained the spurious apocryphal writings, Shepherd of Hermas and the Epistle of Barnabas. Origen had considered these two uninspired and fanciful books as canonical Scripture (Goodspeed, *The Formation of the New Testament*, p. 103).

A classic example of the incremental inclusion of false teaching is to be found in the first century document called The Didache, Its opening statement says, "The teaching of the Lord to the Gentiles by the Twelve Apostles, which gives it the alternative title: The Teachings of the Twelve Apostles. Though it claims Apostolic Authority and has many honourable exhortations to righteous living that can be found in the Gospels and the Letters, it also has some deviant instructions. Concerning baptism you must first fast (Didache 7), it advocates appointed repetitious prayers and special days for fasting (Didache 8), and what is written of the bread and wine we take in remembrance shows that they had already lost the significance of its meaning (Didache 9). These things may seem innocuous, however, they betray a lack of discernment and an absence of the Holy Spirit which is the hallmark of a declining spiritual life. Claims to Apostolic Authority to give credence to their writings is also a feature of some terrible teachings of other early church writers which we will see later in this study.

I could go on about John Chrysostom (347-407AD), Jerome (340-420AD, Cyril (376-444AD) and many others and show that there is more, much much more, but it isn't good for the soul to hear of such nonsense and blasphemy. I do not for one moment suggest a perusal of all the writings of the so called 'church fathers'. However, there is a compendium of their writings which amounts to fully 38 volumes available in hard copy for around $1500 or as a pdf if you are really interested. However, there are many scholars who have documented their heresies and it is probably easier and wiser to go to the critics first and then follow through on the quotations to validate.

The Ecumenical World Council of Churches advocates church unity (otherwise known as submission to the Roman Papacy) through promoting the writings of the 'church fathers', saying that because they were closer to the time of the Apostles, their writings are closer to the true meaning of the Scriptures and thus they convince many to return to Rome. But as can be seen in the documentation above, there was a progression of false doctrines that slowly eroded their discernment and the result was the formation of the Apostate Catholic Church.

It's a miracle that they held onto the Scriptures at all. However, the false teachers come as messengers of righteousness just as Satan comes as an angel of light. They love to appear holy. Tucking a copy of the Scriptures under their arm and upholding it as the Word of God, yet at the same time promoting their own traditions as authoritative and corrupting the Scriptures as much as they think they can get away with is right up their alley.

As mentioned above, several apocryphal books were included in their Latin translation called the Vulgate: Tobit, Judith, Ecclesiasticus, Baruch, Sophonias and 1st and 2nd Maccabees. All these books are mixtures, containing many things true but also teaching doctrines that are contrary to the rest of the Bible. Maccabees, for instance, contains reasonably accurate history of the Jewish nation worthy of reading, but has reference to a practice of praying for the dead without condemning the deed.

It seems to me that the reason spurious books are added to the canon rather than approved books being taken away, is that the enemy knows that if you take away a book from those that are inspired, what remains is still true. Therefore, to inject error, the more effective way to deceive is to introduce deceptive mixtures by adding false teachings and false prophecies. In my online searches I discovered that we have a multitude of contemporary advocates promoting the writings of the early 'church fathers' AND the many books that have been designated apocrypha. The battle against deception continues.

Here we are in our time, and the effects of the deceptions that manifested in the post apostolic age are still with us. Although Martin Luther made much ground against the traditions of the institutional church of his time, there was also plenty that he held onto that included: transubstantiation, a hierarchy clergy laity system with its false form of authority, infant baptism, baptism by sprinkling, liturgically formatted meetings, the perpetuation of a form of godliness that denied the power of the Spirit, and worst of all; the persecution of 'heretics' which happened to include Jews and Christians who recognised and refused to submit to the same authoritarianism of the Catholics being repeated in the new church structure.

As if all the above is not enough, the Apostolic Prophecies also warned of a period of time that has since earned the title: The Apostasy, or The Falling Away.

1 Timothy 4:1-2
Now the Spirit speaketh expressly, that in the latter times some shall depart from the faith, giving heed to seducing spirits, and doctrines of devils; 2 Speaking lies in hypocrisy; having their conscience seared with a hot iron;

2 Timothy 3:1-5
This know also, that in the last days perilous times shall come. 2 For men shall be lovers of their own selves, covetous, boasters, proud, blasphemers, disobedient to parents, unthankful, unholy, 3 Without natural affection, trucebreakers, false accusers, incontinent, fierce, despisers of those that are good, 4 Traitors, heady, highminded, lovers of pleasures more than lovers of God; 5 Having a form of godliness, but denying the power thereof: from such turn away.

2 Timothy 4:1-4
I charge thee therefore before God, and the Lord Jesus Christ, who shall judge the quick and the dead at his appearing and his kingdom; 2 Preach the word; be instant in season, out of season; reprove, rebuke, exhort with all long suffering and doctrine. 3 For the time will come when they will not endure sound doctrine; but after their own lusts shall they heap to themselves teachers, having itching ears; 4 And they shall turn away their ears from the truth, and shall be turned unto fables.

In these letters to Timothy we find the awful promise that people will turn away from the Faith. People that once walked in the Truth will turn aside to fables (2 Timothy 4:4). Whilst there is a list of rather obvious sins listed by Paul, of note there are some not so obvious characteristics of the people we are warned about:

Now, these people are particularly loving: they are lovers of themselves . . . they are lovers of money (covetous) . . . lovers of pleasure . . . having a form of godliness that denies the power thereof . . . (2 Timothy 3:2-4).

It is these sort of people that Paul warns us that we are to avoid saying, "From such people turn away!" (2 Timothy 3:5).But note, those that have but a form of godliness are lumped in with the brutal despisers of good, and the unloving and unforgiving. Is it that one leads to the other? Well, it seems that when persecution comes, history shows that it is religious people that end up doing abominable things to true believers. Not surprising really as it was religious people that plotted the death of Jesus.

In this letter to the Thessalonians, Paul confirms the latter day falling away and links it to being a precursor to the coming of the Antichrist.

2 Thessalonians 2:1-7
Now we beseech you, brethren, by the coming of our Lord Jesus Christ, and by our gathering together unto him, 2 That ye be not soon shaken in mind, or be troubled, neither by spirit, nor by word, nor by letter as from us, as that the day of Christ is at hand.

3 Let no man deceive you by any means: for that day shall not come, except there come a falling away first, and that man of sin be revealed, the son of perdition;

4 Who opposeth and exalteth himself above all that is called God, or that is worshipped; so that he as God sitteth in the temple of God, shewing himself that he is God. 5 Remember ye not, that, when I was yet with you, I told you these things? 6 And now ye know what withholdeth that he might be revealed in his time. 7 For the mystery of iniquity doth already work . . .

Some contend that the great falling away was what led the world into what is historically referred to as the Dark Ages. There are a number of untenable things that negate this assumption. For instance, the final kingdom ruling the earth, that is described in Daniel Chapter 7:21, is going to be persecuting the saints immediately before the end of the age; just prior to "the dividing of time" (Daniel 7:25). Also, Jesus says that because of being hated by all nations, and the abounding lawlessness, the love of many will grow cold. I think this time is yet to come as He mentioned "all nations", which eliminates the period of the Dark Ages when the Gospel had not yet reached much of the world. The dark ages is perhaps a foreshadowing of that which is to come. The warnings we have should be enough to let us know there will constantly be false teachers and persecution in every generation. Therefore, test all things, including what I have written here and hold fast to what is good.

The mystery of iniquity has been working and certain pockets of severe persecution have already had to be endured by believers in many countries. I believe that when the time comes, we will have either the necessary grace to endure to the end, or the grace to be martyred. Here is Paul comforting the saints in their time of trial by reminding them and assuring them of the Resurrection.

2 Thessalonians 1:3-12
We are bound to thank God always for you, brethren, as it is meet, because that your faith groweth exceedingly, and the charity of every one of you all toward each other aboundeth; 4 So that we ourselves glory in you in the churches of God for your patience and faith in all your persecutions and tribulations that ye endure: 5 Which is a manifest token of the righteous judgment of God, that ye may be counted worthy of the kingdom of God, for which ye also suffer: 6 Seeing it is a righteous thing with God to recompense tribulation to them that trouble you;

7 And to you who are troubled rest with us, when the Lord Jesus shall be revealed from heaven with his mighty angels, 8 In flaming fire taking vengeance on them that know not God, and that obey not the gospel of our Lord Jesus Christ: 9 Who shall be punished with everlasting destruction from the presence of the Lord, and from the glory of his power; 10 When he shall come to be glorified in his saints, and to be admired in all them that believe (because our testimony among you was believed) in that day.

11 Wherefore also we pray always for you, that our God would count you worthy of this calling, and fulfil all the good pleasure of his goodness, and the work of faith with power: 12 That the name of our Lord Jesus Christ may be glorified in you, and ye in him, according to the grace of our God and the Lord Jesus Christ.

1 Thessalonians 4:13-18
But I would not have you to be ignorant, brethren, concerning them which are asleep, that ye sorrow not, even as others which have no hope. 14 For if we believe that Jesus died and rose again, even so them also which sleep in Jesus will God bring with him. 15 For this we say unto you by the word of the Lord, that we which are alive and remain unto the coming of the Lord shall not prevent them which are asleep. 16 For the Lord himself shall descend from heaven with a shout, with the voice of the archangel, and with the trump of God: and the dead in Christ shall rise first: 17 Then we which are alive and remain shall be caught up together with them in the clouds, to meet the Lord in the air: and so shall we ever be with the Lord. 18 Wherefore comfort one another with these words.

Yes, there is great comfort in the knowledge of the Resurrection.

1 Corinthians 15:50-54
Now this I say, brethren, that flesh and blood cannot inherit the kingdom of God; neither doth corruption inherit incorruption. 51 Behold, I shew you a mystery; We shall not all sleep, but we shall all be changed, 52 In a moment, in the twinkling of an eye, at the last trump: for the trumpet

shall sound, and the dead shall be raised incorruptible, and we shall be changed. 53 For this corruptible must put on incorruption, and this mortal must put on immortality. 54 So when this corruptible shall have put on incorruption, and this mortal shall have put on immortality, then shall be brought to pass the saying that is written, Death is swallowed up in victory.

1 Thessalonians 4:16
For the Lord himself shall descend from heaven with a shout, with the voice of the archangel, and with the trump of God: and the dead in Christ shall rise first:

2 Thessalonians 2:1-12
Now we beseech you, brethren, by the coming of our Lord Jesus Christ, and by our gathering together unto him, 2 That ye be not soon shaken in mind, or be troubled, neither by spirit, nor by word, nor by letter as from us, as that the day of Christ is at hand. 3 Let no man deceive you by any means: for that day shall not come, except there come a falling away first, and that man of sin be revealed, the son of perdition; 4 Who opposeth and exalteth himself above all that is called God, or that is worshipped; so that he as God sitteth in the temple of God, shewing himself that he is God. 5 Remember ye not, that, when I was yet with you, I told you these things? 6 And now ye know what withholdeth that he might be revealed in his time. 7 For the mystery of iniquity doth already work: only he who now letteth will let, until he be taken out of the way. 8 And then shall that Wicked be revealed, whom the Lord shall consume with the spirit of his mouth, and shall destroy with the brightness of his coming: 9 Even him, whose coming is after the working of Satan with all power and signs and lying wonders, 10 And with all deceivableness of unrighteousness in them that perish; because they received not the love of the truth, that they might be saved. 11 And for this cause God shall send them strong delusion, that they should believe a lie: 12 That they all might be damned who believed not the truth, but had pleasure in unrighteousness.

Praise the Lord, the Antichrist will be destroyed with the brightness of His coming when He comes to take us home, when He comes to raise us up on that last day. With His mighty angels in flaming fire He will burn up all His enemies. Praise the Lord. For an in depth analysis of 2 Thessalonians 2:7 see He Who Now Restrains in the Appendix.

1 Thessalonians 5:1-11
But of the times and the seasons, brethren, ye have no need that I write unto you. 2 For yourselves know perfectly that the day of the Lord so cometh as a thief in the night. 3 For when they shall say, Peace and safety; then sudden destruction cometh upon them, as travail upon a woman with child; and they shall not escape. 4 But ye, brethren, are not in darkness, that that day should overtake you as a thief. 5 Ye are all the children of light, and the children of the day: we are not of the night, nor of darkness. 6 Therefore let us not sleep, as do others; but let us watch and be sober. 7 For they that sleep sleep in the night; and they that be drunken are drunken in the night. 8 But let us, who are of the day, be sober, putting on the breastplate of faith and love; and for an helmet, the hope of salvation. 9 For God hath not appointed us to wrath, but to obtain salvation by our Lord Jesus Christ, 10 Who died for us, that, whether we wake or

sleep, we should live together with him. 11 Wherefore comfort yourselves together, and edify one another, even as also ye do.

2 Peter 3:1-13

This second epistle, beloved, I now write unto you; in both which I stir up your pure minds by way of remembrance: 2 That ye may be mindful of the words which were spoken before by the holy prophets, and of the commandment of us the apostles of the Lord and Saviour: 3 Knowing this first, that there shall come in the last days scoffers, walking after their own lusts, 4 And saying, Where is the promise of his coming? for since the fathers fell asleep, all things continue as they were from the beginning of the creation. 5 For this they willingly are ignorant of, that by the word of God the heavens were of old, and the earth standing out of the water and in the water: 6 Whereby the world that then was, being overflowed with water, perished: 7 But the heavens and the earth, which are now, by the same word are kept in store, reserved unto fire against the day of judgment and perdition of ungodly men. 8 But, beloved, be not ignorant of this one thing, that one day is with the Lord as a thousand years, and a thousand years as one day. 9 The Lord is not slack concerning his promise, as some men count slackness; but is longsuffering to us-ward, not willing that any should perish, but that all should come to repentance.

10 But the day of the Lord will come as a thief in the night; in the which the heavens shall pass away with a great noise, and the elements shall melt with fervent heat, the earth also and the works that are therein shall be burned up. 11 Seeing then that all these things shall be dissolved, what manner of persons ought ye to be in all holy conversation and godliness, 12 Looking for and hasting unto the coming of the day of God, wherein the heavens being on fire shall be dissolved, and the elements shall melt with fervent heat? 13 Nevertheless we, according to his promise, look for new heavens and a new earth, wherein dwelleth righteousness.

Hebrews 12:25-29

See that ye refuse not him that speaketh. For if they escaped not who refused him that spake on earth, much more shall not we escape, if we turn away from him that speaketh from heaven: 26 Whose voice then shook the earth: but now he hath promised, saying, Yet once more I shake not the earth only, but also heaven. 27 And this word, Yet once more, signifieth the removing of those things that are shaken, as of things that are made, that those things which cannot be shaken may remain. 28 Wherefore we receiving a kingdom which cannot be moved, let us have grace, whereby we may serve God acceptably with reverence and godly fear: 29 For our God is a consuming fire.

The resurrection of the dead is recorded to be one of the foundational doctrines.

Hebrews 6:1-2

Therefore leaving the principles of the doctrine of Christ, let us go on unto perfection; not laying again the foundation of repentance from dead works, and of faith toward God, 2 Of the doctrine of baptisms, and of laying on of hands, and of resurrection of the dead, and of eternal judgment.

Ignorance of the doctrine, or teaching about the resurrection got some saints into trouble:

2 Timothy 2:15-19
Study to shew thyself approved unto God, a workman that needeth not to be ashamed, rightly dividing the word of truth. 16 But shun profane and vain babblings: for they will increase unto more ungodliness. 17 And their word will eat as doth a canker: of whom is Hymenaeus and Philetus; 18 Who concerning the truth have erred, saying that the resurrection is past already; and overthrow the faith of some. 19 Nevertheless the foundation of God standeth sure, having this seal, The Lord knoweth them that are his. And, let every one that nameth the name of Christ depart from iniquity.

In the above passage we find that some people had their faith overthrown by false teaching about the timing of the resurrection. These people were the first to fall prey to the devilish deception that convinced them they had been left behind. If there were other circumstances involved, we can but speculate. But one thing is for sure, it is a fiery dart of Satan that can be extinguished through faith in what the Word of God actually says on this subject. Let us take particular note from these Scriptures again:

2 Thessalonians 2:1-3
Now we beseech you, brethren, by the coming of our Lord Jesus Christ, and by our gathering together unto him, 2 That ye be not soon shaken in mind, or be troubled, neither by spirit, nor by word, nor by letter as from us, as that the day of Christ is at hand. 3 Let no man deceive you by any means: for that day shall not come, except there come a falling away first, and that man of sin be revealed, the son of perdition;

2 Thessalonians 1:7-10
And to you who are troubled rest with us, when the Lord Jesus shall be revealed from heaven with his mighty angels, 8 In flaming fire taking vengeance on them that know not God, and that obey not the gospel of our Lord Jesus Christ: 9 Who shall be punished with everlasting destruction from the presence of the Lord, and from the glory of his power; 10 When he shall come to be glorified in his saints . . .

1 Thessalonians 4:16-17
For the Lord himself shall descend from heaven with a shout, with the voice of the archangel, and with the trump of God: and the dead in Christ shall rise first: 17 Then we which are alive and remain shall be caught up together with them in the clouds, to meet the Lord in the air: and so shall we ever be with the Lord.

2 Thessalonians 2:8
And then shall that Wicked be revealed, whom the Lord shall consume with the spirit of his mouth, and shall destroy with the brightness of his coming:

When Christ shall come

With shout of acclamation

To take me home

What joy shall fill my heart

Then I shall bow

With humble adoration

And there proclaim

My God how great thou art

The Kingdom of God that was manifested in power when the nascent church received the Holy Spirit has a very simple and easy to follow path through history. It will be filled with persecutions and tribulations, it will be inundated with false teachers and all manner of deceptions and yet it will eventually preach the gospel to ALL the earth and then the end shall come. And through it all we always have the victory through our Lord and Saviour Jesus Christ IF we never give up on our faith in Him. Hallelujah!

As noted earlier in this chapter, the Apostles speak little of the destiny of Judah and Israel. However, these three statements from the writings of Paul admonish us to simply believe the promises of God that are found in His Word.

2 Timothy 3:16
All scripture is given by inspiration of God, and is profitable for doctrine

2 Corinthians 1:20
For all the promises of God in him are yea, and in him Amen

Romans 11:29
For the gifts and calling of God are without repentance.

We shall pick up the destiny of Judah and Israel in the following chapters and discover what the Born Again Believers of the Kingdom of God will experience happening on the world scene during that period of time known as the latter days.

FROM SOLOMON TO THE FALL OF ROMAN EMPIRE

KING SOLOMON

KINGDOM OF JUDAH   KINGDOM OF ISRAEL

ASSYRIAN EMPIRE   ISRAEL EXILED 740-720BC

JUDAH EXILED 607-586BC   BABYLONIAN EMPIRE   MANY ISRAELITES ATTAIN
                                                                                   FREEDOM BECOME
                                                                               KNOWN AS CIMMERIANS

JUDAH RETURNS 537BC   MEDES AND PERSIAN EMPIRE   MORE ESCAPE
                                                                                          BECOME KNOWN
                                                                                            AS SCYTHIANS

JUDAH AS A VASSAL STATE   GREEK EMPIRE   ISRAEL BEGINS MIGRATING
                                            ALEXANDER THE GREAT   NORTH AND WEST
                                                                                             INTO EUROPE

KING OF NORTH and KING OF SOUTH

JUDAH BREAKS GREEK YOKE   REMAINING ISRAELITES MIGRATE
                                                                          NORTH AND WEST

JESUS BRINGS   ROMAN EMPIRE   ISRAEL SIFTED
KINGDOM OF GOD   THROUGH THE NATIONS

ABOMINATION OF   TIME OF THE GENTILES BEGINS   GOSPEL IS PREACHED
DESOLATION

JUDAH JOINS ISRAEL IN EXILE   RISE OF CATHOLICISM AND THE DARK AGES

THE ROMAN EMPIRE FALLS TO ISLAMIC EMPIRE

Chapter Thirteen

The Second Exodus

In this chapter and in the two that follow, we will be looking at the prophecies that are still future (2017AD) during that period of time that the Bible refers to as the Latter Days.

When one contemplates the prophesied regathering of both Judah and Israel, the staggering scope of that which is yet to come is almost too much for the mind to apprehend. So take particular attention to the contents of these passages and be enlightened to God's Big Plan to glorify Himself among the nations before the end of the age, before Jesus comes, before the dividing of time between this age and the age to come. There are some long portions of Scripture to get through in this chapter which have considerable details of the coming regathering. I hope you don't find it too tedious to wade through. Take your time and soak it in as these verses are generally completely misunderstood or simply overlooked and rarely taken to heart.

Jeremiah 30:1-24
The word that came to Jeremiah from the Lord, saying, 2 Thus speaketh the Lord God of Israel, saying, Write thee all the words that I have spoken unto thee in a book. 3 For, lo, the days come, saith the Lord, that I will bring again the captivity of my people Israel and Judah, saith the Lord: and I will cause them to return to the land that I gave to their fathers, and they shall possess it. 4 And these are the words that the Lord spake concerning Israel and concerning Judah. 5 For thus saith the Lord; We have heard a voice of trembling, of fear, and not of peace. 6 Ask ye now, and see whether a man doth travail with child? wherefore do I see every man with his hands on his loins, as a woman in travail, and all faces are turned into paleness? 7 Alas! for that day is great, so that none is like it: it is even the time of Jacob's trouble, but he shall be saved out of it. 8 For it shall come to pass in that day, saith the Lord of hosts, that I will break his yoke from off thy neck, and will burst thy bonds, and strangers shall no more serve themselves of him: 9 But they shall serve the Lord their God, and David their king, whom I will raise up unto them.

10 Therefore fear thou not, O my servant Jacob, saith the Lord; neither be dismayed, O Israel: for, lo, I will save thee from afar, and thy seed from the land of their captivity; and Jacob shall return, and shall be in rest, and be quiet, and none shall make him afraid. 11 For I am with thee, saith the Lord, to save thee: though I make a full end of all nations whither I have scattered thee, yet I will not make a full end of thee: but I will correct thee in measure, and will not leave thee altogether unpunished.

147

12 For thus saith the Lord, Thy bruise is incurable, and thy wound is grievous. 13 There is none to plead thy cause, that thou mayest be bound up: thou hast no healing medicines. 14 All thy lovers have forgotten thee; they seek thee not; for I have wounded thee with the wound of an enemy, with the chastisement of a cruel one, for the multitude of thine iniquity; because thy sins were increased. 15 Why criest thou for thine affliction? thy sorrow is incurable for the multitude of thine iniquity: because thy sins were increased, I have done these things unto thee. 16 Therefore all they that devour thee shall be devoured; and all thine adversaries, every one of them, shall go into captivity; and they that spoil thee shall be a spoil, and all that prey upon thee will I give for a prey. 17 For I will restore health unto thee, and I will heal thee of thy wounds, saith the Lord; because they called thee an Outcast, saying, This is Zion, whom no man seeketh after.

18 Thus saith the Lord; Behold, I will bring again the captivity of Jacob's tents, and have mercy on his dwelling places; and the city shall be builded upon her own heap, and the palace shall remain after the manner thereof. 19 And out of them shall proceed thanksgiving and the voice of them that make merry: and I will multiply them, and they shall not be few; I will also glorify them, and they shall not be small. 20 Their children also shall be as aforetime, and their congregation shall be established before me, and I will punish all that oppress them. 21 And their nobles shall be of themselves, and their governor shall proceed from the midst of them; and I will cause him to draw near, and he shall approach unto me: for who is this that engaged his heart to approach unto me? saith the Lord. 22 And ye shall be my people, and I will be your God.

23 Behold, the whirlwind of the Lord goeth forth with fury, a continuing whirlwind: it shall fall with pain upon the head of the wicked. 24 The fierce anger of the Lord shall not return, until he hath done it, and until he have performed the intents of his heart: in the latter days ye shall consider it.

Jeremiah 31:1-40
At the same time, saith the Lord, will I be the God of all the families of Israel, and they shall be my people. 2 Thus saith the Lord, The people which were left of the sword found grace in the wilderness; even Israel, when I went to cause him to rest. 3 The Lord hath appeared of old unto me, saying, Yea, I have loved thee with an everlasting love: therefore with lovingkindness have I drawn thee.

4 Again I will build thee, and thou shalt be built, O virgin of Israel: thou shalt again be adorned with thy tabrets, and shalt go forth in the dances of them that make merry. 5 Thou shalt yet plant vines upon the mountains of Samaria: the planters shall plant, and shall eat them as common things. 6 For there shall be a day, that the watchmen upon the mount Ephraim shall cry, Arise ye, and let us go up to Zion unto the Lord our God. 7 For thus saith the Lord; Sing with gladness for Jacob, and shout among the chief of the nations: publish ye, praise ye, and say, O Lord, save thy people, the remnant of Israel.

8 Behold, I will bring them from the north country, and gather them from the coasts of the earth, and with them the blind and the lame, the woman with child and her that travaileth with child together: a great company shall return thither. 9 They shall come with weeping, and with

148

supplications will I lead them: I will cause them to walk by the rivers of waters in a straight way, wherein they shall not stumble: for I am a father to Israel, and Ephraim is my firstborn.

10 Hear the word of the Lord, O ye nations, and declare it in the isles afar off, and say, He that scattered Israel will gather him, and keep him, as a shepherd doth his flock. 11 For the Lord hath redeemed Jacob, and ransomed him from the hand of him that was stronger than he. 12 Therefore they shall come and sing in the height of Zion, and shall flow together to the goodness of the Lord, for wheat, and for wine, and for oil, and for the young of the flock and of the herd: and their soul shall be as a watered garden; and they shall not sorrow any more at all. 13 Then shall the virgin rejoice in the dance, both young men and old together: for I will turn their mourning into joy, and will comfort them, and make them rejoice from their sorrow. 14 And I will satiate the soul of the priests with fatness, and my people shall be satisfied with my goodness, saith the Lord.

15 Thus saith the Lord; A voice was heard in Ramah, lamentation, and bitter weeping; Rachel weeping for her children refused to be comforted for her children, because they were not. 16 Thus saith the Lord; Refrain thy voice from weeping, and thine eyes from tears: for thy work shall be rewarded, saith the Lord; and they shall come again from the land of the enemy. 17 And there is hope in thine end, saith the Lord, that thy children shall come again to their own border.

18 I have surely heard Ephraim bemoaning himself thus; Thou hast chastised me, and I was chastised, as a bullock unaccustomed to the yoke: turn thou me, and I shall be turned; for thou art the Lord my God. 19 Surely after that I was turned, I repented; and after that I was instructed, I smote upon my thigh: I was ashamed, yea, even confounded, because I did bear the reproach of my youth. 20 Is Ephraim my dear son? is he a pleasant child? for since I spake against him, I do earnestly remember him still: therefore my bowels are troubled for him; I will surely have mercy upon him, saith the Lord. 21 Set thee up waymarks, make thee high heaps: set thine heart toward the highway, even the way which thou wentest: turn again, O virgin of Israel, turn again to these thy cities. 22 How long wilt thou go about, O thou backsliding daughter? for the Lord hath created a new thing in the earth, A woman shall compass a man.

23 Thus saith the Lord of hosts, the God of Israel; As yet they shall use this speech in the land of Judah and in the cities thereof, when I shall bring again their captivity; The Lord bless thee, O habitation of justice, and mountain of holiness. 24 And there shall dwell in Judah itself, and in all the cities thereof together, husbandmen, and they that go forth with flocks. 25 For I have satiated the weary soul, and I have replenished every sorrowful soul. 26 Upon this I awaked, and beheld; and my sleep was sweet unto me.

27 Behold, the days come, saith the Lord, that I will sow the house of Israel and the house of Judah with the seed of man, and with the seed of beast. 28 And it shall come to pass, that like as I have watched over them, to pluck up, and to break down, and to throw down, and to destroy, and to afflict; so will I watch over them, to build, and to plant, saith the Lord. 29 In those days they shall say no more, The fathers have eaten a sour grape, and the children's teeth are set on

edge. 30 But every one shall die for his own iniquity: every man that eateth the sour grape, his teeth shall be set on edge.

31 Behold, the days come, saith the Lord, that I will make a new covenant with the house of Israel, and with the house of Judah: 32 Not according to the covenant that I made with their fathers in the day that I took them by the hand to bring them out of the land of Egypt; which my covenant they brake, although I was an husband unto them, saith the Lord: 33 But this shall be the covenant that I will make with the house of Israel; After those days, saith the Lord, I will put my law in their inward parts, and write it in their hearts; and will be their God, and they shall be my people. 34 And they shall teach no more every man his neighbour, and every man his brother, saying, Know the Lord: for they shall all know me, from the least of them unto the greatest of them, saith the Lord: for I will forgive their iniquity, and I will remember their sin no more.

35 Thus saith the Lord, which giveth the sun for a light by day, and the ordinances of the moon and of the stars for a light by night, which divideth the sea when the waves thereof roar; The Lord of hosts is his name: 36 If those ordinances depart from before me, saith the Lord, then the seed of Israel also shall cease from being a nation before me for ever. 37 Thus saith the Lord; If heaven above can be measured, and the foundations of the earth searched out beneath, I will also cast off all the seed of Israel for all that they have done, saith the Lord.

38 Behold, the days come, saith the Lord, that the city shall be built to the Lord from the tower of Hananeel unto the gate of the corner. 39 And the measuring line shall yet go forth over against it upon the hill Gareb, and shall compass about to Goath. 40 And the whole valley of the dead bodies, and of the ashes, and all the fields unto the brook of Kidron, unto the corner of the horse gate toward the east, shall be holy unto the Lord; it shall not be plucked up, nor thrown down any more for ever.

There is SO MUCH in these two chapters, but for this study it will suffice to highlight a few verses. Early in Chapter 30, the prophet makes mention of "Jacob's Trouble". In the context it clearly refers to both Judah and Israel (verses 3-7). After a lengthy discourse describing this trouble, we find these words at the end of chapter 30, "in the latter days ye shall consider it." Then after giving all the woes of this time of affliction we find at the beginning of Chapter 31 these words of comfort, "At the same time," says the Lord, "I will be the God of all the families of Israel, and they shall be My people." Oh, Hallelujah! All Israel will be saved.

Jeremiah 31:9 in particular refers to Ephraim as His firstborn. This hearkens back to the promise given by Jacob to the sons of Joseph when the Birthright Blessing which originally belonged to Reuben, Jacob's firstborn, was instead placed upon Ephraim.

9 They shall come with weeping, and with supplications will I lead them: I will cause them to walk by the rivers of waters in a straight way, wherein they shall not stumble: for I am a father to Israel, and Ephraim is my firstborn.

Also note this promise of the continuation of Israel as a nation.

35 Thus saith the Lord, which giveth the sun for a light by day, and the ordinances of the moon and of the stars for a light by night, which divideth the sea when the waves thereof roar; The Lord of hosts is his name: 36 If those ordinances depart from before me, saith the Lord, then the seed of Israel also shall cease from being a nation before me for ever. 37 Thus saith the Lord; If heaven above can be measured, and the foundations of the earth searched out beneath, I will also cast off all the seed of Israel for all that they have done, saith the Lord.

Hosea and Amos also speak of this great exodus to come.

Hosea 3:4-5

For the children of Israel shall abide many days without a king, and without a prince, and without a sacrifice, and without an image, and without an ephod, and without teraphim: 5 Afterward shall the children of Israel return, and seek the Lord their God, and David their king; and shall fear the Lord and his goodness in the latter days.

The mention of a future "David their king" in the above verse also appears in Ezekiel 34:23 and Ezekiel 37:24. In Jeremiah 3:9 we find it with these words added, ". . . whom I will raise up for them." In the same way that John the Baptist was referred to as Elijah because he carried the same kind of anointing, "David" in these verses is referring to Christ, not a reincarnation of King David. It is Jesus who has been raised up to reign over Israel. He is the King who sits on the Throne of David. Hallelujah!

Amos 9:9-15

For, lo, I will command, and I will sift the house of Israel among all nations, like as corn is sifted in a sieve, yet shall not the least grain fall upon the earth. 10 All the sinners of my people shall die by the sword, which say, The evil shall not overtake nor prevent us. 11 In that day will I raise up the tabernacle of David that is fallen, and close up the breaches thereof; and I will raise up his ruins, and I will build it as in the days of old: 12 That they may possess the remnant of Edom, and of all the heathen, which are called by my name, saith the Lord that doeth this. 13 Behold, the days come, saith the Lord, that the plowman shall overtake the reaper, and the treader of grapes him that soweth seed; and the mountains shall drop sweet wine, and all the hills shall melt. 14 And I will bring again the captivity of my people of Israel, and they shall build the waste cities, and inhabit them; and they shall plant vineyards, and drink the wine thereof; they shall also make gardens, and eat the fruit of them. 15 And I will plant them upon their land, and they shall no more be pulled up out of their land which I have given them, saith the Lord thy God.

Since the Romans uprooted Judah following their return from Babylon, this prophecy, like that of Jeremiah 30-31, cannot refer to the Kingdom of Judah prior to 70AD. It must therefore refer to a subsequent time: "they shall no more be pulled up out of their land".

Ezekiel 37:1-14

The hand of the Lord was upon me, and carried me out in the spirit of the Lord, and set me down in the midst of the valley which was full of bones, 2 And caused me to pass by them round about:

and, behold, there were very many in the open valley; and, lo, they were very dry. 3 And he said unto me, Son of man, can these bones live? And I answered, O Lord God, thou knowest. 4 Again he said unto me, Prophesy upon these bones, and say unto them, O ye dry bones, hear the word of the Lord. 5 Thus saith the Lord God unto these bones; Behold, I will cause breath to enter into you, and ye shall live: 6 And I will lay sinews upon you, and will bring up flesh upon you, and cover you with skin, and put breath in you, and ye shall live; and ye shall know that I am the Lord.

7 So I prophesied as I was commanded: and as I prophesied, there was a noise, and behold a shaking, and the bones came together, bone to his bone. 8 And when I beheld, lo, the sinews and the flesh came up upon them, and the skin covered them above: but there was no breath in them. 9 Then said he unto me, Prophesy unto the wind, prophesy, son of man, and say to the wind, Thus saith the Lord God; Come from the four winds, O breath, and breathe upon these slain, that they may live. 10 So I prophesied as he commanded me, and the breath came into them, and they lived, and stood up upon their feet, an exceeding great army.

11 Then he said unto me, Son of man, these bones are the whole house of Israel: behold, they say, Our bones are dried, and our hope is lost: we are cut off for our parts. 12 Therefore prophesy and say unto them, Thus saith the Lord God; Behold, O my people, I will open your graves, and cause you to come up out of your graves, and bring you into the land of Israel.

13 And ye shall know that I am the Lord, when I have opened your graves, O my people, and brought you up out of your graves, 14 And shall put my spirit in you, and ye shall live, and I shall place you in your own land: then shall ye know that I the Lord have spoken it, and performed it, saith the Lord.

In this symbolic vision of the valley of dry bones we find in verses 11-13 that the Lord again does not leave it to our imaginations, but gives the interpretation saying, "Son of man, these bones are the whole house of Israel." The Lord declares that there will be a time when Israel will cry out, "Our hope is lost . . . we are cut off!" Although this passage uses resurrection imagery, it is obviously not The Resurrection being spoken of. All indications are that this is the time of "Jacob's Trouble". He will reply by bringing them into their own land and they shall have the Spirit of God in them (verse 14).

Many prophecy teachers proclaim that Jacob's Trouble is something that happens only to the Jews sometime in the latter days during a tribulation that is supposed to happen after the rapture. Some say it was the holocaust of World War Two. Both of these views fail to appreciate that when the name Jacob or Israel is used in the Word of God to address a people group that includes the Jews, it automatically includes ALL the descendants of Jacob. It never is applied referring to the Jews alone. And as mentioned previously, it is the Northern Kingdom exclusive of the Jews who are consistently referred to as Jacob or Israel when not called Joseph or Ephraim.

Back to Ezekiel. Immediately following the Dry Bones Vision, which culminates with the Lord saying He will bring them into their own land, the prophet continues with a vision of the two sticks becoming one:

Ezekiel 37:15-28

The word of the Lord came again unto me, saying, 16 Moreover, thou son of man, take thee one stick, and write upon it, For Judah, and for the children of Israel his companions: then take another stick, and write upon it, For Joseph, the stick of Ephraim and for all the house of Israel his companions: 17 And join them one to another into one stick; and they shall become one in thine hand. 18 And when the children of thy people shall speak unto thee, saying, Wilt thou not shew us what thou meanest by these?

19 Say unto them, Thus saith the Lord God; Behold, I will take the stick of Joseph, which is in the hand of Ephraim, and the tribes of Israel his fellows, and will put them with him, even with the stick of Judah, and make them one stick, and they shall be one in mine hand. 20 And the sticks whereon thou writest shall be in thine hand before their eyes.

21 And say unto them, Thus saith the Lord God; Behold, I will take the children of Israel from among the heathen, whither they be gone, and will gather them on every side, and bring them into their own land: 22 And I will make them one nation in the land upon the mountains of Israel; and one king shall be king to them all: and they shall be no more two nations, neither shall they be divided into two kingdoms any more at all.

23 Neither shall they defile themselves any more with their idols, nor with their detestable things, nor with any of their transgressions: but I will save them out of all their dwelling places, wherein they have sinned, and will cleanse them: so shall they be my people, and I will be their God. 24 And David my servant shall be king over them; and they all shall have one shepherd: they shall also walk in my judgments, and observe my statutes, and do them.

25 And they shall dwell in the land that I have given unto Jacob my servant, wherein your fathers have dwelt; and they shall dwell therein, even they, and their children, and their children's children for ever: and my servant David shall be their prince for ever. 26 Moreover I will make a covenant of peace with them; it shall be an everlasting covenant with them: and I will place them, and multiply them, and will set my sanctuary in the midst of them for evermore. 27 My tabernacle also shall be with them: yea, I will be their God, and they shall be my people. 28 And the heathen shall know that I the Lord do sanctify Israel, when my sanctuary shall be in the midst of them for evermore.

In this latter vision of Ezekiel 37, one "stick" is clearly identified as representing the tribe of Joseph and his companions i.e. the Ten Tribes, and the other "stick" represents the tribe of Judah and his companions i.e. the tribe of Benjamin and the Levites. This important prophecy is obviously yet future to us, and could not have been fulfilled in 2nd Temple times (5th century BC through to 70AD). The latter verses of the chapter make this clear as it says again that they will be in the land that He gave to Jacob. Further, as chapters 38 and 39 show, the 'joining of the two sticks' is just preceding the invasion by Gog and Magog. (More on Gog and Magog later). To apply Ezekiel 37 to any time in the past is to rob it of any sensible meaning. And note the promise of the new covenant in verses 26-28. God's sanctuary will be in the very midst of His people, the Kingdom of God within, just as it is with us who believe. Hallelujah! Note again, David as servant and king referring to Christ.

Isaiah 11:11-14

And it shall come to pass in that day, that the Lord shall set his hand again the second time to recover the remnant of his people, which shall be left, from Assyria, and from Egypt, and from Pathros, and from Cush, and from Elam, and from Shinar, and from Hamath, and from the islands of the sea. 12 And he shall set up an ensign for the nations, and shall assemble the outcasts of Israel, and gather together the dispersed of Judah from the four corners of the earth.

13 The envy also of Ephraim shall depart, and the adversaries of Judah shall be cut off: Ephraim shall not envy Judah, and Judah shall not vex Ephraim.

The antagonism between Israel and Judah will end. As mentioned elsewhere, Israel is referred to as Ephraim as they were the leading tribe.

14 But they shall fly upon the shoulders of the Philistines toward the west; they shall spoil them of the east together: they shall lay their hand upon Edom and Moab; and the children of Ammon shall obey them.

Don't try and present this scenario to the Anti-God Squad United Nation Security Council as the solution to peace in the Middle East. They would just hate these verses.

Jeremiah 50:4-5

In those days, and in that time, saith the Lord, the children of Israel shall come, they and the children of Judah together, going and weeping: they shall go, and seek the Lord their God. 5 They shall ask the way to Zion with their faces thitherward, saying, Come, and let us join ourselves to the Lord in a perpetual covenant that shall not be forgotten.

Jeremiah 3:18

In those days the house of Judah shall walk with the house of Israel, and they shall come together out of the land of the north to the land that I have given for an inheritance unto your fathers.

Hosea 1:10-11

Yet the number of the children of Israel shall be as the sand of the sea, which cannot be measured nor numbered; and it shall come to pass, that in the place where it was said unto them, Ye are not my people, there it shall be said unto them, Ye are the sons of the living God. 11 Then shall the children of Judah and the children of Israel be gathered together, and appoint themselves one head, and they shall come up out of the land: for great shall be the day of Jezreel.

Jeremiah 30:21-22

And their nobles shall be of themselves, and their governor shall proceed from the midst of them; and I will cause him to draw near, and he shall approach unto me: for who is this that engaged his heart to approach unto me? saith the Lord. 22 And ye shall be my people, and I will be your God.

Note in these passages just mentioned how it is that Judah and Israel are coming together. At least half the world's population of Jews are still living outside of the Promised Land and for the most part they are content to dwell in those lands. Something's going to happen . . . It also appears from the last two Scriptures just mentioned that their form of government may still be democracy. Yet Christ shall be their King. Hmmmmmmm . . .

The prophets offer us an incredibly vivid picture of this coming union of the 'lost ten tribes', the sons of Joseph and his companions, with those we know today as the Jewish people. The animosity that has prevailed down through the ages will finally be removed and the two shall become one. The family feud between the Jews and the Joes will be over. The prophets make it clear that this reunion happens around the same time as they are brought out of the nations.

Jeremiah 3:11-18

And the Lord said unto me, The backsliding Israel hath justified herself more than treacherous Judah. 12 Go and proclaim these words toward the north, and say, Return, thou backsliding Israel, saith the Lord; and I will not cause mine anger to fall upon you: for I am merciful, saith the Lord, and I will not keep anger for ever. 13 Only acknowledge thine iniquity, that thou hast transgressed against the Lord thy God, and hast scattered thy ways to the strangers under every green tree, and ye have not obeyed my voice, saith the Lord. 14 Turn, O backsliding children, saith the Lord; for I am married unto you: and I will take you one of a city, and two of a family, and I will bring you to Zion: 15 And I will give you pastors according to mine heart, which shall feed you with knowledge and understanding. 16 And it shall come to pass, when ye be multiplied and increased in the land, in those days, saith the Lord, they shall say no more, The ark of the covenant of the Lord: neither shall it come to mind: neither shall they remember it; neither shall they visit it; neither shall that be done any more. 17 At that time they shall call Jerusalem the throne of the Lord; and all the nations shall be gathered unto it, to the name of the Lord, to Jerusalem: neither shall they walk any more after the imagination of their evil heart.

18 In those days the house of Judah shall walk with the house of Israel, and they shall come together out of the land of the north to the land that I have given for an inheritance unto your fathers.

Just a little dig at those who claim to know the whereabouts of the Ark of the Lord. Here it is a little plainer in the New King James:

Jeremiah 3:16 NKJV

"The ark of the covenant of the Lord.' It shall not come to mind, nor shall they remember it, nor shall they visit *it,* nor shall it be made anymore."

155

Ooops, slightly off topic but never mind. Let's get back to the regathering:

Jeremiah 16:14-15
Therefore, behold, the days come, saith the Lord, that it shall no more be said, The Lord liveth, that brought up the children of Israel out of the land of Egypt; 15 But, The Lord liveth, that brought up the children of Israel from the land of the north, and from all the lands whither he had driven them: and I will bring them again into their land that I gave unto their fathers.

Jeremiah 23:7-8
Therefore, behold, the days come, saith the Lord, that they shall no more say, The Lord liveth, which brought up the children of Israel out of the land of Egypt; 8 But, The Lord liveth, which brought up and which led the seed of the house of Israel out of the north country, and from all countries whither I had driven them; and they shall dwell in their own land.

Lest anyone doubt the contents of these verses, Jeremiah repeated the proclamation. The language could not be plainer. The future restoration of all the Tribes of Israel is absolutely mind boggling. It will involve an unprecedented geopolitical and demographic upheaval. It is to surpass the Exodus from Egypt in magnitude and significance. By no stretch of language or imagination can any of these texts be applied to the hopeful but limited return of the Jews from Babylon in 586BC.

It has been my experience that those who maintain that the Jewish people today represent the fulfilment of the biblical prophecies regarding the restoration of ALL Israel have not carefully read the many portions of Scripture dealing with that restoration. The texts we have just reviewed make it very plain that a great awakening lies ahead; Judah and Israel together coming out of the nations.

Take a break and get ready for another long and detailed prophecy.

Ezekiel 36:1-38
Also, thou son of man, prophesy unto the mountains of Israel, and say, Ye mountains of Israel, hear the word of the Lord: 2 Thus saith the Lord God; Because the enemy hath said against you, Aha, even the ancient high places are ours in possession: 3 Therefore prophesy and say, Thus saith the Lord God; Because they have made you desolate, and swallowed you up on every side, that ye might be a possession unto the residue of the heathen, and ye are taken up in the lips of talkers, and are an infamy of the people:

4 Therefore, ye mountains of Israel, hear the word of the Lord God; Thus saith the Lord God to the mountains, and to the hills, to the rivers, and to the valleys, to the desolate wastes, and to the cities that are forsaken, which became a prey and derision to the residue of the heathen that are round about; 5 Therefore thus saith the Lord God; Surely in the fire of my jealousy have I spoken against the residue of the heathen, and against all Idumea, which have appointed my land into their possession with the joy of all their heart, with despiteful minds, to cast it out for a prey.

6 Prophesy therefore concerning the land of Israel, and say unto the mountains, and to the hills, to the rivers, and to the valleys, Thus saith the Lord God; Behold, I have spoken in my jealousy and in my fury, because ye have borne the shame of the heathen: 7 Therefore thus saith the Lord God; I have lifted up mine hand, Surely the heathen that are about you, they shall bear their shame. 8 But ye, O mountains of Israel, ye shall shoot forth your branches, and yield your fruit to my people of Israel; for they are at hand to come. 9 For, behold, I am for you, and I will turn unto you, and ye shall be tilled and sown:

10 And I will multiply men upon you, all the house of Israel, even all of it: and the cities shall be inhabited, and the wastes shall be builded: 11 And I will multiply upon you man and beast; and they shall increase and bring fruit: and I will settle you after your old estates, and will do better unto you than at your beginnings: and ye shall know that I am the Lord. 12 Yea, I will cause men to walk upon you, even my people Israel; and they shall possess thee, and thou shalt be their inheritance, and thou shalt no more henceforth bereave them of men. 13 Thus saith the Lord God; Because they say unto you, Thou land devourest up men, and hast bereaved thy nations: 14 Therefore thou shalt devour men no more, neither bereave thy nations any more, saith the Lord God. 15 Neither will I cause men to hear in thee the shame of the heathen any more, neither shalt thou bear the reproach of the people any more, neither shalt thou cause thy nations to fall any more, saith the Lord God.

16 Moreover the word of the Lord came unto me, saying, 17 Son of man, when the house of Israel dwelt in their own land, they defiled it by their own way and by their doings: their way was before me as the uncleanness of a removed woman. 18 Wherefore I poured my fury upon them for the blood that they had shed upon the land, and for their idols wherewith they had polluted it: 19 And I scattered them among the heathen, and they were dispersed through the countries: according to their way and according to their doings I judged them. 20 And when they entered unto the heathen, whither they went, they profaned my holy name, when they said to them, These are the people of the Lord, and are gone forth out of his land.

21 But I had pity for mine holy name, which the house of Israel had profaned among the heathen, whither they went. 22 Therefore say unto the house of Israel, thus saith the Lord God; I do not this for your sakes, O house of Israel, but for mine holy name's sake, which ye have profaned among the heathen, whither ye went.

23 And I will sanctify my great name, which was profaned among the heathen, which ye have profaned in the midst of them; and the heathen shall know that I am the Lord, saith the Lord God, when I shall be sanctified in you before their eyes. 24 For I will take you from among the heathen, and gather you out of all countries, and will bring you into your own land. 25 Then will I sprinkle clean water upon you, and ye shall be clean: from all your filthiness, and from all your idols, will I cleanse you.

26 A new heart also will I give you, and a new spirit will I put within you: and I will take away the stony heart out of your flesh, and I will give you an heart of flesh. 27 And I will put my spirit

within you, and cause you to walk in my statutes, and ye shall keep my judgments, and do them. 28 And ye shall dwell in the land that I gave to your fathers; and ye shall be my people, and I will be your God. 29 I will also save you from all your uncleannesses: and I will call for the corn, and will increase it, and lay no famine upon you. 30 And I will multiply the fruit of the tree, and the increase of the field, that ye shall receive no more reproach of famine among the heathen. 31 Then shall ye remember your own evil ways, and your doings that were not good, and shall lothe yourselves in your own sight for your iniquities and for your abominations.

32 Not for your sakes do I this, saith the Lord God, be it known unto you: be ashamed and confounded for your own ways, O house of Israel. 33 Thus saith the Lord God; In the day that I shall have cleansed you from all your iniquities I will also cause you to dwell in the cities, and the wastes shall be builded. 34 And the desolate land shall be tilled, whereas it lay desolate in the sight of all that passed by. 35 And they shall say, This land that was desolate is become like the garden of Eden; and the waste and desolate and ruined cities are become fenced, and are inhabited. 36 Then the heathen that are left round about you shall know that I the Lord build the ruined places, and plant that that was desolate: I the Lord have spoken it, and I will do it. 37 Thus saith the Lord God; I will yet for this be enquired of by the house of Israel, to do it for them; I will increase them with men like a flock. 38 As the holy flock, as the flock of Jerusalem in her solemn feasts; so shall the waste cities be filled with flocks of men: and they shall know that I am the Lord.

Some people look at these prophecies and declare that because of the sinfulness of the tribes of Israel, they no longer qualify to live in the Promised Land. However, this gathering is wholly for the Glory of the Lord as these verses repeated below make clear:

22 Therefore say unto the house of Israel, thus saith the Lord God; I do not this for your sakes, O house of Israel, but for mine holy name's sake, which ye have profaned among the heathen, whither ye went.

32 Not for your sakes do I this, saith the Lord God, be it known unto you: be ashamed and confounded for your own ways, O house of Israel.

Ezekiel 20:33-44
As I live, saith the Lord God, surely with a mighty hand, and with a stretched out arm, and with fury poured out, will I rule over you: 34 And I will bring you out from the people, and will gather you out of the countries wherein ye are scattered, with a mighty hand, and with a stretched out arm, and with fury poured out. 35 And I will bring you into the wilderness of the people, and there will I plead with you face to face. 36 Like as I pleaded with your fathers in the wilderness of the land of Egypt, so will I plead with you, saith the Lord God. 37 And I will cause you to pass under the rod, and I will bring you into the bond of the covenant:

38 And I will purge out from among you the rebels, and them that transgress against me: I will bring them forth out of the country where they sojourn, and they shall not enter into the land

of Israel: and ye shall know that I am the Lord. 39 As for you, O house of Israel, thus saith the Lord God; Go ye, serve ye every one his idols, and hereafter also, if ye will not hearken unto me: but pollute ye my holy name no more with your gifts, and with your idols. 40 For in mine holy mountain, in the mountain of the height of Israel, saith the Lord God, there shall all the house of Israel, all of them in the land, serve me: there will I accept them, and there will I require your offerings, and the firstfruits of your oblations, with all your holy things. 41 I will accept you with your sweet savour, when I bring you out from the people, and gather you out of the countries wherein ye have been scattered; and I will be sanctified in you before the heathen. 42 And ye shall know that I am the Lord, when I shall bring you into the land of Israel, into the country for the which I lifted up mine hand to give it to your fathers. 43 And there shall ye remember your ways, and all your doings, wherein ye have been defiled; and ye shall lothe yourselves in your own sight for all your evils that ye have committed. 44 And ye shall know that I am the Lord when I have wrought with you for my name's sake, not according to your wicked ways, nor according to your corrupt doings, O ye house of Israel, saith the Lord God.

This work of God, as mentioned above, is totally for His Glory. God will demonstrate to the nations His faithfulness to the Patriarchs. What He promised them He will surely bring to pass.

Micah 5:7-15
And the remnant of Jacob shall be in the midst of many people as a dew from the Lord, as the showers upon the grass, that tarrieth not for man, nor waiteth for the sons of men. 8 And the remnant of Jacob shall be among the Gentiles in the midst of many people as a lion among the beasts of the forest, as a young lion among the flocks of sheep: who, if he go through, both treadeth down, and teareth in pieces, and none can deliver. 9 Thine hand shall be lifted up upon thine adversaries, and all thine enemies shall be cut off.

Right at the time of their great strength the following is proclaimed against them. Hear the continuation of this passage:

10 And it shall come to pass in that day, saith the Lord, that I will cut off thy horses out of the midst of thee, and I will destroy thy chariots: 11 And I will cut off the cities of thy land, and throw down all thy strong holds: 12 And I will cut off witchcrafts out of thine hand; and thou shalt have no more soothsayers: 13 Thy graven images also will I cut off, and thy standing images out of the midst of thee; and thou shalt no more worship the work of thine hands. 14 And I will pluck up thy groves out of the midst of thee: so will I destroy thy cities. 15 And I will execute vengeance in anger and fury upon the heathen, such as they have not heard.

That last verse is a little clearer in the New King James:

Micah 5:15 NKJV
And I will execute vengeance in anger and fury on the nations that have not heard. Note: Micah 5:15 "heard" is literally *obeyed* or *listened*.

The KJV makes the last verse at odds with the rest of the prophecy by using the word "heathen" for the Hebrew word *goyim*, which most English translations have rendered as "nations" as per the NKJV. The KJV's choice to translate *goyim* to "heathen" alters the meaning considerably, and does not make good grammar as it changes the subject of the paragraph. This prophecy is actually addressed to Jacob/Israel (Micah 5:7-8) and it is they who are "the nations that have not obeyed". They are the remnant that was to become a multitude of nations, Israel that was to be like a lion among the sheep, conquering all their adversaries according to the promises made to the Patriarchs. Here they are yet again in apostasy, Israel again in disobedience because they would not listen.

Jeremiah 16:16-18
Behold, I will send for many fishers, saith the Lord, and they shall fish them; and after will I send for many hunters, and they shall hunt them from every mountain, and from every hill, and out of the holes of the rocks. 17 For mine eyes are upon all their ways: they are not hid from my face, neither is their iniquity hid from mine eyes. 18 And first I will recompense their iniquity and their sin double; because they have defiled my land, they have filled mine inheritance with the carcases of their detestable and abominable things.

Jeremiah 3:14
Turn, O backsliding children, saith the Lord; for I am married unto you: and I will take you one of a city, and two of a family, and I will bring you to Zion:

Ezekiel 20:38
And I will purge out from among you the rebels, and them that transgress against me: I will bring them forth out of the country where they sojourn, and they shall not enter into the land of Israel: and ye shall know that I am the Lord.

This verse from Ezekiel is taken from its context above to highlight the manner of God's dealing with Israel in the day that He starts to bring them back; He will purge the rebels from among them.

Isaiah 10:20-23
And it shall come to pass in that day, that the remnant of Israel, and such as are escaped of the house of Jacob, shall no more again stay upon him that smote them; but shall stay upon the Lord, the Holy One of Israel, in truth. 21 The remnant shall return, even the remnant of Jacob, unto the mighty God. 22 For though thy people Israel be as the sand of the sea, yet a remnant of them shall return: the consumption decreed shall overflow with righteousness. 23 For the Lord God of hosts shall make a consumption, even determined, in the midst of all the land.

Ezekiel 39:28
Then shall they know that I am the Lord their God, which caused them to be led into captivity among the heathen: but I have gathered them unto their own land, and have left none of them any more there.

Jeremiah 30:11
For I am with thee, saith the Lord, to save thee: though I make a full end of all nations whither I have scattered thee, yet I will not make a full end of thee: but I will correct thee in measure, and will not leave thee altogether unpunished.

Jeremiah 30:7
Alas! for that day is great, so that none is like it: it is even the time of Jacob's trouble, but he shall be saved out of it.

Jeremiah 46:28
Fear thou not, O Jacob my servant, saith the Lord: for I am with thee; for I will make a full end of all the nations whither I have driven thee: but I will not make a full end of thee, but correct thee in measure; yet will I not leave thee wholly unpunished.

Did you note Ezekiel 39:28? God will not leave any of them behind.

Many will think it is the end of the age. Because of the overwhelming wickedness, all the Israelite nations around the world where the Lord has scattered them will be destroyed. Their cities will be destroyed. Their military strongholds will be destroyed. It will certainly be **TEOTWAWKI:** The End Of The World As We Know It.

The regathering of Israel and Judah does not look pretty. In fact it looks VERY SERIOUS. A righteous remnant will most likely endure a catastrophic world war type scenario, perhaps even nuclear war. It did take the Second World War and the holocaust to get the Jews motivated to get their 'foot in the door' and to have them taking possession of at least a portion of the Promised Land. With fury poured out the Ten Tribes of Israel along with the remainder of Judah in Diaspora could be reduced to the status of refugees and there will be only one place on earth where they will be welcome.

The Christians among the nations will no doubt be helping them return as Christians did for the Jews escaping the Nazis during the Second World War. Get ready Church! Those with love in their hearts, the true members the Kingdom of God on earth will be assisting the restoration of the Kingdom of Israel. Many of them will only then begin to realise their own heritage. What an amazing time this will be.

Isaiah 49:22 NKJV
Thus says the Lord God: "Behold, I will lift My hand in an oath to the nations, And set up My standard for the peoples; They shall bring your sons in *their* arms, And your daughters shall be carried on *their* shoulders;

Isaiah 60:9 NKJV
Surely the coastlands shall wait for Me; And the ships of Tarshish *will come* first, To bring your sons from afar, Their silver and their gold with them, To the name of the Lord your God, And to the Holy One of Israel, Because He has glorified you.

Isaiah 66:20 NKJV
Then they shall bring all your brethren for an offering to the Lord out of all nations, on horses and in chariots and in litters, on mules and on camels, to My holy mountain Jerusalem," says the Lord, "as the children of Israel bring an offering in a clean vessel into the house of the Lord.

Jeremiah 16:16
Behold, I will send for many fishers, saith the Lord, and they shall fish them; and after will I send for many hunters, and they shall hunt them from every mountain, and from every hill, and out of the holes of the rocks.

The end result will be that the descendants of Abraham, Isaac and Jacob, both the House of Judah and the House of Israel, will be united together with each other, and more importantly, restored completely to the Lord God Almighty.

Jeremiah 3:14
Turn, O backsliding children, saith the Lord; for I am married unto you: and I will take you one of a city, and two of a family, and I will bring you to Zion:

Isaiah 10:20-22
And it shall come to pass in that day, that the remnant of Israel, and such as are escaped of the house of Jacob, shall no more again stay upon him that smote them; but shall stay upon the Lord, the Holy One of Israel, in truth. 21 The remnant shall return, even the remnant of Jacob, unto the mighty God. 22 For though thy people Israel be as the sand of the sea, yet a remnant of them shall return: the consumption decreed shall overflow with righteousness.

The regathering of Israel is going to be a MAJOR EVENT. When it will take place, and how it will take place, and how long it will take to happen; I can but speculate as I am but a student of the Word. From the Word I can say that it is prophesied. It will surely come to pass. As they say, "Coming to a city near you." And for the Word of the Lord to be found true, this must all happen before Jesus returns.

Chapter Fourteen
Back in the Promised Land

The reality of Judah and Israel being brought back into the Promised Land should by now be well established in the hearts of all who have come this far following the Lion and the Unicorn on the Road to Zion. But what is it going to be like? What kind of kingdom is it going to be?

In approaching this subject, we must remember the words of Jesus and the Apostles and not allow the revelation of the Gospel of the Kingdom of God to be excluded from the context wherein these prophecies we are about to study are to be understood: Christ's Kingdom is not of this world; it is in the world but not of it; and the New Covenant is an everlasting Covenant.

Unbelieving Jews are still waiting for their Messiah, but they are not looking for a spiritual kingdom. The Messiah of their imagination is not Jesus ruling and reigning in the hearts of men, women and children from His throne in Heaven. A charismatic, Torah keeping Jew with a brilliant military mind, whose wisdom delivers a victory against incredible odds is more like what they are waiting for. They are waiting for some sort of combination of perhaps Moses, David and Elijah to appear in their midst, someone that can be seen with the natural eye, not someone that you must exercise faith in without seeing. The words of Jesus about the necessity of being born of the Spirit is foreign to them.

Unfortunately, many Christians have adopted this Jewish idea of a Messiah physically ruling an earthly kingdom and have constructed a theory that Jesus will then come to rule and reign bodily from Jerusalem. Effectively they have been persuaded to believe that during the reign of this Messiah, being in the world but not of the world would no longer apply to His Kingdom. Jesus said it was going to be better for His disciples that He go away and send the Holy Spirit. By being present, He would be presenting to those that are alive during that period of time a way of salvation that was somehow depreciated. Presently, we believe in the resurrection of our Lord and Saviour without seeing Him and He was only ever revealed in His Glorified Body to His disciples who already believed who He was. It would no longer be faith as the substance of things unseen if Jesus was in His Glorified Body revealed for everyone to see. Not only that, some who hold to this theory also have resurrected saints ruling and reigning with Him over people who have not even been saved. Glorified people living on the planet with mere mortals? Bizarre theology! The whole idea of Him being bodily in Jerusalem runs contrary to the Gospel.

Along with all the above, this earthly kingdom eschatology supports the idea that there will be a restoration of the sacrificial system in a rebuilt temple. I'm not saying a temple won't be built (Again, I'm not a prophet), in fact it's highly likely (in my opinion) that the Jews will build another temple as soon as the geopolitical and demographic circumstances allow. However, the only person the Scriptures speak about that will appear in any future temple dedicated to God and calling himself God is a character known as 'the man of sin' (2 Thessalonians 2:3-4).

To support their view, the proponents of the Jesus reigning from Jerusalem theory draw on a vast array of Scriptures that they interpret according to their own understanding. Two of the prominent passages used in presenting this particular eschatological viewpoint are Zechariah's prophecy mentioning the feet of the Lord standing on the Mount of Olives and Ezekiel's long description of a temple that has never been built. Later in this chapter we will examine these same Scriptures to see what the Word is actually saying about the future conditions that Judah and Israel will be experiencing.

Every member of every earthly kingdom who will ever enter into the Kingdom of God and become a Born Again Believer will do so in exactly the same way every other man, woman or child has done since the Gospel was first preached. They will repent and enter in by faith and faith alone. There is never going to be a different path into the Kingdom of God. There is only one Gospel.

2 Corinthians 11:3-4
But I fear, lest by any means, as the serpent beguiled Eve through his subtilty, so your minds should be corrupted from the simplicity that is in Christ. 4 For if he that cometh preacheth another Jesus, whom we have not preached, or if ye receive another spirit, which ye have not received, or another gospel, which ye have not accepted, ye might well bear with him.

Galatians 1:6-9
I marvel that ye are so soon removed from him that called you into the grace of Christ unto another gospel: 7 Which is not another; but there be some that trouble you, and would pervert the gospel of Christ. 8 But though we, or an angel from heaven, preach any other gospel unto you than that which we have preached unto you, let him be accursed. 9 As we said before, so say I now again, if any man preach any other gospel unto you than that ye have received, let him be accursed.

I suspect the enemy has already sown this false teaching with the express purpose of setting people up to accept a false Christ, possibly one of many in times to come. I also suspect that this teaching is somewhat anti-Semitic as it does not encourage evangelism toward the Jews, leaving them to be dealt with separately in a period of tribulation while the church is 'raptured away'. Terrible theology.

When we are looking at the restoration of the Kingdom of Israel, we are not looking at it as a manifestation of the Kingdom of God, EXCEPT that we are definitely looking to see the natural kingdom enter into the Spiritual Kingdom and as a consequence they will experience the many temporal benefits that pertain to those who have entered the Kingdom of God through faith in our Lord Jesus Christ. We are also looking at it as the fulfilment of the promises of God to the descendants of Abraham, Isaac and Jacob. God will be demonstrating to the world His faithfulness in keeping His promises so that His Name is glorified and all might know that He is God. Amen.

Romans 11:5
Even so then at this present time also there is a remnant according to the election of grace.

This statement is part of an answer to the rhetorical question Paul asked, "Has God cast away His people?" He goes on to say later in the passage:

Romans 11:25-29
For I would not, brethren, that ye should be ignorant of this mystery, lest ye should be wise in your own conceits; that blindness in part is happened to Israel, until the fulness of the Gentiles be come in. 26 And so all Israel shall be saved: as it is written, There shall come out of Sion the Deliverer, and shall turn away ungodliness from Jacob: 27 For this is my covenant unto them, when I shall take away their sins. 28 As concerning the gospel, they are enemies for your sakes: but as touching the election, they are beloved for the father's sakes. 29 For the gifts and calling of God are without repentance.

It is important to see the distinction in the Word of God between the election of grace (Romans 11:5) and the election of race (Romans 11:28). The election of grace is that which grants Judah and Israel and all the Gentiles repentance from dead works and faith in our Lord Jesus Christ. The election of grace is that which God gives to the humble who turn from their wicked ways and through faith become part of the Kingdom of His Son. This election will never change. No one can claim entry into the Kingdom of God based on the fact that they are children of Abraham. Let that be clearly understood.

However, the election of race is based on the promises God made to the Patriarchs. On account of them, Israelites are called and chosen of God to receive certain blessings given to Abraham, Isaac, Jacob, Joseph and Ephraim. In particular, the promise of the Promised Land.

Romans 11:28 NKJV
Concerning the gospel *they are* enemies for your sake, but concerning the election *they are* beloved for the sake of the fathers.

On account of the promises made to the fathers, all Israelites are partakers of an election (the parameters of which are found in His Word), and out of the elect race, God has always found a remnant to enter into the election of grace in every age for the blindness is only in part. With regard to the promise that all Israel shall be saved, God is able. With regard to the promise to restore Judah and Israel back in the Land, God is able. To do both at the same time, God is able, AND WILL, bring a remnant of the election of race, the remnant of Judah and Israel who will survive Jacob's Trouble, into the election of grace. To do this He will have purged the rebels out from among them (Ezekiel 20:38).

According to Paul, the partial blindness will continue "until the fullness of the Gentiles be come in". There is some speculation as to what that actually means. Some say that it is when all the Gentile Church has been saved, however, there is not sufficient information in the passage to come to a dogmatic conclusion. Another possible thought is that it refers to an Old Testament Scripture where Jacob is blessing Ephraim.

Genesis 48:17-19 NKJV
Now when Joseph saw that his father laid his right hand on the head of Ephraim, it displeased him; so he took hold of his father's hand to remove it from Ephraim's head to Manasseh's head. 18 And Joseph said to his father, "Not so, my father, for this one *is* the firstborn; put your right hand on his head." 19 But his father refused and said, "I know, my son, I know. He also shall become a people, and he also shall be great; but truly his younger brother shall be greater than he, and his descendants shall become a multitude of nations.

In the last few words of this prophecy we find the phrase: "multitude of nations". The Hebrew phrase is *melo ha'goyim*. 'Melo' according to Strong's #4393 is literally 'fullness', and *'ha'goyim'* according to Strong's #1471 is literally 'the nations'. Thus the phrase reads, literally: "the fullness of the nations". Thus Paul could have been quoting from the Scriptures as he often did.

Translators and editors have chosen to render 'fullness' as 'multitude' in verse 19 to correspond with the Birthright Promise to Abraham in Genesis 17:1-7 where he is told his seed will become "many nations". Hebrew for 'many' is *hamon* which is sometimes used in Hebrew as a synonym for *melo*, making 'fullness' and 'multitude' contextually synonymous.

This alternative translation of Genesis 48:19 to read "fullness of the nations" is also confirmed in Brown-Driver-Briggs Hebrew Lexicon. Thus Paul's prophecy in Romans 11:25-26 paraphrased could read as follows: A partial hardening has happened to Israel until the fullness of the nations (as promised to Ephraim the leading tribe of Israel) has come in; and thus all Israel will be saved. We shall see what we shall see. Either way, they shall be saved.

And I believe it. There will come a time when all Israel shall be saved. It shall be a time when all of natural Israel finally becomes part of Spiritual Israel, part of the world wide Body of Christ. They shall become believers in *Yeshua Ha Mashiach*. The whole unified twelve tribes of Israel will all know Jesus as Lord and shall know Him as their Messiah King as all believers have done since the Gospel first went forth. They shall receive the Promise of the Spirit, the indwelling presence of the Holy Ghost living in their midst. They will be Born Again. And as a consequence, many material blessings will overtake them, just as many have experienced temporal blessings during the last two thousand years who have believed in the Lord with all their heart. Here is the promise of God to His people:

2 Chronicles 7:14

If my people, which are called by my name, shall humble themselves, and pray, and seek my face, and turn from their wicked ways; then will I hear from heaven, and will forgive their sin, and will heal their land.

Let us now look at the Scriptures and see what this looks like from the Word of God. First we will look at another long passage from Ezekiel, the prophecy concerning the attempted attack on Israel by Gog and Magog and we shall glean some notable details of Israel's future blessing.

Ezekiel 38:1-23

And the word of the Lord came unto me, saying, 2 Son of man, set thy face against Gog, the land of Magog, the chief prince of Meshech and Tubal, and prophesy against him, 3 And say, Thus saith the Lord God; Behold, I am against thee, O Gog, the chief prince of Meshech and Tubal: 4 And I will turn thee back, and put hooks into thy jaws, and I will bring thee forth, and all thine army, horses and horsemen, all of them clothed with all sorts of armour, even a great company with bucklers and shields, all of them handling swords: 5 Persia, Ethiopia, and Libya with them; all of them with shield and helmet: 6 Gomer, and all his bands; the house of Togarmah of the north quarters, and all his bands: and many people with thee. 7 Be thou prepared, and prepare for thyself, thou, and all thy company that are assembled unto thee, and be thou a guard unto them.

8 After many days thou shalt be visited: in the latter years thou shalt come into the land that is brought back from the sword, and is gathered out of many people, against the mountains of Israel, which have been always waste: but it is brought forth out of the nations, and they shall dwell safely all of them. 9 Thou shalt ascend and come like a storm, thou shalt be like a cloud to cover the land, thou, and all thy bands, and many people with thee. 10 Thus saith the Lord God; It shall also come to pass, that at the same time shall things come into thy mind, and thou shalt think an evil thought: 11 And thou shalt say, I will go up to the land of unwalled villages; I will go to them that are at rest, that dwell safely, all of them dwelling without walls, and having neither bars nor gates, 12 To take a spoil, and to take a prey; to turn thine hand upon the desolate places that are now inhabited, and upon the people that are gathered out of the nations, which have gotten cattle and goods, that dwell in the midst of the land. 13 Sheba, and Dedan, and the merchants of Tarshish, with all the young lions thereof, shall say unto thee, Art thou come to take a spoil? hast thou gathered thy company to take a prey? to carry away silver and gold, to take away cattle and goods, to take a great spoil?

14 Therefore, son of man, prophesy and say unto Gog, Thus saith the Lord God; In that day when my people of Israel dwelleth safely, shalt thou not know it? 15 And thou shalt come from thy place out of the north parts, thou, and many people with thee, all of them riding upon horses, a great company, and a mighty army: 16 And thou shalt come up against my people of Israel, as a cloud to cover the land; it shall be in the latter days, and I will bring thee against my land, that the heathen may know me, when I shall be sanctified in thee, O Gog, before their eyes. 17 Thus saith the Lord God; Art thou he of whom I have spoken in old time by my servants the prophets of Israel, which prophesied in those days many years that I would bring thee against them?

18 And it shall come to pass at the same time when Gog shall come against the land of Israel, saith the Lord God, that my fury shall come up in my face. 19 For in my jealousy and in the fire of my wrath have I spoken, Surely in that day there shall be a great shaking in the land of Israel; 20 So that the fishes of the sea, and the fowls of the heaven, and the beasts of the field, and all creeping things that creep upon the earth, and all the men that are upon the face of the earth, shall shake at my presence, and the mountains shall be thrown down, and the steep places shall fall, and every wall shall fall to the ground. 21 And I will call for a sword against him throughout all my mountains, saith the Lord God: every man's sword shall be against his brother. 22 And I will plead against him with pestilence and with blood; and I will rain upon him, and upon his bands, and upon the many people that are with him, an overflowing rain, and great hailstones, fire, and brimstone. 23 Thus will I magnify myself, and sanctify myself; and I will be known in the eyes of many nations, and they shall know that I am the Lord.

Ezekiel 39:1-29
Therefore, thou son of man, prophesy against Gog, and say, Thus saith the Lord God; Behold, I am against thee, O Gog, the chief prince of Meshech and Tubal: 2 And I will turn thee back, and leave but the sixth part of thee, and will cause thee to come up from the north parts, and will bring thee upon the mountains of Israel: 3 And I will smite thy bow out of thy left hand, and will cause thine arrows to fall out of thy right hand. 4 Thou shalt fall upon the mountains of Israel, thou, and all thy bands, and the people that is with thee: I will give thee unto the ravenous birds of every sort, and to the beasts of the field to be devoured. 5 Thou shalt fall upon the open field: for I have spoken it, saith the Lord God.

6 And I will send a fire on Magog, and among them that dwell carelessly in the isles: and they shall know that I am the Lord. 7 So will I make my holy name known in the midst of my people Israel; and I will not let them pollute my holy name any more: and the heathen shall know that I am the Lord, the Holy One in Israel. 8 Behold, it is come, and it is done, saith the Lord God; this is the day whereof I have spoken.

9 And they that dwell in the cities of Israel shall go forth, and shall set on fire and burn the weapons, both the shields and the bucklers, the bows and the arrows, and the handstaves, and the spears, and they shall burn them with fire seven years: 10 So that they shall take no wood out of the field, neither cut down any out of the forests; for they shall burn the weapons with fire: and they shall spoil those that spoiled them, and rob those that robbed them, saith the Lord God. 11 And it shall come to pass in that day, that I will give unto Gog a place there of graves in Israel, the valley of the passengers on the east of the sea: and it shall stop the noses of the passengers: and there shall they bury Gog and all his multitude: and they shall call it The valley of Hamongog. 12 And seven months shall the house of Israel be burying of them, that they may cleanse the land. 13 Yea, all the people of the land shall bury them; and it shall be to them a renown the day that I shall be glorified, saith the Lord God. 14 And they shall sever out men of continual employment, passing through the land to bury with the passengers those that remain upon the face of the earth, to cleanse it: after the end of seven months shall they search. 15 And the passengers that pass through the land, when any seeth a man's bone, then shall he set

up a sign by it, till the buriers have buried it in the valley of Hamongog. 16 And also the name of the city shall be Hamonah. Thus shall they cleanse the land.

17 And, thou son of man, thus saith the Lord God; Speak unto every feathered fowl, and to every beast of the field, Assemble yourselves, and come; gather yourselves on every side to my sacrifice that I do sacrifice for you, even a great sacrifice upon the mountains of Israel, that ye may eat flesh, and drink blood. 18 Ye shall eat the flesh of the mighty, and drink the blood of the princes of the earth, of rams, of lambs, and of goats, of bullocks, all of them fatlings of Bashan. 19 And ye shall eat fat till ye be full, and drink blood till ye be drunken, of my sacrifice which I have sacrificed for you. 20 Thus ye shall be filled at my table with horses and chariots, with mighty men, and with all men of war, saith the Lord God.

21 And I will set my glory among the heathen, and all the heathen shall see my judgment that I have executed, and my hand that I have laid upon them. 22 So the house of Israel shall know that I am the Lord their God from that day and forward. 23 And the heathen shall know that the house of Israel went into captivity for their iniquity: because they trespassed against me, therefore hid I my face from them, and gave them into the hand of their enemies: so fell they all by the sword. 24 According to their uncleanness and according to their transgressions have I done unto them, and hid my face from them.

25 Therefore thus saith the Lord God; Now will I bring again the captivity of Jacob, and have mercy upon the whole house of Israel, and will be jealous for my holy name; 26 After that they have borne their shame, and all their trespasses whereby they have trespassed against me, when they dwelt safely in their land, and none made them afraid. 27 When I have brought them again from the people, and gathered them out of their enemies' lands, and am sanctified in them in the sight of many nations; 28 Then shall they know that I am the Lord their God, which caused them to be led into captivity among the heathen: but I have gathered them unto their own land, and have left none of them any more there. 29 Neither will I hide my face any more from them: for I have poured out my spirit upon the house of Israel, saith the Lord God.

Let's pull a few Scriptures from the above passage and take note of the blessings that Israel is going to be enjoying when this attempt by Gog and Magog comes to pass.

Ezekiel 38:8
After many days thou shalt be visited: in the latter years thou shalt come into the land that is brought back from the sword, and is gathered out of many people, against the mountains of Israel, which have been always waste: but it is brought forth out of the nations, and they shall dwell safely all of them.

Ezekiel 38:11-12
And thou shalt say, I will go up to the land of unwalled villages; I will go to them that are at rest, that dwell safely, all of them dwelling without walls, and having neither bars nor gates, 12 To take a spoil, and to take a prey; to turn thine hand upon the desolate places that are now inhabited,

and upon the people that are gathered out of the nations, which have gotten cattle and goods, that dwell in the midst of the land.

Ezekiel 38:13
Art thou come to take a spoil? hast thou gathered thy company to take a prey? to carry away silver and gold, to take away cattle and goods, to take a great spoil?

When Gog and Magog come to plunder, it is in the "latter years". Israel is described as a peaceful people, dwelling safely, at rest, living in prosperity, with "silver and gold" and "cattle and goods" and "great spoil." They are without walls and at peace, quite unlike the present circumstances that the Jews are experiencing at this point in time (2017AD) where they are armed to the teeth and building walls to protect themselves from the constant threat of Islamic terrorism.

Ezekiel 38:16
It shall be in the latter days, and I will bring thee against my land, that the heathen may know me, when I shall be sanctified in thee, O Gog, before their eyes.

Ezekiel 38:21-23
And I will call for a sword against him throughout all my mountains, saith the Lord God: every man's sword shall be against his brother. 22 And I will plead against him with pestilence and with blood; and I will rain upon him, and upon his bands, and upon the many people that are with him, an overflowing rain, and great hailstones, fire, and brimstone. 23 Thus will I magnify myself, and sanctify myself; and I will be known in the eyes of many nations, and they shall know that I am the Lord.

Again take note that this prophecy is concerning the "latter days" and is not the end of the age. There is a difference. After God has supernaturally destroyed the armies of Gog and Magog, the people of Israel are burying bodies for seven months to cleanse the land and burning weapons for seven years as firewood (Ezekiel 39:9-16). It is details like these that are commonly overlooked. When it comes to pass, this experience of Israel's supernatural protection gets the attention of many other nations so that they too know that He is Lord (Ezekiel 38:23, 39:7). Let's also look at what Isaiah has to say about this future time of blessing for Israel.

Isaiah 65:17-25
For, behold, I create new heavens and a new earth: and the former shall not be remembered, nor come into mind.

18 But be ye glad and rejoice for ever in that which I create: for, behold, I create Jerusalem a rejoicing, and her people a joy. 19 And I will rejoice in Jerusalem, and joy in my people: and the voice of weeping shall be no more heard in her, nor the voice of crying.

20 There shall be no more thence an infant of days, nor an old man that hath not filled his days: for the child shall die an hundred years old; but the sinner being an hundred years old shall be accursed.

21 And they shall build houses, and inhabit them; and they shall plant vineyards, and eat the fruit of them. 22 They shall not build, and another inhabit; they shall not plant, and another eat: for as the days of a tree are the days of my people, and mine elect shall long enjoy the work of their hands. 23 They shall not labour in vain, nor bring forth for trouble; for they are the seed of the blessed of the Lord, and their offspring with them. 24 And it shall come to pass, that before they call, I will answer; and while they are yet speaking, I will hear. 25 The wolf and the lamb shall feed together, and the lion shall eat straw like the bullock: and dust shall be the serpent's meat. They shall not hurt nor destroy in all my holy mountain, saith the Lord.

We all know there will be no death in the new earth, nor will there be any sinners in the new creation as this passage has in verse 20, therefore, if the new heavens and the new earth mentioned at the beginning of the above passage are to be taken literally, they cannot be connected to the following verses. If it is to be taken literally, that particular verse would have to be a one line prophecy of the new heavens and the new earth that is promised in the New Testament. If we do not take that verse literally we could perhaps consider it as speaking symbolically of the time of great blessing that the following verses describe. If we choose the latter, perhaps we could accept it as a two-fold promise and that it is one of many examples of God 'hiding' a promise of that which is spiritual inside that which is natural. What we cannot accept is the idea of sin and death in the new creation.

Many people who have accepted this earthly reign theory quote this passage in support of their teaching. But having read it carefully, we find that it says nothing of the sort. There is not one hint of mention of Messiah, let alone His supposed time of ruling from Jerusalem. It simply describes a time of wonderful blessings from God, the likes of which have been experienced frequently in times of revival when God has healed the land. A documentary of a number of outpourings of the Holy Spirit put out by the Sentinel Group (sentinelgroup.org) is worth watching. Examples of the land being healed include: unusually bountiful crops, fish returning to reefs, visible glory resting on houses, and more . . . Here is another look at the coming period of blessing for the people of Israel.

Zechariah 14:16-21
And it shall come to pass, that every one that is left of all the nations which came against Jerusalem shall even go up from year to year to worship the King, the Lord of hosts, and to keep the feast of tabernacles. 17 And it shall be, that whoso will not come up of all the families of the earth unto Jerusalem to worship the King, the Lord of hosts, even upon them shall be no rain. 18 And if the family of Egypt go not up, and come not, that have no rain; there shall be the plague, wherewith the Lord will smite the heathen that come not up to keep the feast of tabernacles. 19 This shall be the punishment of Egypt, and the punishment of all nations that come not up to keep the feast of tabernacles. 20 In that day shall there be upon the bells of the horses, Holiness Unto The Lord; and the pots in the Lord's house shall be like the bowls before the altar. 21 Yea, every pot in Jerusalem and in Judah shall be holiness unto the Lord of hosts: and all they that sacrifice shall come and take of them, and seethe therein: and in that day there shall be no more the Canaanite in the house of the Lord of hosts.

The International Christian Embassy of Jerusalem (ICEJ), founded in 1980, hosts internationally attended events incorporating worship to the King of Kings to celebrate the Feast of Tabernacles in Jerusalem every year. Perhaps this is a foretaste of the fulfilment of that prophecy. As all those Christians know when they worship Him in Jerusalem at the ICEJ events, He is both in their hearts and in Heaven, but not on earth. It is only unbelief that makes people think He has to be physically in Jerusalem for people to worship Him in Jerusalem. Let's face it, even under the Old Covenant when they were required to make their sacrifices in Jerusalem, Jesus was not physically there, yet He has always been the express image of the unseen God.

Isaiah 2:1-4
The word that Isaiah the son of Amoz saw concerning Judah and Jerusalem. 2 And it shall come to pass in the last days, that the mountain of the Lord's house shall be established in the top of the mountains, and shall be exalted above the hills; and all nations shall flow unto it. 3 And many people shall go and say, Come ye, and let us go up to the mountain of the Lord, to the house of the God of Jacob; and he will teach us of his ways, and we will walk in his paths: for out of Zion shall go forth the law, and the word of the Lord from Jerusalem. 4 And he shall judge among the nations, and shall rebuke many people: and they shall beat their swords into plowshares, and their spears into pruning hooks: nation shall not lift up sword against nation, neither shall they learn war any more.

We actually have to come with a preconceived viewpoint to these portions of Scripture to see a bodily presence of Jesus in Jerusalem. Does He not already teach us of His ways? Does not the Gospel already make us peace loving people? All the Scriptures used to support this Messiah reigning in Jerusalem theology, which has its roots in Judaism, do not in truth prove anything other than what can be and is experienced by individuals, families, villages, and as I recall at least one large city, during conditions of revival.

However, there is this one passage that really needs to have the light of the rest of God's Word to shine upon a couple of verses. Let's look at the Scripture that the whole Jesus in Jerusalem theory is based on. This one is the Goliath of the earthly Kingdom of God idea. I'll just pause for a moment and pick up my stones . . .

Zechariah 14:1-5
Behold, the day of the Lord cometh, and thy spoil shall be divided in the midst of thee. 2 For I will gather all nations against Jerusalem to battle; and the city shall be taken, and the houses rifled, and the women ravished; and half of the city shall go forth into captivity, and the residue of the people shall not be cut off from the city. 3 Then shall the Lord go forth, and fight against those nations, as when he fought in the day of battle.

4 And his feet shall stand in that day upon the mount of Olives, which is before Jerusalem on the east, and the mount of Olives shall cleave in the midst thereof toward the east and toward the west, and there shall be a very great valley; and half of the mountain shall remove toward the north, and half of it toward the south.

5 And ye shall flee to the valley of the mountains; for the valley of the mountains shall reach unto Azal: yea, ye shall flee, like as ye fled from before the earthquake in the days of Uzziah king of Judah: and the Lord my God shall come, and all the saints with thee.

From this passage we find these two statements:

Verse 4: "And his feet shall stand in that day upon the mount of Olives"

Verse 5: "The Lord my God shall come, and all the saints with thee."

First of all, who are these saints? If we say they are risen from the dead (for the dead in Christ shall rise first), does it fit with the understanding from the New Testament about the resurrection when Jesus comes? When we read the remainder of Zechariah Chapter 14, does it match the New Testament accounts of the Coming of the Lord?

1 Thessalonians 4:17
Then we which are alive and remain shall be caught up together with them in the clouds, to meet the Lord in the air: and so shall we ever be with the Lord.

2 Thessalonians 1:6-10
Seeing it is a righteous thing with God to recompense tribulation to them that trouble you; 7 And to you who are troubled rest with us, when the Lord Jesus shall be revealed from heaven with his mighty angels, 8 In flaming fire taking vengeance on them that know not God, and that obey not the gospel of our Lord Jesus Christ: 9 Who shall be punished with everlasting destruction from the presence of the Lord, and from the glory of his power; 10 When he shall come to be glorified in his saints, and to be admired in all them that believe (because our testimony among you was believed) in that day.

2 Thessalonians 2:8
And then shall that Wicked be revealed, whom the Lord shall consume with the spirit of his mouth, and shall destroy with the brightness of his coming:

From Paul's letters to the Thessalonians we see Jesus when He comes to be glorified in His saints. He is accompanied by mighty angels with the dead in Christ who have first risen from their graves and He is destroying those who do not know God with flaming fire. We who are alive and remain are caught up to meet Him in the air. This scene in Zechariah 14 is entirely different for it portrays those who are alive and are in Jerusalem as fleeing through a newly formed valley!

So who are the saints in Zechariah? A look at some other Old Testament Scriptures about the subject of saints will be helpful in getting the understanding. We shall take a look at this verse from Daniel and to help with understanding this subject, a number of different translations are presented.

Elihu Ben Ephraim

Daniel 8:13 KJV
Then I heard one saint speaking, and another saint said unto that certain saint which spake, How long shall be the vision concerning the daily sacrifice, and the transgression of desolation, to give both the sanctuary and the host to be trodden under foot?

Daniel 8:13 MEV
Then I heard one saint speaking, and another saint said to that certain saint which spoke, "How long shall be the vision concerning the daily sacrifice and the transgression of desolation, the giving of both the sanctuary and the host to be trodden under foot?"

Daniel 8:13 NKJV
Then I heard a holy one speaking; and *another* holy one said to that certain *one* who was speaking, "How long *will* the vision *be, concerning* the daily *sacrifices* and the transgression of desolation, the giving of both the sanctuary and the host to be trampled underfoot?"

Daniel 8:13 GNT
Then I heard one angel ask another, "How long will these things that were seen in the vision continue? How long will an awful sin replace the daily sacrifices? How long will the army of heaven and the Temple be trampled on?"

Daniel 8:13 ICB
Then I heard one angel speaking. Another angel asked the first one, "How long will the things in this vision last? The vision is about the daily sacrifices. It is about the turning away from God that brings destruction. It is about the Temple being pulled down. It is about the army of heaven being walked on."

The Hebrew word translated 'saint' here in the King James Version and in the Modern English Version is *qadosh* and it is rendered as 'holy one' in most English Bibles. However, in this verse in Daniel, the context reveals that Daniel is referring to the angels that are explaining the vision to him. This is a classic case of where the context determines the meaning of a word, and so the Good News Translation (GNT) and the International Children's Bible (ICB) are quite correct in translating the Hebrew word *qadosh* as 'angel' instead of the literal 'holy one' and instead of the word 'saint'.

Another verse that has in its context the Lord coming down with 'saints' is found in the writings of Moses.

Deuteronomy 33:2
And he said, The Lord came from Sinai, and rose up from Seir unto them; he shined forth from mount Paran, and he came with ten thousands of saints: from his right hand went a fiery law for them.

174

This Scripture is speaking about the time when Moses was receiving the Law. Again the majority of English Bibles translate the Hebrew word *qadosh* as 'holy ones' where the KJV has 'saints'. The ICB and the GNT are again correct in allowing the context to render the word *qadosh* as angels along with a few other versions (EXB, TLB, MSG, NCV, NIRV).

That the Lord moves in the affairs of men with angels, and in particular at times of war is revealed by this story from the life of the prophet Elisha.

2 Kings 6:8, 14-17
Then the king of Syria warred against Israel . . .

14 Therefore sent he thither horses, and chariots, and a great host: and they came by night, and compassed the city about. 15 And when the servant of the man of God was risen early, and gone forth, behold, an host compassed the city both with horses and chariots. And his servant said unto him, Alas, my master! how shall we do?

16 And he answered, Fear not: for they that be with us are more than they that be with them. 17 And Elisha prayed, and said, Lord, I pray thee, open his eyes, that he may see. And the Lord opened the eyes of the young man; and he saw: and, behold, the mountain was full of horses and chariots of fire round about Elisha.

Awesome! A host of angels ready to do battle. The Lord has definitely come with angels on other occasions. With these examples from God's Word, it is not unreasonable to suggest that these saints mentioned in Zechariah are in fact angels. The situation is a battle scene in Jerusalem and the Lord is rescuing His people. In the New Testament it is recorded that Jesus said He could have called for twelve legions of angels to assist Him if He had so desired. He also said that when He comes He will send forth His angels to gather His elect from the uttermost part of earth to the uttermost part of heaven (Mark 13:27). One thing is for sure, this passage in Zechariah does not equate with the New Testament Scriptures regarding the circumstances that accompany the resurrection.

The writings of Zechariah are filled with symbolic language, and so it is with the imagery of the Lord's feet standing on the Mount of Olives to split it in two. When the Lord says His hand will be heavy upon a nation, or when He calls the earth His footstool, or Jerusalem His footstool, does he mean to say He is reclining and putting His feet up to relax? Why do we accept one hyper-literal interpretation from the prophecies of a man who regularly used symbols in his proclamations?

In support of the literal interpretation of Jesus landing on the Mount of Olives, some argue from the New Testament that the angels said Jesus would return in like manner to the way he departed and therefore He will return to the Mount of Olives and land on His feet.

Acts 1:9-11
And when he had spoken these things, while they beheld, he was taken up; and a cloud received him out of their sight. 10 And while they looked stedfastly toward heaven as he went up, behold, two men stood by them in white apparel; 11 Which also said, Ye men of Galilee, why stand ye gazing up into heaven? this same Jesus, which is taken up from you into heaven, shall so come in like manner as ye have seen him go into heaven.

If we take the statement "come in like manner" to mean in exactly the same way, as many propose, then when Jesus returns there should be but a small group of disciples watching and a couple of angels giving comments. This kind of reasoning is foolish to say the least. A careful look at the context reveals that they were all looking at a cloud receiving Him out of their sight when the angel spoke those words. That is how they saw Him "go into Heaven." Nothing more should be taken from it, for He Himself describes His actual coming:

Matthew 24:30-31
And then shall appear the sign of the Son of man in heaven: and then shall all the tribes of the earth mourn, and they shall see the Son of man coming in the clouds of heaven with power and great glory. 31 And he shall send his angels with a great sound of a trumpet, and they shall gather together his elect from the four winds, from one end of heaven to the other.

We also note that the angel's comment to the disciples was concerning Him being taken into Heaven, not His 'take off' from the Mount of Olives for they were all gazing at the sky when the angel spoke. We can search through all the gospels and all the letters and find there is no mention of a touch down, there is no splitting of a mountain and there is no fleeing through a valley. When He comes in the clouds with power and glory, we are caught up to meet Him in the air by the angels whom He sends out to gather His elect. And then it's Judgment Day before His Throne followed by a New Heaven and a New Earth. Hallelujah!

Here is a similar passage in Micah which we will analyse:

Micah 1:1-9
The word of the Lord that came to Micah the Morasthite in the days of Jotham, Ahaz, and Hezekiah, kings of Judah, which he saw concerning Samaria and Jerusalem. 2 Hear, all ye people; hearken, O earth, and all that therein is: and let the Lord God be witness against you, the Lord from his holy temple. 3 For, behold, the Lord cometh forth out of his place, and will come down, and tread upon the high places of the earth.

Again we have the Lord's feet touching the mountain tops, otherwise described as "tread upon the high places of the earth". In this passage the context confirms that it is the land of Israel that is intended as the prophecy is directed at Samaria and Jerusalem. Translating the Hebrew word *eretz* as 'earth' is to mislead the modern-day reader into picturing Planet Earth. The most frequently used English equivalent for *eretz* is 'land'. *Eretz Israel* is how the Jews refer to the state of Israel. That aside, the passage continues and note its format: totally symbolic.

4 And the mountains shall be molten under him, and the valleys shall be cleft, as wax before the fire, and as the waters that are poured down a steep place. 5 For the transgression of Jacob is all this, and for the sins of the house of Israel. What is the transgression of Jacob? is it not Samaria? and what are the high places of Judah? are they not Jerusalem?

6 Therefore I will make Samaria as an heap of the field, and as plantings of a vineyard: and I will pour down the stones thereof into the valley, and I will discover the foundations thereof. 7 And all the graven images thereof shall be beaten to pieces, and all the hires thereof shall be burned with the fire, and all the idols thereof will I lay desolate: for she gathered it of the hire of an harlot, and they shall return to the hire of an harlot. 8 Therefore I will wail and howl, I will go stripped and naked: I will make a wailing like the dragons, and mourning as the owls. 9 For her wound is incurable; for it is come unto Judah; he is come unto the gate of my people, even to Jerusalem.

Samaria has long been judged and there were no literal molten mountains or valleys cleft like wax. If it is a literal melting of mountains, it could possibly be the end of the earth mentioned by Peter when the elements melt with fervent heat, but apart from that we would have to take these verses as symbolic language. The Lord Himself tells us to command mountains to be cast into the sea. Does He mean literal mountains? There is a time to take things literally and there is a time to take things metaphorically. We must let the Scriptures decide for us or else we will end up with endless confusion.

So then, Zechariah's prophecy, along with the entire Old Testament, is best approached from a New Testament perspective. If there is anything literal we are to take from it, it is simply that there will be a supernatural intervention by the Lord on Jerusalem's behalf sometime. Amen. There may indeed be a massive earthquake. I'm inclined to think so but of course I'm not dogmatic. And this particular incident may be but one of many, as the nascent Jewish nation that has re-established itself in the Middle East has already seen some remarkable deliverances from destruction which anyone who has read the documentation of the Six Day War and the Yom Kippur War can testify. By the way, many supernatural experiences of miraculous protection including visions of angels were seen during those wars too.

Perhaps if we want to stretch our imaginations, we could say that when Jesus walked on the Mount of Olives this Scripture was fulfilled and the Mount of Olives was split with the earthquake that happened at the resurrection and the great valley is the way made for the escape of the church that was rent through His Blood. I am taking foolish liberties, however, it actually takes less effort to accept such an interpretation than wrapping one's mind around a different gospel for Israel and Judah in the latter days.

If we combine Micah's prophecy and Zechariah's prophecy with this one from Isaiah, we will perhaps appreciate the use of symbolic prophecies a little more:

Isaiah 31:4-5
For thus hath the Lord spoken unto me, Like as the lion and the young lion roaring on his prey, when a multitude of shepherds is called forth against him, he will not be afraid of their voice, nor abase himself for the noise of them: so shall the Lord of hosts come down to fight for mount Zion, and for the hill thereof. 5 As birds flying, so will the Lord of hosts defend Jerusalem; defending also he will deliver it; and passing over he will preserve it.

This time He comes as "birds flying". We know that Jerusalem is going to be a cup of drunkenness to the surrounding nations (Zechariah 12:2) and all these Scriptures speak symbolically about the Lord Himself coming to defend the Holy City and deliver it from those who will attempt to destroy it. Hallelujah! These 'comings' of the Lord are not to be equated with The Coming at the end of the age, but are speaking metaphorically of His Hand helping His people or on other occasions when judgment is or was to come. At the end of the age it will be both.

Now, as for the temple described in Chapters 40-48 of Ezekiel, it is often looked upon as 'proof' for the theory that a temple will be built in Jerusalem from which Messiah will reign when the Jews are back in the Land. I'll not quote the entire nine chapters, leaving you to read through the passage in your own Bibles and I will draw your attention to some key verses that will give the necessary understanding.

Now, are you ready? Have you read Chapters 40-48 of Ezekiel? Then look again at these verses:

Ezekiel 42:13
Then said he unto me . . . there shall they lay the most holy things, and the meat offering, and the sin offering, and the trespass offering; for the place is holy.

Ezekiel 44:29
They shall eat the meat offering, and the sin offering, and the trespass offering: and every dedicated thing in Israel shall be theirs.

Ezekiel 45:19
And the priest shall take of the blood of the sin offering, and put it upon the posts of the house, and upon the four corners of the settle of the altar, and upon the posts of the gate of the inner court.

These three Scriptures clearly show that sacrifices for sin were intended to be made in this temple. Now, I can fully understand the Jews to be expecting to perform these sacrifices as it is beyond dispute that these instructions are according to the Law of the Levitical Priesthood. But as a Christian, we must first of all understand the reality that God has made a New Covenant in the Blood of His Son and it is an Everlasting Covenant through which He has put an end to sacrifice and offering for sin. The thorough teaching that compares the Old Covenant to the New Covenant found in the Book of Romans and the Book of Hebrews leaves us fully convinced that the symbolic works of the law are made completely obsolete. So what is going on here?

At the beginning of this very long passage, Ezekiel was given some instructions:

Ezekiel 40:4
And the man said unto me, Son of man, behold with thine eyes, and hear with thine ears, and set thine heart upon all that I shall shew thee; for to the intent that I might shew them unto thee art thou brought hither: declare all that thou seest to the house of Israel.

Ezekiel was a priest. That means he was from the tribe of Levi and was part of the Kingdom of Judah. He is called to declare to the house of Israel everything he saw. At this point of time in history, the house of Judah was in captivity in Babylon, and the majority of Israel was still in exile in the northern reaches of the Babylonian Empire where the Assyrians had previously deported them. Again the Lord gives Ezekiel his instructions, but in this verse he also gives the purpose of the instructions.

Ezekiel 43:10 NKJV
Son of man, describe the temple to the house of Israel, that they may be ashamed of their iniquities; and let them measure the pattern.

The Lord was looking for repentance from the house of Israel; that they might "be ashamed of their iniquities." Let us look at the beginning of the Book of Ezekiel and hear a bit more about his mission.

Ezekiel 2:2-5
And the spirit entered into me when he spake unto me, and set me upon my feet, that I heard him that spake unto me. 3 And he said unto me, Son of man, I send thee to the children of Israel, to a rebellious nation that hath rebelled against me: they and their fathers have transgressed against me, even unto this very day. 4 For they are impudent children and stiff hearted. I do send thee unto them; and thou shalt say unto them, Thus saith the Lord God. 5 And they, whether they will hear, or whether they will forbear, (for they are a rebellious house,) yet shall know that there hath been a prophet among them.

Ezekiel 2:6-8
And thou, son of man, be not afraid of them, neither be afraid of their words, though briers and thorns be with thee, and thou dost dwell among scorpions: be not afraid of their words, nor be dismayed at their looks, though they be a rebellious house. 7 And thou shalt speak my words unto them, whether they will hear, or whether they will forbear: for they are most rebellious. 8 But thou, son of man, hear what I say unto thee; Be not thou rebellious like that rebellious house: open thy mouth, and eat that I give thee.

Ezekiel 3:4-9
And he said unto me, Son of man, go, get thee unto the house of Israel, and speak with my words unto them. 5 For thou art not sent to a people of a strange speech and of an hard language, but to the house of Israel; 6 Not to many people of a strange speech and of an hard language, whose

words thou canst not understand. Surely, had I sent thee to them, they would have hearkened unto thee.

7 But the house of Israel will not hearken unto thee; for they will not hearken unto me: for all the house of Israel are impudent and hardhearted.

8 Behold, I have made thy face strong against their faces, and thy forehead strong against their foreheads. 9 As an adamant harder than flint have I made thy forehead: fear them not, neither be dismayed at their looks, though they be a rebellious house.

What a mission! To go to a people that would not listen. So then, Ezekiel is to show them the details of the temple that they might be ashamed and repent. The following two passages explain Ezekiel's mission more completely:

Ezekiel 3:17-21
Son of man, I have made thee a watchman unto the house of Israel: therefore hear the word at my mouth, and give them warning from me. 18 When I say unto the wicked, Thou shalt surely die; and thou givest him not warning, nor speakest to warn the wicked from his wicked way, to save his life; the same wicked man shall die in his iniquity; but his blood will I require at thine hand. 19 Yet if thou warn the wicked, and he turn not from his wickedness, nor from his wicked way, he shall die in his iniquity; but thou hast delivered thy soul.

20 Again, When a righteous man doth turn from his righteousness, and commit iniquity, and I lay a stumbling-block before him, he shall die: because thou hast not given him warning, he shall die in his sin, and his righteousness which he hath done shall not be remembered; but his blood will I require at thine hand. 21 Nevertheless if thou warn the righteous man, that the righteous sin not, and he doth not sin, he shall surely live, because he is warned; also thou hast delivered thy soul.

Ezekiel 33:1-20
Again the word of the Lord came unto me, saying, 2 Son of man, speak to the children of thy people, and say unto them, When I bring the sword upon a land, if the people of the land take a man of their coasts, and set him for their watchman: 3 If when he seeth the sword come upon the land, he blow the trumpet, and warn the people; 4 Then whosoever heareth the sound of the trumpet, and taketh not warning; if the sword come, and take him away, his blood shall be upon his own head. 5 He heard the sound of the trumpet, and took not warning; his blood shall be upon him. But he that taketh warning shall deliver his soul. 6 But if the watchman see the sword come, and blow not the trumpet, and the people be not warned; if the sword come, and take any person from among them, he is taken away in his iniquity; but his blood will I require at the watchman's hand.

7 So thou, O son of man, I have set thee a watchman unto the house of Israel; therefore thou shalt hear the word at my mouth, and warn them from me. 8 When I say unto the wicked, O wicked man, thou shalt surely die; if thou dost not speak to warn the wicked from his way, that

wicked man shall die in his iniquity; but his blood will I require at thine hand. 9 Nevertheless, if thou warn the wicked of his way to turn from it; if he do not turn from his way, he shall die in his iniquity; but thou hast delivered thy soul.

10 Therefore, O thou son of man, speak unto the house of Israel; Thus ye speak, saying, If our transgressions and our sins be upon us, and we pine away in them, how should we then live? 11 Say unto them, As I live, saith the Lord God, I have no pleasure in the death of the wicked; but that the wicked turn from his way and live: turn ye, turn ye from your evil ways; for why will ye die, O house of Israel? 12 Therefore, thou son of man, say unto the children of thy people, The righteousness of the righteous shall not deliver him in the day of his transgression: as for the wickedness of the wicked, he shall not fall thereby in the day that he turneth from his wickedness; neither shall the righteous be able to live for his righteousness in the day that he sinneth. 13 When I shall say to the righteous, that he shall surely live; if he trust to his own righteousness, and commit iniquity, all his righteousnesses shall not be remembered; but for his iniquity that he hath committed, he shall die for it.

14 Again, when I say unto the wicked, Thou shalt surely die; if he turn from his sin, and do that which is lawful and right; 15 If the wicked restore the pledge, give again that he had robbed, walk in the statutes of life, without committing iniquity; he shall surely live, he shall not die. 16 None of his sins that he hath committed shall be mentioned unto him: he hath done that which is lawful and right; he shall surely live.

17 Yet the children of thy people say, The way of the Lord is not equal: but as for them, their way is not equal. 18 When the righteous turneth from his righteousness, and committeth iniquity, he shall even die thereby. 19 But if the wicked turn from his wickedness, and do that which is lawful and right, he shall live thereby. 20 Yet ye say, The way of the Lord is not equal. O ye house of Israel, I will judge you every one after his ways.

Again the Lord calls out to Israel.

Ezekiel 44:6
And thou shalt say to the rebellious, even to the house of Israel, Thus saith the Lord God; O ye house of Israel, let it suffice you of all your abominations,

Ezekiel 44:6 NKJV
Now say to the rebellious, to the house of Israel, 'Thus says the Lord God: "O house of Israel, let Us have no more of all your abominations.

Israel did not respond to the Lord. Just as the Lord said to Ezekiel, they did not listen. God's plans for the temple and the instructions regarding the sacrifices were for that time period when **God would cover their sin with the blood of lambs symbolic of the coming of Christ,** but the call to repentance fell upon deaf ears. Therefore the temple was not built for they never came to build it. They were being offered atonement for their sin but they would not come to the party and therefore they were left to their own devices and God brought a remnant of the Jews back into the Land by themselves. God in His mercy was reaching out to Israel despite their hardened hearts. Oh, what a gracious and merciful God we serve!

The temple plans as described by Ezekiel were never going to be built. Apart from a few individuals and perhaps some families who settled in Samaria, Israel never returned. A tiny remnant of Judah returned and built a much smaller temple. Note that the Jews had the details of the temple in Ezekiel's writings but they obviously never felt obliged to build accordingly. I suggest they understood that the message was to Israel. Since then, God has proceeded with His plan to build a temple made of flesh and blood on the foundation stone of His Son, a temple built of living stones like me, and you; if you have faith in our Lord Jesus Christ. He has come and made His sanctuary within our very midst. Hallelujah!

Whether there will be an attempt by the Jews or returning Israelites to build according to the pattern given by Ezekiel is another matter altogether. Even if there is, God is certainly not going to be blessing any sacrifices that deny the Sacrifice that He has already made. Deny the Son and you deny the Father. Jesus will certainly not be present in Jerusalem blessing that kind of rebellion.

In summary, Israel and Judah will be brought back into the land and into the Kingdom of His Son. The blessings of belonging to Him will become theirs and all the Scriptures that describe those blessings will surely come to pass as they continue to trust in Him in Spirit and in Truth. How long will that last? Long enough for Gog and Magog to do their thing. Long enough for Israel to burn their weapons for seven years. Long enough for nations to be coming to the Feast of Tabernacles for a few years? This verse from Chapter 37 gives us some idea.

Ezekiel 37:25
And they shall dwell in the land that I have given unto Jacob my servant, wherein your fathers have dwelt; and they shall dwell therein, even they, and their children, and their children's children for ever . . .

Looks like, with the words "for ever" that it's until the end of the age, but how long that will be I have no idea, except it does mention "children's children" which would indicate at least a couple of generations. Isaiah 65:20 mentions a child dying at a hundred years and a sinner living to a hundred years being accursed. WOW. This world could be around for a while if we are to take this literally. But like all of us, their faith will be subject to trial. If they are going to be there long enough for there to be following generations, those generations would have to come to faith themselves.

Isaiah 65:22 NKJV
They shall not build and another inhabit; They shall not plant and another eat; For as the days of a tree, *so shall be* the days of My people, And My elect shall long enjoy the work of their hands.

How long are the days of a tree? As a friend of mine would reply, "How long is a piece of string?" The general impression is that this is quite a long time, maybe even two or three hundred years . . . or more? I really don't know, we shall just have to wait and see . . .

At the same time, the powers of darkness will be continuing in the world to bring about The Antichrist. The redeemed Israelites who will then be Christians, or if you prefer, Messianic Believers, together with the people of God from all over the world, will still have a final tribulation to endure before the Resurrection and Rapture when death is finally destroyed and we inherit a New Heaven and a New Earth where righteousness dwells. And we will still have the Gospel to preach.

Here's one more passage that encapsulates God's plan for the whole of Israel in the Latter Days.

Zephaniah 3:8-20 NKJV
"Therefore wait for Me," says the Lord,
"Until the day I rise up for plunder;
My determination is to gather the nations
To My assembly of kingdoms,
To pour on them My indignation,
All My fierce anger;
All the earth shall be devoured
With the fire of My jealousy.
9 "For then I will restore to the peoples a pure language,
That they all may call on the name of the Lord,
To serve Him with one accord.
10 From beyond the rivers of Ethiopia
My worshipers,
The daughter of My dispersed ones,
Shall bring My offering.
11 In that day you shall not be shamed for any of your deeds
In which you transgress against Me;
For then I will take away from your midst
Those who rejoice in your pride,
And you shall no longer be haughty
In My holy mountain.
12 I will leave in your midst
A meek and humble people,
And they shall trust in the name of the Lord.
13 The remnant of Israel shall do no unrighteousness
And speak no lies,
Nor shall a deceitful tongue be found in their mouth;
For they shall feed their flocks and lie down,
And no one shall make them afraid."

14 Sing, O daughter of Zion!
Shout, O Israel!
Be glad and rejoice with all your heart,
O daughter of Jerusalem!
15 The Lord has taken away your judgments,
He has cast out your enemy.
The King of Israel, the Lord, is in your midst;
You shall see disaster no more.
16 In that day it shall be said to Jerusalem:
"Do not fear;
Zion, let not your hands be weak.
17 The Lord your God in your midst,
The Mighty One, will save;
He will rejoice over you with gladness,
He will quiet you with His love,
He will rejoice over you with singing."
18 "I will gather those who sorrow over the appointed assembly,
Who are among you,
To whom its reproach is a burden.
19 Behold, at that time
I will deal with all who afflict you;
I will save the lame,
And gather those who were driven out;
I will appoint them for praise and fame
In every land where they were put to shame.
20 At that time I will bring you back,
Even at the time I gather you;
For I will give you fame and praise
Among all the peoples of the earth,
When I return your captives before your eyes,"
Says the Lord.

Again we need to look at this through the understanding of the New Covenant or we will come to a wrong conclusion of what this Scripture means.

John 14:16-20
I will pray the Father, and he shall give you another Comforter, that he may **abide with you for ever**; 17 Even the Spirit of truth; whom the world cannot receive, because it seeth him not, neither knoweth him: but ye know him; for **he dwelleth with you**, and shall be in you. 18 I will not leave you comfortless: I will come to you. 19 Yet a little while, and the world seeth me no more; but ye see me: because I live, ye shall live also. 20 At that day ye shall know that **I am in my Father, and ye in me, and I in you**. (Emphasis mine)

Again from the passage in Zephaniah, followed by verses from Luke and Matthew so that we truly get the New Testament interpretation of the Old Testament writing:

Zephaniah 3:15,17
The King of Israel, the Lord, is **in your midst**;

17 The Lord your God **in your midst** . . .(Emphasis mine)

Luke 17:21
nor will they say, 'See here!' or 'See there!' For indeed, the kingdom of God **is within you**." (Emphasis mine)

Matthew 18:20
For where two or three are gathered together in my name, there am I **in the midst** of them." (Emphasis mine)

Oh, Hallelujah! All Israel will be singing . . .

He's living in you

He's living in me

The Kingdom of God has set us free

He's in our midst

If you believe

He's living in you

He's living in me

Chapter Fifteen
Latter Day Middle East Scenarios

The Prophetic War of Psalm 83; Egypt, Israel and Assyria together as one; Damascus no longer a city; Jerusalem a cup of drunkeness. A brief discussion on these and some other very interesting prophetic scenarios that have not yet been fulfilled and which will surely come to pass in the latter days.

The Prophetic War of Psalm 83

Psalm 83:1-18
Keep not thou silence, O God: hold not thy peace, and be not still, O God. 2 For, lo, thine enemies make a tumult: and they that hate thee have lifted up the head. 3 They have taken crafty counsel against thy people, and consulted against thy hidden ones. 4 They have said, Come, and let us cut them off from being a nation; that the name of Israel may be no more in remembrance.

5 For they have consulted together with one consent: they are confederate against thee: 6 The tabernacles of Edom, and the Ishmaelites; of Moab, and the Hagarenes; 7 Gebal, and Ammon, and Amalek; the Philistines with the inhabitants of Tyre; 8 Assur also is joined with them: they have holpen the children of Lot. Selah.

9 Do unto them as unto the Midianites; as to Sisera, as to Jabin, at the brook of Kison: 10 Which perished at Endor: they became as dung for the earth. 11 Make their nobles like Oreb, and like Zeeb: yea, all their princes as Zebah, and as Zalmunna: 12 Who said, Let us take to ourselves the houses of God in possession. 13 O my God, make them like a wheel; as the stubble before the wind. 14 As the fire burneth a wood, and as the flame setteth the mountains on fire; 15 So persecute them with thy tempest, and make them afraid with thy storm. 16 Fill their faces with shame; that they may seek thy name, O Lord.

17 Let them be confounded and troubled for ever; yea, let them be put to shame, and perish: 18 That men may know that thou, whose name alone is Jehovah, art the most high over all the earth.

This Psalm employs a unusual literary format, rarely found in all of Scripture, in that it is a prophecy in the form of a prayer (also employed in Psalm 22). It speaks of a time when all the surrounding nations that have been enemies of Israel in ages past form a confederacy with the intent to destroy Israel forever.

4 They have said, Come, and let us cut them off from being a nation; that the name of Israel may be no more in remembrance. 5 For they have consulted together with one consent: they are confederate against thee: 6 The tabernacles of Edom, and the Ishmaelites; of Moab, and the Hagarenes; 7 Gebal, and Ammon, and Amalek; the Philistines with the inhabitants of Tyre; 8 Assur also is joined with them: they have holpen the children of Lot. Selah.

Here are the modern day equivalents of the nations mentioned:

The Tents of Edom	Southern Jordan
The Ishmaelites	Saudi Arabia and parts of Jordan
Moab	Central Jordan
The Hagarenes	Egypt (or NW Jordan?)
Gebal	Lebanon
Ammon	Jordan
Amalek	Sinai
Philistines	Gaza
The Inhabitants of Tyre	Lebanon
Assur	Syria, NW Iraq, SW Turkey
The Children of Lot	Jordan

Whilst being antagonistic towards Israel and Judah in days gone by, these nations have never historically been a unified force against Israel. The confederacy that has formed between these nations has come about in recent times through the common ideology they now share in the religion of Islam. Now they all chant, "Death to Israel" in their streets.

As the Psalmist continues, we find there is a call for God to deal with those enemies in a particular way. The examples cited in verses 9 and 10 are significantly similar and give us a clear picture of the sort of deliverance Israel should expect. In every case, the Lord gives their foes into their hand. From this it is plain to see that this prophetic prayer is foretelling God's hand delivering their present day enemies into the hands of the Israeli Defence Force. A perusal of the documentation of the Six Day War reveals a foretaste of the kind of victory we should expect against this confederacy.

A Rebuilt Temple

2 Thessalonians 2:3-4
Let no one deceive you by any means; for *that Day will not come* unless the falling away comes first, and the man of sin is revealed, the son of perdition, 4 who opposes and exalts himself above all that is called God or that is worshiped, so that he sits as God in the temple of God, showing himself that he is God.

Prevailing Jewish theology does not allow them to rebuild their temple until Messiah comes as Zechariah 6:12 says, "He shall build the temple of the Lord." One day the Jews will realise that the temple Messiah came to build is made of living stones (1 Peter 2:5). In the meantime the Jews are waiting for their own version of Messiah. A major victory led by a charismatic Torah keeping military leader could result in the Orthodox Sanhedrin recognising such a man as their Messiah. The Psalm 83 war could provide just such a geopolitical scenario. They may then have the necessary political and demographic authority to clear the temple mount of its present structures and proceed with their dreams.

Some protest saying, "How is it then the 'Temple of God' when in fact the one calling himself God and sitting in it is in fact The Antichrist?" Even though the Jews intend to build this future temple in their unbelief, because it will be dedicated to God and presented to God by the to-be-formed priesthood, God will still accept it and call it His. We have an example of God doing just such a thing in Numbers Chapter 16. Read the whole chapter in your own Bible if you like as I won't quote the whole passage here, just the relevant verse:

Numbers 16:37-38 NKJV
"Tell Eleazar, the son of Aaron the priest, to pick up the censers out of the blaze, for they are holy, and scatter the fire some distance away. 38 The censers of these men who sinned against their own souls, let them be made into hammered plates as a covering for the altar. **Because they presented them before the Lord, therefore they are holy;** and they shall be a sign to the children of Israel." (Emphasis mine)

Yes, there will be a Temple of God, even though the Lord does not live in temples made by the hands of man (Acts 7:48; 17:24).

Egypt, Israel and Assyria Together as One

Isaiah 19:18-25
In that day shall five cities in the land of Egypt speak the language of Canaan, and swear to the Lord of hosts; one shall be called, The city of destruction. (some manuscripts have *city of Righteousness)*

19 In that day shall there be an altar to the Lord in the midst of the land of Egypt, and a pillar at the border thereof to the Lord. 20 And it shall be for a sign and for a witness unto the Lord of hosts in the land of Egypt: for they shall cry unto the Lord because of the oppressors, and he shall send them a saviour, and a great one, and he shall deliver them. 21 And the Lord shall be known to Egypt, and the Egyptians shall know the Lord in that day, and shall do sacrifice and oblation; yea, they shall vow a vow unto the Lord, and perform it. 22 And the Lord shall smite Egypt: he shall smite and heal it: and they shall return even to the Lord, and he shall be entreated of them, and shall heal them. 23 In that day shall there be a highway out of Egypt to Assyria, and the Assyrian shall come into Egypt, and the Egyptian into Assyria, and the Egyptians shall serve with the Assyrians. 24 In that day shall Israel be the third (one of three) with Egypt and with

Assyria, even a blessing in the midst of the land: 25 Whom the Lord of hosts shall bless, saying, Blessed be Egypt my people, and Assyria the work of my hands, and Israel mine inheritance.

How this is going to come about is anyone's guess. This passage is another one of those Scriptures that should perhaps not be mentioned to the United Nations Security Council. On the other hand, maybe we should advise them not to worry about it as God has got it all under control. That aside, Scriptures like these are off the radar for most Christians.

Damascus No Longer A City

Look at this verse from Isaiah concerning Damascus, a city which is reported to be the longest continuously inhabited city of all time with some dating its origins back to around 4000BC, possibly contemporary or shortly after the tower of Babel incident recorded in Genesis 11:1-9.

Isaiah 17:1
The burden of Damascus. Behold, Damascus is taken away from being a city, and it shall be a ruinous heap.

For Damascus to come to an end was and is unheard of and how it will come about is again anyone's guess. But with the civil war in Syria showing us what has happened in Allepo, another large city of that nation, the possibility of it becoming a heap of ruins is not such a far out expectation. Maybe it gets nuked . . . or otherwise totally bombed to smithereens. Not wishing anything upon them, but anyone with knowledge of this Scripture should absent themselves from the city and sell their real estate now.

Jerusalem A Cup of Drunkeness

Zechariah 12:1-9
The burden of the word of the Lord against Israel. Thus says the Lord, who stretches out the heavens, lays the foundation of the earth, and forms the spirit of man within him: 2 "Behold, I will make Jerusalem a cup of drunkenness to all the surrounding peoples, when they lay siege against Judah and Jerusalem. 3 And it shall happen in that day that I will make Jerusalem a very heavy stone for all peoples; all who would heave it away will surely be cut in pieces, though all nations of the earth are gathered against it. 4 In that day," says the Lord, "I will strike every horse with confusion, and its rider with madness; I will open My eye on the house of Judah, and will strike every horse of the peoples with blindness. 5 And the governors of Judah shall say in their heart, 'The inhabitants of Jerusalem *are* my strength in the Lord of hosts, their God.' 6 In that day I will make the governors of Judah like a firepan in the woodpile, and like a fiery torch in the sheaves; they shall devour all the surrounding peoples on the right hand and on the left, but Jerusalem shall be inhabited again in her own place—Jerusalem.

7 "The Lord will save the tents of Judah first, so that the glory of the house of David and the glory of the inhabitants of Jerusalem shall not become greater than that of Judah. 8 In that day the Lord will defend the inhabitants of Jerusalem; the one who is feeble among them in that day shall be like David, and the house of David *shall be* like God, like the Angel of the Lord before them. 9 It shall be in that day *that* I will seek to destroy all the nations that come against Jerusalem.

The above may be a parallel of Psalm 83, though the prophecy seems to focus on Judah, so it could be before the Ten Tribes return. The following verses could be describing the event that prepares the hearts of the people of Judah to enter into the Kingdom of God as the latter part of the passage seems to indicate.

Zechariah 12:10-14
"And I will pour on the house of David and on the inhabitants of Jerusalem the Spirit of grace and supplication; then they will look on Me whom they pierced. Yes, they will mourn for Him as one mourns for *his* only *son,* and grieve for Him as one grieves for a firstborn. 11 In that day there shall be a great mourning in Jerusalem, like the mourning at Hadad Rimmon in the plain of Megiddo. 12 And the land shall mourn, every family by itself: the family of the house of David by itself, and their wives by themselves; the family of the house of Nathan by itself, and their wives by themselves; 13 the family of the house of Levi by itself, and their wives by themselves; the family of Shimei by itself, and their wives by themselves; 14 all the families that remain, every family by itself, and their wives by themselves.

With the passing of time and the other prophetic wars already mentioned in this book, Judah will open their hearts to the real Messiah who bore their sins and rose from the dead for their justification. It is likely that as a result of their victories, their present borders will be enlarged and the Ten Tribes of Israel would then find sufficient space to settle in when God gathers them back from the nations where they had been scattered.

Remember this passage from a previous chapter:

Isaiah 11:11-14
It shall come to pass in that day *that* the Lord shall set His hand again the second time to recover the remnant of His people who are left, from Assyria and Egypt, from Pathros and Cush, from Elam and Shinar, from Hamath and the islands of the sea. 12 He will set up a banner for the nations, and will assemble the outcasts of Israel, and gather together the dispersed of Judah from the four corners of the earth.

13 Also the envy of Ephraim shall depart, and the adversaries of Judah shall be cut off; Ephraim shall not envy Judah, and Judah shall not harass Ephraim. 14 But they shall fly down upon the shoulder of the Philistines toward the west; together they shall plunder the people of the East; they shall lay their hand on Edom and Moab; and the people of Ammon shall obey them.

I guess that will finally solve the Palestinian Peace Problem.

The End of the World is Near?

As you can see, there are a lot of prophecies that are yet to be fulfilled, so many that this author does not believe that the end of the age is imminent. Whilst many say that things can happen quickly, it is also true that some things simply grind along slowly and inexorably. In the Gospel of Luke, Jesus warned that many people would come saying that the "time is near" or as some translations say, "the time is at hand" and He called them deceivers, so I am not inclined to be persuaded by contemporary prophecy pundits proclaiming that the end of the age is just around the corner.

Luke 21:8 NKJV
And He said: "Take heed that you not be deceived. For many will come in My name, saying, 'I am *He*,' and, 'The time has drawn near.' Therefore do not go after them.

Those who proclaim that Jesus could return at any moment are certainly included in that category. Although we will not know the hour or the day, Jesus said that we are to look up and know when the time is near by the signs He gave us. (Matthew 24:33). And Paul writes that this Day will not overtake us like a thief in the night. He asserts that only those walking in darkness will be taken unawares (1 Thessalonians 5:4). Nevertheless, each one of us should always be prepared at any time for we do not know the number of our days. It's worth repeating: although we may become aware that the time is nigh, no one will know the hour or the day.

One might ask, "Where are we (2017AD) in Bible prophecy?" My answer is simple: some time before the great regathering of Israel and a long way from when the sun, moon and stars start losing their light. And because there are untold people who have not yet heard the Gospel we are still some distance from fulfilling the great commission. So whilst we can be filled with the knowledge of His will for the nations and in particular Judah and Israel, let us not forget His will for us individually. Let us aspire to always and without partiality speak the truth in love. Let us be busy with our Father's business so that we may be able to hear those words, "Well done, good and faithful servant. Enter into the joy of the Lord."

THE TIME OF THE GENTILES
and
THE LATTER DAYS

**Most likely progression of events from 1900 to the End of the Age.
Some of the following could overlap or be a slightly different order.**

JUDAH SCATTERED------------------ISLAM IN THE MIDDLE EAST----------------ISRAEL SCATTERED

JUDAH CREATES------------------------------ISLAM GROWS------------------------TEN TRIBES ISRAEL
JEWISH STATE 1948   DOMINATES WORLD

JUDAH SURVIVES ATTACKS-----ISLAM INFILTRATES THE NATIONS--------ISRAEL IN APOSTASY

JERUSALEM A CUP OF DRUNKENESS TO ALL SURROUNDING NATIONS

JUDAH IN DIRE STRAITS RECEIVES MESSIAH-----------JACOBS TROUBLE OVERTAKES ISRAEL

THIS COULD RESULT IN A WORLD WAR WITH MAJOR GEOPOLITICAL UPHEAVAL

JUDAH AND ISRAEL HAVE A GREAT AWAKENING TO THEIR JOINT IDENTITY

REMNANT OF JUDAH AND ISRAEL RECONCILED TO EACH OTHER AND TO GOD

JUDAH AND ISRAEL IN EXILE GATHERED BY GOD TO PROMISED LAND IN GREAT EXODUS

JUDAH AND ISRAEL RESTORED TO EXPERIENCE PEACE AND PROSPERITY

GOG AND MAGOG DESTROYED

THE GOSPEL CONTINUES TO BE PREACHED IN ALL THE WORLD

NATIONS SEND DELEGATES TO FEAST OF TABERNACLES

ISLAMIC EMPIRE PRODUCES TEN KINGS

ANTICHRIST KINGDOM ARISES

FINAL TRIAL AND TRIBULATION OF THE SAINTS BOTH IN ISRAEL AND THE WORLD

JESUS RETURNS FOR HIS SAINTS AND DESTROYS HIS ENEMIES

THE RESURRECTION

JUDGMENT DAY

NEW HEAVENS AND A NEW EARTH

Chapter Sixteen

The End of the Road

I guess you all know by now why I chose The Lion and The Unicorn on the Road to Zion as the alternative title for this book. And perhaps you have found yourself riding on the back of the Unicorn? Well . . . that one might still be too cryptic, but I'm not going to explain it as some riddles are better unexplained. Anyway, congratulations on completing the journey with me through the Scriptures. Most of you will have probably gone through a considerable paradigm shift and for some of you it may have been a hard going tedious exercise. Others may have found it easier, it being but a confirmation of things known intuitively. A few will have gone to the trouble of double checking my findings in order to be satisfied that all is kosher. Some of you may even need to read the whole thing over again to let it all sink in. Whatever is your natural ability, the very fact that you have come this far in this study, is to me evidence of a persistent character that is intent on pursuing the knowledge of the truth that is only found in God's Word.

What follows is a summation of the entire prophetic destiny of Judah, Israel and the Kingdom of God. For those of you who may be wanting to communicate these truths to others, with each chapter summary I have put the pertinent Scripture references that would enable you to easily direct people's attention to the promises of God's Word on this subject. Hopefully, you will find this this to be a handy tool.

In Chapter One we examined the Patriarchal Prophecies where God laid the foundation of His plan for the descendants of Abraham, Isaac and Jacob. We saw that the promise of the Sceptre was given to the tribe of Judah and promise of the Birthright Blessing was given the sons of Joseph; in particular Ephraim.

Genesis 17:1-7; Genesis 48:12-20; Genesis 49:26; Genesis 49:10; 1 Chronicles 5:1-2; Deuteronomy 33:16-17; Genesis 48:16.

In Chapter Two we traced the separation of Israel from Judah so that they became two kingdoms and we took note of their ongoing animosity toward one another. More than 180 verses testifying to the reality of two houses, two kingdoms, two destinies.

Joshua 11:21; 1 Samuel 11:8; 17:52; 18:16; 2 Samuel 2:10; 3:10; 5:5; 11:11; 12:8; 19:11,40,41,42,43; 20:2; 21:2; 24:1,9; 1 Kings 1:35; 2:32; 4:20,25; 12:17,20,21; 15:9,17,25,33; 16:8,23,29; 22:2,10,29,41,51; 2 Kings 3:1,9; 8:16,25; 9:21; 13:1,10,12; 14:1,9,11,12,13,15,17,23,28; 15:1,8,17,23,27,32; 17:1,13,18,19; 18:1,5; 22:18; 23:22,27; 1 Chronicles 5:17; 9:1; 13:6; 21:5; 28:4; 2 Chronicles 10:17; 11:1,3;

13:15,16,18; 15:9; 16:1,11; 18:3,9,28; 20:35; 21:13; 23:2; 24:5,6,9; 25:17,18,21,22,23,25,26; 27:7; 28:19,26; 30:1,6,25; 31:1,6; 32:32; 34:9,21; 35:18,27; 36:8; Psalms 76:1; 114:2; Isaiah 5:7; 7:1; 11:12; 48:1; Jeremiah 3:8,11,18; 5:11; 9:26; 11:10,17; 12:14; 13:11; 23:6; 30:3,4; 31:23,27,31; 32:30,32; 33:7,14; 36:2; 50:4,20,33; 51:5; Lamentations 2:5; Ezekiel 9:9; 25:3; 27:17; 37:16,19; Daniel 9:7; Hosea 1:1,11; 4:15; 5:5; 8:14; 11:12; Amos 1:1; Micah 1:5; 5:2; Zechariah 1:19; 8:13; 11:14; Malachi 2:11. Have you read through that list yet? . . . (; -)

In Chapter Three the rebellion against God by the Northern Kingdom of Israel, led by the tribe of Ephraim, became so bad that He allowed them to be taken captive and carried away into exile. Yet even at that time, God made further promises to them about their eventual return and blessing.

1 Chronicles 5:26; 2 Kings 17:5, 16-18, 21-24; Hosea 1:9-10, 3:4, 5:7, 8:8; Ezekiel 4:13, 11:16, 12:16, 12:1-28, 20:23; Amos 9:8-9; Micah 5:7-9.

In Chapters Four and Five we examined the prophecies of Daniel that gave us our first glimpse of the end of the age. In the dream of the statue we found the prophesied history of the nations that would prevail over the Middle East from the time of the Babylonians. In the vision of the four beasts we learnt about the prevailing spiritual powers of darkness that would influence the whole world and how the fourth spiritual power was also the fifth and final geopolitical power at the end of the age portrayed in Nebuchadnezzar's dream.

Daniel 2:31-45; Daniel 7:1-28.

In Chapters Six through Nine, we took a synoptic view of the three prophecies of Daniel that covered the period of history of the Kingdom of Judah from the time of Daniel through to the Abomination of Desolation and the fall of Jerusalem that culminated with the Kingdom of Judah being taken into exile. In the Seventy Week Prophecy we found the promise of the coming of Messiah and the details of His mission.

Daniel Chapters 8, 9, 11 and 12.

In Chapter Ten we presented the Kingdom of God; its manner of manifestation and its power. It became clear that the Jews were not expecting a spiritual Kingdom that was to be in the world but not of the world. Jesus came as Prophet, Priest and King to take up the Throne of David, also known as the Throne of the LORD.

Matthew, Mark, Luke and John.

In Chapter Eleven we saw that the prophecies of Jesus were to be understood synoptically which enabled us to see that the Abomination of Desolation and the destruction of Jerusalem was the beginning of that period of time Jesus referred to as "the time of the Gentiles" (Luke 21:24). We also learnt that the end of the age would not come until the Gospel had been preached in all the world. We saw with clarity that the harvest at the end of the age included both the "wheat and the tares", the "good fish and the bad fish", the "sheep and the goats", and that we who believe will be raised up to be with Him on the "last day".

Matthew 13 and 24, Mark 13, Luke 21 and John 6:39,40,44,54.

In Chapter Twelve we heard from the Apostles that the Church would be subjected to deceptions leading to apostasy and be afflicted with false prophets and false teachers. We looked briefly at the steady decline of the early 'church fathers' from apostolic times into the dark ages. We also saw clearly that the Antichrist arises right before the end of the age and prevails against the saints (Daniel 7:21-25), but is utterly vanquished when Jesus comes with flaming fire to destroy His enemies.

Jude 1:3-4; 1 Timothy 6:9-11; Acts 20:28-31; 3 John 1:9-10; 2 Peter 2:1-3; Matthew 20:25-28; Matthew 23:8-11; 1 Peter 5:1-4; 1 Timothy 4:1-2; 2 Timothy 3:1-5; 2 Timothy 4:1-4; 2 Thessalonians 2:1-12; 2 Thessalonians 1:3-12; 1 Thessalonians 4:13-18; 1 Corinthians 15:50-54 1 Thessalonians 4:16; 1 Thessalonians 5:1-11; 2 Peter 3:1-13; 2 Timothy 2:15-19; Daniel 7:21-25.

We got valuable insight into the coming events of the Latter Days in Chapters Thirteen, Fourteen and Fifteen where we saw that there are many prophecies concerning Judah, Israel and the Middle East that are yet to be fulfilled before the end of the age, things that will surely come to pass despite the resolutions emanating from the United Nations Security Council. Along with some very interesting Scriptures foretelling geopolitical scenarios in the Middle East, we learnt of a predicted exodus of tremendous proportions that is mind boggling in its scope. After thousands of years of animosity, Judah and Israel become reconciled to each other and they come together out of the nations and back into the Promised Land. But more importantly they get reconciled to God, and upon entering into the Kingdom of God they experience many blessings common to those who believe. The Scriptures reveal that after being gathered from all the nations where He had scattered them (from the east and the west, the north and the south) and after some attempts by enemies to dislodge them, they will be living for a time in prosperity and peace. During that time of being "at peace and without walls", they will experience being protected supernaturally by God when Gog and Magog attempt to attack them to plunder their wealth.

Chapter Thirteen: The Second Exodus. Jeremiah 30-31; Hosea 3:4-5; Amos 9:9-15; Ezekiel 37:15-38; Isaiah 11:11-14; Jeremiah 50:4-5; Jeremiah 3:18; Hosea 1:10-11; Jeremiah 3:11-18; Jeremiah 16:14-15; Jeremiah 23:7-8; Ezekiel 36; Ezekiel 20:33-44; Isaiah 10:20-23; Ezekiel 39:28; Jeremiah 46:28.

Chapter Fourteen: Back in the Promised Land. Romans 11:5, 25-29; Ezekiel 38-39; Isaiah 65:17-25; Zechariah 14:16-21; Isaiah 2:1-4.

Chapter Fifteen: Latter Day Middle East Scenarios. Psalm 83; 2 Thessalonians 2:3-4; Isaiah 19:18-25; Isaiah 17:1; Zechariah 12:1-14; Isaiah 11:1-14.

An unspecified period of time called the Latter Days approaches the inhabitants of this world, the majority of whom are totally unaware of the plans of God for Judah AND Israel to end up back in the Land with their hearts turned to their Messiah. Like people from every generation, the believers in the restored nation will be tested. The forces of evil at large in the world will continue on their wicked way to produce the manifestation of that final kingdom whose reign is portrayed in the Book of Daniel Chapters 2 and 7. These powers of darkness who are at work on the mystery of lawlessness will eventually bring forth the Antichrist.

At the same time, the people of the Kingdom of God both in Israel and in the rest of the world, will be busy seeking first the Kingdom of God and His righteousness and ensuring that the Gospel will be preached in ALL the earth. I believe that when that is accomplished, every person on earth will have heard The Word. Whilst the very young will not be held accountable (to whom little is given little is required) everyone alive with a conscience will then have made their choice. Then the final hour will come, the Lord Jesus Christ will be accompanied by all His angels and all His saints when He comes with flaming fire to destroy the wicked and to raise up those who have believed and received His salvation.

On the Day of the Lord, on that last day, the dead in Christ will rise first (The Resurrection) and we who are in Christ and are still alive on the earth will meet Him in the air (The Rapture). Our natural bodies will be transformed in the twinkling of an eye into that which is immortal and then we will all appear before the Lord. He will then be seated on His Throne and we will all have to give an account of our lives lived and to receive or lose rewards according to His justice and mercy (The Judgment); the wicked will go into everlasting condemnation and the righteous into eternal life where we will inherit a new Earth and a new Heaven where only righteousness dwells, the place that Jesus said He was going to prepare for us. Hallelujah! The Lion and the Unicorn complete their journey to Zion, together with many companions who joined with them along the way. Many of those reading this will solve the riddle and find themselves riding on the back of the Unicorn. Praise the Lord.

Most of you will have ventured into the Appendix and read the relative articles as prompted during this study. Don't forget to read through the remaining articles: How to Find the Lost Ten Tribes, and The Revelation of Revelation.

Love joy and peace to you in Jesus Mighty Name.

Appendix

I Believe in Unicorns

A quote from the King James Version of the Bible: Deuteronomy 33:17, mentions the word "unicorns". The KJV is not alone in this; all the earliest English translations mention unicorns. Of course, this brings ridicule from the secular critics, "You know, them Christians believe in unicorns . . ." Well, I believe in unicorns, and when you have finished reading this little chapter, you will too. Mind you, it won't be the fairy-tale white horse with a horn on its forehead that has its origins in Greek mythology. No, the unicorn I am speaking of is quite a different creature.

In the King James Version of the Bible there are actually nine references to a creature called the unicorn.

Numbers 23:22
God brought them out of Egypt; he hath as it were the strength of an unicorn.

Numbers 24:8
God brought him forth out of Egypt; he hath as it were the strength of an unicorn: he shall eat up the nations his enemies, and shall break their bones, and pierce them through with his arrows.

Deuteronomy 33:17
His glory is like the firstling of his bullock, and his horns are like the horns of unicorns: with them he shall push the people together to the ends of the earth: and they are the ten thousands of Ephraim, and they are the thousands of Manasseh.

Job 39:9
Will the unicorn be willing to serve thee, or abide by thy crib?

Job 39:10
Canst thou bind the unicorn with his band in the furrow? Or will he harrow the valleys after thee?

Psalm 22:21
Save me from the lion's mouth: for thou hast heard me from the horns of the unicorns.

Psalm 29:6
He maketh them also to skip like a calf; Lebanon and Sirion like a young unicorn.

Psalm 92:10
But my horn shalt thou exalt like the horn of an unicorn: I shall be anointed with fresh oil.

Isaiah 34:7

And the unicorns shall come down with them, and the bullocks with the bulls; and their land shall be soaked with blood, and their dust made fat with fatness.

The biblical description of the unicorn is rather scant, but what it does say gives one the impression that this animal is something to be respected on account of its strength. Despite being described as a powerful beast, the unicorn is not portrayed as the kind of animal that can be harnessed to work in the fields. We are left convinced that it cannot be trained. Relatively few contemporary translators have bothered to do the scholarly research necessary to identify this creature. The popular mythical image associated with the mention of a unicorn has shied the majority away. Instead of pressing on to the discovery of the mystery, they have chosen to translate the Hebrew word *reem* that represents this creature, as "wild ox", a choice which this author considers to be an epic fail, for there are Hebrew words for both ox and wild if such a creature were originally intended.

Young's Literal Translation of the Bible has simply transliterated the original Hebrew word *reem* without any effort to translate it, which perhaps is their honest admission that they didn't know what a *reem* is. Other English transliterations include: reyn, r'en, ren, or re'en; probably pronounced 'reh-ehn' or 'reh-ehm'.

Of over fifty modern and popular English translations and versions of the Bible available on biblegateway.com published since the year 1900, forty-five have rendered the Hebrew word *reem* as wild ox, five have it as a wild bull and one has it as a buffalo. Yet prior to the year 1900, NOT ONE English translation can be found with the words wild ox, bull or buffalo representing the Hebrew word *reem*. With the exception of one and only one (mentioned later), the early English Bibles all uniformly used the word "unicorn".

Edit: Since writing this article I have discovered a list of other Bibles that have used the word "unicorn": The Bill Bible 1671; The Smith Bible 1876; The Brenton Translation 1851; The Thompson Bible 1808; Daniel Webster's Bible 1833; The Longman Version 1841; Darby's translation of 1890; Lamsa's 1933 Bible translation of the Syraic Peshitta; the 1936 Masoretic Scriptures Hebrew Publishing Company, New York, the Catholic Douay version of 1950; The Word of JAH translation 1993; The 21st Century King James Version 1994; The Revised Webster Bible 1995; the Third Millennium Bible 1998; God's First Truth 1999; The Apostolic Bible Polyglot English of 2003; The Revised Geneva Bible 2005; The Complete Apostles' Bible of 2005; The Apostolic Bible 2006; English Jubilee Bible 2010; Biblos Interlinear Bible 2013; The Hebraic Transliteration Scriptures 2010 by Yerusha Shen; The Work of God's Children's Illustrated Bible 2011; The New Brenton Translation 2012 and The New English Septuagint Translation 2014. Also the Modern Greek translation of the Old Testament has translated the Hebrew word *reem* to *monoceros* or *monokeros* as per the Septuagint of old. Looks like they still believe in unicorns.

I have not found any record among Hebrew scholastic works as to what this creature called *reem* is. The *reem* it seems, is considered to be like the behemoth and the leviathan mentioned in the

Book of Job; animals that are presumed to be extinct. Modern Hebrew, although based on Biblical Hebrew, has had to invent new words for things not found in the Holy Scriptures and with the identity of this creature lost in antiquity, they have invented a new word for the actual animal that the *reem* represents. (Later in this article for the new word) This is completely understandable as the *reem* did not exist in the Holy Land for a very long time, long enough for all knowledge of what this creature is to be completely forgotten. Along with many other scholars, Jewish researchers have guessed that perhaps the extinct auroch (which is an ancient cattle beast also known as the urus) could be the intended animal. But as this study will reveal, the *reem* is certainly not extinct.

Twentieth Century English dictionaries uniformly give a mythological meaning to the word unicorn. This has possibly been motivated by the use of the horned horse image on the Heraldry of England and Scotland. Here are a few examples of the contemporary meaning assigned to the word unicorn:

The American Heritage Dictionary of the English Language defines unicorn as: "A fabled creature symbolic of virginity and usually represented as a horse with a single straight spiralled horn projecting from its forehead."

Dictionary.com defines unicorn as: "A mythical creature resembling a horse, with a single horn in the centre of its forehead: often symbolic of chastity or purity."

Merriam-Webster's Learner's Dictionary definition of unicorn is: "An imaginary animal that looks like a horse and has a straight horn growing from the middle of its forehead."

The Financial Times Lexicon defines unicorn as: "A private company valued at more than $1 billion dollars."

Noah Webster's Dictionary 1913: "Unicorn 1. A fabulous animal with one horn; the monoceros; often represented in heraldry as a supporter. 2. A two-horned animal of some unknown kind, so called in the Authorized Version of the Scriptures. 3. The unicorn mentioned in the Scripture was probably the urus. 4. Any large beetle having a hornlike prominence on the head or prothorax. 5. The kamichi; called also *unicorn bird*. 6. A howitzer."

The question remains, how then did the early translators of the Bible come to use the word "unicorn" as their translation of the word *reem*? The answer to that question begins with the ancient Greek translation of the Hebrew Scriptures known as the Septuagint (*septuaginta* Latin for 'seventy'). "The Translation of the Seventy" is the literal Greek title for this copy of what we now call the Old Testament which was completed sometime during the third century BC. In this Greek translation, the word *reem* is translated into Greek as *monokeros* or *monoceros*, which means in English: one-horned. It seems that the seventy Jewish scholars who were commissioned to do the translation believed in unicorns too.

The following two verses from the King James Version are at the centre of the considerable confusion that surrounds the identity of this particular creature.

Psalm 92:10
But my horn shalt thou exalt like the horn of an unicorn . . ."

Deuteronomy 33:17
His glory is like the firstling of his bullock, and his horns are like the horns of unicorns: with them he shall push the people together to the ends of the earth: and they are the ten thousands of Ephraim, and they are the thousands of Manasseh."

In Psalm 92:10, the language is clear, a singular horn on a singular unicorn, but in Deuteronomy 33:17 the English word "unicorns" is plural with a margin note that says; "literally a unicorn" (singular). This is how it reads in Young's Literal Translation:

Deuteronomy 33:17 YLT
His honour [is] a firstling of his ox, And his horns [are] horns of a reem; By them peoples he doth push together to the ends of earth; And they [are] the myriads of Ephraim, And they [are] the thousands of Manasseh."

The Hebrew word *reem* is definitely in its singular form and by using the singular, Young's agrees with the ancient translators of the Septuagint. But how can we have plural horns on a one-horned beast? Isn't the definition in the 1913 dictionary mentioned above a bit of an oxymoron: a unicorn (a one-horned beast) is "a two-horned animal of some unknown kind" . . . Duh? Talk about confusion. However, there are two possible explanations to the enigma of this verse that we will now explore.

This first attempt requires a little knowledge of Hebrew and English grammar, in particular the difference in the use of the words 'a' and 'the'. The 'a' being the indefinite article and the 'the' being the definite article. In the Hebrew language there is no indefinite article. Whenever a noun is indefinite, the context is all there is to define what is meant. Therefore, whether it's *reem* or a *reem* depends on the context. When the noun is definite, the Hebrew always uses the definite article with the exception of proper nouns which are not prefaced with either a definite or an indefinite article. What follows will illustrate how this information helps us understand the seeming incongruity of this particular verse.

Take this statement: "The Return of the Lion and the Unicorn". In my mind, the Unicorn refers to the whole multitude of unicorns. But without the context of what I have written, the sentence itself could refer to a single unicorn. In my case, the word "Unicorn" is used in the singular to represent a proper noun, to speak of the plurality of unicorns. In English we use a definite article, 'the', but in Hebrew when a word is used as a proper noun, no definite article is used. They would say, "The Return of Unicorn", and the context would determine what is meant. The plurality of horns upon the *reem* is therefore appropriate IF it is speaking of the *reem* as a species. The context in Deuteronomy 33:17 certainly allows for it to be referring to the "ten thousands of Ephraim" and the "thousands of Manasseh", not just the two horns representing Joseph's sons, but a myriad of horns representing their descendants that are imbued with strength to push the peoples to the ends of the earth.

This explanation is of course based on the presumption that the plurality of unicorns is intended. Perhaps it is with this in mind that the KJV translators chose to insert the plural proper noun in the main text with a centre column reference noting the singular. Likewise the translators of the Septuagint using the term *monoceros* in the singular, using it as a proper noun referring to the multitude.

However, there is another explanation that is equally plausible. In the Greek (*monoceros*) and in the Latin based English word (unicorn), the name of the creature is also descriptive of the creature. It is one-horned. But the Hebrew word *reem* is not descriptive at all. What description is available to us from the Hebrew is limited to the context of the Scriptures If we dismiss the possibility just offered that the species is intended, and accept that the *reem* mentioned in the two verses is the same beast, we can come to but one conclusion; that the *reem* can be a one-horned creature AND it can be a two-horned creature.

And nature itself provides us with just such an animal. It is the rhinoceros. The one-horned rhinoceros is called in Latin, *rhinoceros unicornis*, and this creature is found alive today in northern India and Nepal. Its relative, the two-horned rhinoceros is called in Latin, *diceros bicornis* and is mostly living in the southern regions of the African continent. The gradual reduction and/or change of their range, which previously included Northern Africa and the Land of Israel according to archaeological findings, has been going on for thousands of years. The lion and the bear are examples of other animals that used to be living in Israel according to Scripture (1 Samuel 17:34-36), that are now only found in Zoos in the Holy Land.

In 2015 a total of over 3,500 Indian one-horned rhinoceros were estimated to be living in the wild. These unicorns are considered a threatened species, possibly becoming endangered because of illegal hunting for their horns that are prized in Asian countries for so called medicinal reasons; Vietnam apparently being the prime culprit. There is also a sub species called the Javan rhinoceros that is also known as the lesser one-horned rhinoceros. This smaller variety of unicorn is on the extremely endangered list as their numbers are now less than a hundred. The Javan unicorn was until recent times found in Vietnam but they have been hunted to extinction in that country. With powdered unicorn horn being more expensive by weight than gold, it's a real problem trying to thwart those that are involved in the poaching of these beasts.

As mentioned above, all English Bible translations before the year 1900 used the word unicorn. So let's take a look at a couple of English dictionaries from the nineteenth century and see what we find.

Noah Webster's Dictionary 1828

U'NICORN, n. [L. unicornis; unus, one, and cornu, horn.] 1. An animal with one horn; the monoceros; this name is often applied to the rhinoceros. 2. The sea unicorn is a fish of the whale kind, called narwal, remarkable for a horn growing out at his nose. 3. A fowl.

Noah Webster's Dictionary 1844

U'NI-CORN, n. [L. *unicornis*; *unus*, one, and *cornu*, horn.] 1. An animal with one horn; the monoceros. This name often applied to the rhinoceros. 2. The sea unicorn, called narwal, is of the whale kind, and is remarkable for a horn growing out at his nose. 3. A fowl. Grew. *Fossil unicorn*, or *fossil unicorn's horn*, a substance used in medicine, a terrene crustaceous spar. Cyc.

Note: "narwal" is now spelt narwhal or narwhale.

According to these nineteenth century dictionaries, the word unicorn was often applied to the rhinoceros and there was no hint of mythology. Although the Greek mythological creature was probably known, its prominence in the English language was insufficient to gain a mention in the compendium of English words. We see here a classic example of how the definition of a word can change over time. With regards to the word "unicorn", that change, which is recorded in the editions of most English dictionaries, was rather rapid toward the end of the nineteenth century. Around that time, the change of the translation of the Hebrew word *reem* in most of our more popular modern Bibles also changed. This change in the common usage of the word unicorn, to become associated with the mythical image of an imaginary horned horse, was most likely the catalyst that caused the modern translators to shy away and retranslate the word to "wild ox" as found in our contemporary Bibles, perhaps to avoid embarrassment.

What shall we presume? Certainly we cannot presume the *reem* to be a "wild ox". A wild horse can be trained and a wild ox can be trained but no one has ever trained the rhinoceros to work in the fields. God's portrait of this animal in the Scriptures suitably describes this beast so we are left with the choice of which rhinoceros was intended by Moses when he wrote Deuteronomy 33:17.

Early Latin translations used five different words to represent the word *reem* that appears in the Hebrew: Rinoceros; Rinocerotis; Rinocerota; Unicornium; Unicornis. Were they using the term interchangeably, or did they discern a difference? The King James translators were not entirely ignorant of the term either because in Isaiah 34:7 they included a centre column reference regarding the word "unicorns" stating: "or rhinocerots". As I mentioned above, there happens to be one English Bible translation (that I know of) that has translated the word *reem* into both unicorn and rhinoceros in their main text, and that is the Douay-Rheims 1899 American Edition. Here are the two verses in question:

Deuteronomy 33:17 DRA

His beauty as of the firstling of a bullock, his horns as the horns of a rhinoceros: with them shall he push the nations even to the ends of the earth. These are the multitudes of Ephraim and these the thousands of Manasses.

Note the different verse numbering in this translation, took me a while to find the text.

Psalm 91:11 DRA

But my horn shall be exalted like that of the unicorn . . ."

If we now presume that the two-horned rhinoceros is what is intended in Deuteronomy 33:17, the context also allows for a plausible interpretation. Ephraim and Manasseh being the tribes descended from Joseph were to become great, but Ephraim was to become greater than Manasseh. The two-horned rhinoceros has one horn greater than the other, thus the ten thousands of Ephraim could be symbolised by the greater horn and Manasseh symbolised by the lesser horn, yet their oneness and closeness to each other is preserved for the context in this particular verse reveals that together they represent Joseph.

This whole mystery of the unicorn is somewhat symbolic and probably prophetic. It was a variety of rhinoceros that symbolized the strength of the descendants of Joseph's sons, Ephraim and Manasseh. They became the leading tribes of the Kingdom of Israel after they separated themselves from Judah. It not only symbolized their strength, it probably symbolises their stubbornness in that they can't be trained, and also the peak of their destiny in that nothing in the animal kingdom stands against them. In the wild they don't get on with lions, and lions sometimes have a go at the rhinoceros but to no avail. The rhinoceros just drives them off (I've seen wildlife videos of their interaction online). Just as the identity and whereabouts of the *reem* became mostly lost, the identity and the whereabouts of Ephraim and Manasseh were likewise mostly lost.

The modern day Hebrew word for rhinoceros is *karnaf* a compound word meaning 'horn' and 'nose', probably a translation back to Hebrew of the Latin *rhinoceros* which itself is actually a transliteration from the ancient Greek *rhino* and *keros* meaning 'nose' and 'horn'. To my knowledge, *karnaf* has not yet been linked to the original word *reem*, which is remarkable considering the seventy Jewish scholars of antiquity clearly identified the *reem* as a one horned creature (*monoceros* or *monokeros*) in their Greek translation.

This disconnect is amazingly symbolic of the ongoing breach between Israel and Judah that is prevalent to this day. When I am reminded that Manasseh means forgetfulness, and I see the forgotten identity of the descendants of Joseph and the forgotten identity of the *reem*, it not only blows my mind, it also makes it hard to believe that God didn't have a hand in these parallel lost identities. Join with me in declaring: Oh my God, you are amazing.

The Abomination of Desolation

What was the Abomination of Desolation? Was it a statue or some sort of idol? Was it a man calling himself God in the Temple of God? Or was it something else entirely that merely brought desolation? Most scholars simply speculate, saying that the Word of God is not specific about what it actually is. They thus presume that it would have been obvious to the believers at the time and they would have been able to respond accordingly. A careful study of the Scriptures reveals that God did not leave it up to the entire community of believers to figure this out on their own, but made it abundantly clear what He was referring to and that it was going to be obvious to all concerned. The Scriptures speak for themselves so let's see what we shall see.

The passages that speak of an Abomination of Desolation are to be found in the Book of Daniel Chapters 8, 9, 11 and 12 and in the Gospels of Matthew, Mark and Luke. If you have come to this chapter without having read Chapter Eleven of this study, you would do well to read it through before continuing so as to have a proper understanding of the synoptic prophecies of Jesus. That said, we will now look at the Gospel Scriptures first:

Matthew 24:15-16
When ye therefore shall see the abomination of desolation, spoken of by Daniel the prophet, stand in the holy place, (whoso readeth, let him understand:) 16 Then let them which be in Judaea flee into the mountains:

Mark 13:14
But when ye shall see the abomination of desolation, spoken of by Daniel the prophet, standing where it ought not, (let him that readeth understand,) then let them that be in Judaea flee to the mountains:

Luke 21:20-21
And when ye shall see Jerusalem compassed with armies, then know that the desolation thereof is nigh. 21 Then let them which are in Judaea flee to the mountains; and let them which are in the midst of it depart out; and let not them that are in the countries enter thereinto.

If we were to accept that it was some sort of idol erected in the Temple, we have got all sorts of problems reconciling that scenario with the instructions of Jesus. How were the people in the country who were told not to enter the city to know that the abomination had been set up in the temple in the city? And how were the Romans able to set up some idol when the Jews had completely taken control over the city? The Roman armies were outside the city walls laying siege, not inside erecting idols.

When the final battle was fought and the fortress at the temple was overtaken, the Romans did not do anything but set the temple on fire that day and slaughter over a million people in a massive massacre. How could any abomination set up in the Temple then become a sign to the disciples for them to flee? It would be too late. The whole idea simply doesn't fit.

Clearly, the Abomination of Desolation was not something that required one to be in Jerusalem or near the Temple in order to see it. If you were out in the country when you saw this abomination you were not to enter the city, but to flee to the mountains.

Luke 21:20 lets us know that the Abomination of Desolation was the presence of armies around Jerusalem. With all their idolatrous emblems, that were an abomination to the Jews, they were standing in the Holy Land where they ought not, set up and ready to make the city a desolation. This was the sign for the disciples to FLEE.

You may recall from this study that there are two Abomination of Desolations mentioned in Daniel Chapters 11 and 12. While there are two abominations mentioned, there are actually three desolations of Jerusalem which appear in the Scriptures that we shall now look at and see what God's Word says about desolation.

Daniel 9:1-2
In the first year of Darius the son of Ahasuerus, of the seed of the Medes, which was made king over the realm of the Chaldeans; 2 In the first year of his reign I Daniel understood by books the number of the years, whereof the word of the Lord came to Jeremiah the prophet, that he would accomplish seventy years in the desolations of Jerusalem.

Jeremiah 25:11
And this whole land shall be a desolation, and an astonishment; and these nations shall serve the king of Babylon seventy years.

The destruction of the Temple and the removal of Judah from the city by the Babylonians for seventy years was referred to as a desolation, or desolations. As Daniel continues in his prayer, he again bewails the desolation of Jerusalem.

Daniel 9:17-18
Now therefore, O our God, hear the prayer of thy servant, and his supplications, and cause thy face to shine upon thy sanctuary that is desolate, for the Lord's sake. 18 O my God, incline thine ear, and hear; open thine eyes, and behold our desolations, and the city which is called by thy name: for we do not present our supplications before thee for our righteousnesses, but for thy great mercies.

After Daniel's prayer, we have the Seventy Sevens prophecy wherein we find mention of the Abomination of Desolation.

Daniel 9:26b NKJV
And the people of the prince who is to come shall destroy the city and the sanctuary. The end of it *shall be* with a flood, and till the end of the war desolations are determined.

Daniel 9:27b NKJV
And on the wing of abominations shall be one who makes desolate, even until the consummation, which is determined, is poured out on the desolate.

The above two quotes are a parallelism which make for a clear understanding. The one who made desolate was the Roman general Titus who led the people of the prince who was to come in a war filled with abominable desolations. There is no mention of idolatry being a factor.

Speaking of this same "prince", we have another confirmation from Daniel 8.

Daniel 8:11-12 NKJV
He even exalted *himself* as high as the Prince of the host; and by him the daily *sacrifices* were taken away, and the place of His sanctuary was cast down. 12 Because of transgression, an army was given over *to the horn* to oppose the daily *sacrifices;* and he cast truth down to the ground. He did *all this* and prospered. 13 Then I heard a holy one speaking; and *another* holy one said to that certain *one* who was speaking, "How long *will* the vision *be, concerning* the daily *sacrifices* and the transgression of desolation, the giving of both the sanctuary and the host to be trampled underfoot?"

Instead of calling the desolation an abomination, in this passage it is called the transgression of desolation and the context reveals that it is the giving of both the sanctuary and the host to be trampled.

The only possible act of idolatry which could be associated with an abomination of desolation is that which occurred earlier in history during the reign of Antiochus IV that we find in this part of Daniel's prophecy.

Daniel 11:31 NKJV
And forces shall be mustered by him, and they shall defile the sanctuary fortress; then they shall take away the daily *sacrifices,* and place *there* the abomination of desolation.

As mentioned previously in this study, the Greeks certainly defiled the Sanctuary with their idolatrous practices. They also prohibited the daily sacrifices and set troops to completely exclude Jews from the Temple so that it remained desolate for over three years. However, we would be making a presumption to assume that the abomination was some form of idolatry when the prophecy itself only makes provision for any idolatrous act to be described as defilement rather than the actual Abomination of Desolation. The verse says, "They shall defile the sanctuary . . .AND place there the abomination of desolation." Thus alerting us to two different acts.

When Daniel again mentions an Abomination of Desolation in Chapter 12 verses 8-12, we find that there is no indication of what it is, only a question about the timing.

From all the above I believe it is clear that it is the armies and the desolation they brought which are the abomination and not any erected idol or image and certainly not any person. Not saying there won't be some person sitting in a Temple calling himself God sometime in the future, in fact I'm sure there will be, just saying that that is not what is described as the Abomination of Desolation in Daniel or the Gospels. Hope you found this enlightening.

First Fruits Resurrection

Matthew 27:51-53 NKJV
Then, behold, the veil of the temple was torn in two from top to bottom; and the earth quaked, and the rocks were split, 52 and the graves were opened; and many bodies of the saints who had fallen asleep were raised; 53 and coming out of the graves after his resurrection, they went into the holy city and appeared to many.

It has always amazed me that Matthew only gives this one sentence to cover this momentous event. If it had happened in our time, we would have written books on the subject, with interviews of those who talked with them, what they said, who they were, how long they stayed, how many there were . . . It hardly needs to be said that this was not the final resurrection from the dead, however, it is certainly one of the encouraging signs that God has given that there will indeed be a more complete resurrection. This article will set forth this event recorded in Matthew as the fulfilment of the symbolic offering of the Feast of First Fruits.

Leviticus 23:9-14 NKJV
And the Lord spoke to Moses, saying, 10 "speak to the children of Israel, and say to them: 'when you come into the land which I give to you, and reap its harvest, then you shall bring a sheaf of the first fruits of your harvest to the priest. 11 he shall wave the sheaf before the Lord, to be accepted on your behalf; on the day after the Sabbath the priest shall wave it. 12 and you shall offer on that day, when you wave the sheaf, a male lamb of the first year, without blemish, as a burnt offering to the Lord.

Before the harvest began, the owners were to go through the field and select enough to form a sheaf and bring it as an offering to the temple. It has been suggested there were always a few heads of grain that ripened early. Along with the sheaf a young male lamb without blemish was also sacrificed. As surely as the Passover feast was fulfilled, the other feasts were too, as they all pointed towards Christ. However, not many people take much notice of the first fruit resurrection in the New Testament. Most scholars recognize Jesus as being the first fruits, citing Paul's letter to the Corinthians, but they overlook the detailed instructions in Leviticus just mentioned; the lamb was to be offered with a sheaf from the coming harvest. Both the lamb and the sheaf are the first fruits.

1 Corinthians 15:22-24 NKJV
For as in Adam all die, even so in Christ all shall be made alive. 23 But each one in his own order: Christ, the firstfruits, afterward those *who are* Christ's at His coming. 24 Then *comes* the end, when He delivers the kingdom to God the Father,

213

In the above verse, I have added a comma to the text between "Christ" and "the firstfruits". The original Greek supplies no punctuation, and so all commas, speech marks etc., are at the discretion of the editors. I believe this suggested edit of mine conforms better with the reality of the first fruit resurrection cited in Matthew and in Leviticus. He rose first, the many saints very soon after as per the Feast of First Fruits (recorded in Matthew 27:52-53) and later, the final future resurrection being the harvest at the end of the age.

The word "appeared" is used 73 times in Scripture and about 60 of those times it speaks of the Lord appearing to his people, either in the Old or the New Testaments. On occasion it's used of an angel or a cherub, twice for a star and never for a mortal person. In particular in the New Testament it is used again and again concerning Jesus appearing to his disciples after the resurrection and included amongst the Scriptures using this word is the reference to those who appeared from the grave. It is not used in any other way. All of these appearances are short and temporary, indicating that these saints did not hang around to live and later die again.

Ephesians 4:8 NKJV
Therefore He says: "When He ascended on high, He led captivity captive,

I suspect Daniel was among those who were raised and appeared at that time because he was told he would be raised at the end of the days. Our study revealed that the days mentioned were the days of the end of the prophecy (Daniel 12:13). These saints, although they were in "Abraham's bosom" (Luke 16:22), they were still captive in Sheol. Jesus leading "captivity captive" would seem to indicate Him raising all the saints in "captivity" as First Fruits when He Himself "ascended on high".

There is debate over whether this resurrection included all the saints that had gone before or just a selection of them, noting that the word "many" might not mean "all". On the other hand it mentions "the graves being opened" and that phrase on its own could very well be all inclusive. It would seem strange to me to consider that He would have treated some of the saints of old differently when He "took captivity captive" (Ephesians 4:8). However, there is not enough given in the Word to make a dogmatic statement. My thoughts are that they were all resurrected (the graves were opened) but only "many" of them stopped by in Jerusalem where they showed themselves to "many" in the city. Whether they showed themselves anywhere else we can but speculate.

These saints that came out of their graves did not hang about and later die. They appeared, and then ascended so that when He presented Himself on High as the Lamb sacrificed, He would then, as our High Priest, have also presented the First Fruits from the Harvest. Thus Jesus has fulfilled the Feast of First Fruits just as surely as He has fulfilled every other aspect of the Law. Hallelujah!

The Two Genealogies

Almost every Christian who has read their Bible will sooner or later become aware of the differences between the two genealogies of Jesus Christ found in Matthew 1:1-17 and Luke.3:23-38. Secular critics consider these differences to be evidence of the Bible contradicting itself. As a consequence, some of their unbelieving questions have provoked scholars to find suitable answers in order to satisfy and silence the voices of doubt that attack the integrity of the Word of God. In pursuing this subject I discovered just how thoroughly God has crossed every 'T' and dotted every 'I', or as Jesus put it, "Not one jot or tittle of the Law shall pass away to all is fulfilled."

Most if not all of the Church has accepted the explanation that the genealogy listed in Matthew pertains to Joseph and the genealogy listed in Luke pertains to Mary. Closer examination of both the genealogies exposes a number of mysteries that could still be unsettling for some and so with this article I hope to show how these apparent anomalies can be satisfactorily and plausibly resolved.

Here we have the genealogy from the Gospel of Matthew:

Matthew 1:1-17 NKJV
The book of the genealogy of Jesus Christ, the Son of David, the Son of Abraham: 2 Abraham begot Isaac, Isaac begot Jacob, and Jacob begot Judah and his brothers. 3 Judah begot Perez and Zerah by Tamar, Perez begot Hezron, and Hezron begot Ram. 4 Ram begot Amminadab, Amminadab begot Nahshon, and Nahshon begot Salmon. 5 Salmon begot Boaz by Rahab, Boaz begot Obed by Ruth, Obed begot Jesse, 6 and Jesse begot David the king.

David the king begot Solomon by her *who had been the wife* of Uriah. 7 Solomon begot Rehoboam, Rehoboam begot Abijah, and Abijah begot Asa. 8 Asa begot Jehoshaphat, Jehoshaphat begot Joram, and Joram begot Uzziah. 9 Uzziah begot Jotham, Jotham begot Ahaz, and Ahaz begot Hezekiah. 10 Hezekiah begot Manasseh, Manasseh begot Amon, and Amon begot Josiah. 11 Josiah begot Jeconiah and his brothers about the time they were carried away to Babylon.

12 And after they were brought to Babylon, Jeconiah begot Shealtiel, and Shealtiel begot Zerubbabel. 13 Zerubbabel begot Abiud, Abiud begot Eliakim, and Eliakim begot Azor. 14 Azor begot Zadok, Zadok begot Achim, and Achim begot Eliud. 15 Eliud begot Eleazar, Eleazar begot Matthan, and Matthan begot Jacob. 16 And Jacob begot Joseph the husband of Mary, of whom was born Jesus who is called Christ.

17 So all the generations from Abraham to David *are* fourteen generations, from David until the captivity in Babylon *are* fourteen generations, and from the captivity in Babylon until the Christ *are* fourteen generations.

And here we have the genealogy from the Gospel of Luke:

Luke 3:23-38 NKJV
Now Jesus Himself began *His ministry at* about thirty years of age, being (as was supposed) *the* son of Joseph, *the son* of Heli, 24 *the son* of Matthat, *the son* of Levi, *the son* of Melchi, *the son* of Janna, *the son* of Joseph, 25 *the son* of Mattathiah, *the son* of Amos, *the son* of Nahum, *the son* of Esli, *the son* of Naggai, 26 *the son* of Maath, *the son* of Mattathiah, *the son* of Semei, *the son* of Joseph, *the son* of Judah, 27 *the son* of Joannas, *the son* of Rhesa, *the son* of Zerubbabel, *the son* of Shealtiel, *the son* of Neri, 28 *the son* of Melchi, *the son* of Addi, *the son* of Cosam, *the son* of Elmodam, *the son* of Er, 29 *the son* of Jose, *the son* of Eliezer, *the son* of Jorim, *the son* of Matthat, *the son* of Levi, 30 *the son* of Simeon, *the son* of Judah, *the son* of Joseph, *the son* of Jonan, *the son* of Eliakim, 31 *the son* of Melea, *the son* of Menan, *the son* of Mattathah, *the son* of Nathan, *the son* of David, 32 *the son* of Jesse, *the son* of Obed, *the son* of Boaz, *the son* of Salmon, *the son* of Nahshon, 33 *the son* of Amminadab, *the son* of Ram, *the son* of Hezron, *the son* of Perez, *the son* of Judah, 34 *the son* of Jacob, *the son* of Isaac, *the son* of Abraham, *the son* of Terah, *the son* of Nahor, 35 *the son* of Serug, *the son* of Reu, *the son* of Peleg, *the son* of Eber, *son* of Shelah, 36 *the son* of Cainan, *the son* of Arphaxad, *the son* of Shem, *the son* of Noah, *the son* of Lamech, 37 *the son* of Methuselah, *the son* of Enoch, *the son* of Jared, *the son* of Mahalalel, *the son* of Cainan, 38 *the son* of Enosh, *the son* of Seth, *the son* of Adam, *the son* of God.

Matthew's account of the genealogy of Joseph begins with Abraham and follows the ancestry through King David and King Solomon and ends with noting Joseph as "the husband of Mary of whom was born Jesus." Matthew is writing primarily to the Jews and the genealogy he listed was to communicate to them the legal ancestry of Jesus' right to the Throne of David because He is the son of David and the seed of Abraham. Matthew uses the term "begot" to indicate a biological descendant, usually the immediate son but sometimes it can mean progeny a few generations distant. Begot also refers to the rare practice of a brother raising up a son on behalf of a childless deceased sibling and so it is more concerned with the legality of the inheritance than the specific bloodline. It therefore extends to adoptions and step children. More on that later.

Luke's account of Mary's ancestry begins with Jesus and goes all the way back to Adam. We have Jesus "as was supposed" the son of Joseph. Thereafter you will note that the words *"the son"* are in italics throughout the rest of the passage. This indicates in the NKJV that the words are added to the text by the editors for clarification. The actual original only says "of".

Luke does not use the term "begot", but the much broader term "son". While it certainly includes begotten children and progeny in general, it also includes such things as adoption, sons in law, the fact of being created and even those of like character, as in the term "sons of the devil". Although Luke's Gospel is written primarily to the Gentiles, Luke's genealogy is according to Jewish tradition that always identified the man and rarely his wife, even when the wife's blood line is being noted. Thus Joseph is recorded as "of Heli" when that was actually Mary's father, Joseph being the son in law. Joseph's actual father was called Jacob (Matthew 1:16). To our way of thinking, this seems rather misogynistic but in reality it was done to keep track of the inheritance according to the Law. Complicated business sorting it all out in our day.

At the time of the writing of these two genealogies, the records were available to be confirmed as the registry was kept in storage by the priesthood. The record was probably recorded when the presentation of a child was done at the temple with the offerings under the Law. Because the genealogy could have been easily verified when the Gospels were originally written, secular critics have no legitimate reason to dispute the Gospel records as it would have been simply silly for anyone to claim a direct lineage falsely when the records were so readily available. However, these temple records were all later destroyed at the destruction of Jerusalem in 70AD which incidentally presents a tremendous dilemma for Orthodox Jews who are now not able to give credibility to the bloodline and inheritance of any son of David, which means they could never legitimately confirm the identity of the Messiah they are waiting for. For Christians, this loss of the records leaves us leaning on the written Word of God and the witness of the Holy Spirit in our hearts.

A notable difference in the two genealogies is the number of people listed in Matthew's Gospel compared to the number listed in Luke's, particularly for the period of time from the captivity in Babylon to the time of Christ. Critics point out that there are not enough people listed for the 500 years that this lineage covers. They also note that some of the descendants of David are simply left out of Matthew's list when the bloodline is compared to other genealogical recordings in the Hebrew Scriptures. Four rather wicked kings are simply omitted.

As mentioned above, the term "begot", is used in a broad manner. We can all see that Jesus is referred to as the son of David even though it is many generations later. Later in this article you will see a prophecy given to Hezekiah that speaks of sons he will beget a hundred years into the future. It appears that Matthew, perhaps for the sake of easy memorising, has limited the account of the genealogy to fourteen for each period of time and so he has left out four of the more wicked kings from his account. Likewise with the time from the captivity to Christ, all the characters are not mentioned. It appears the Jews were more interested in descent and it was not out of order for them to omit unseemly characters from their genealogy. As we have no records covering this period of time, we can but speculate as to the reasons why certain people were skipped over.

Luke on the other hand has given a fuller record in the genealogy of Mary. But there is one thing that really does need explanation and that is the fact that both genealogies mention the same two characters: Shealtiel and Zerubbabel. And it is regarding Shealtiel and Zerubbabel that we find incredibly confusing details. In both Matthew and Luke, Shealtiel is recorded as the father of Zerubbabel, but in Chronicles we have a different character listed as father:

1 Chronicles 3:19 NKJV
The sons of Pedaiah *were* Zerubbabel and Shimei.

Here we have Pedaiah as Zerubbabel's father. To add to the confusion, Matthew 1:12 records Shealtiel as the son of Jeconiah, but Luke 3:27 lists him as the son of Neri. And the portion of the genealogy mentioned in 1 Chronicles 3 that recorded Zerubbabel's children does not mention either of the names found in Matthew or Luke.

Scholars have offered many attempts at reconciling those starkly different accounts in the ancestral records. With a combination of many people's insights and some of my own analytical thinking I believe I can present a likely solution to this conundrum.

Let's lay out this portion of the different genealogies so you can see this easily.

Matthew's Genealogy:
Jeconiah, Shealtiel, Zerubbabel, Abiud

Luke's Genealogy:
Neri, Shealtiel, Zerubbabel, Rhesa

1 Chronicles Genealogy:
Jeconiah, Shealtiel of whom there is no record of any children
Jeconiah, Pedaiah, Zerubabbel who had several children but neither Rhesa or Abiud are mentioned

We note with this following Scripture that Shealtiel and Pedaiah are brothers.

1 Chronicles 3:17-18 NKJV
And the sons of Jeconiah *were* Assir, Shealtiel his son, 18 *and* Malchiram, Pedaiah, Shenazzar, Jecamiah, Hoshama, and Nedabiah.

Okay, it's time to start sorting this mess out. Let's do the easy one first. With regard to Zerubbabel's children, we can easily accept the idea that the genealogy is accurate but not exhaustive so that the Chronicles account of his children is simply incomplete due to the Babylonian captivity being fraught with geopolitical turmoil. To address the other apparent contradictions we must first have a look at the historical context and also some prophetic statements about the descendants of David that were to be in the captivity in Babylon that have a bearing on this matter.

2 Kings 20:16-18 NKJV

Then Isaiah said to Hezekiah, "Hear the word of the Lord: 17 'Behold, the days are coming when all that *is* in your house, and what your fathers have accumulated until this day, shall be carried to Babylon; nothing shall be left,' says the Lord. 18 'And they shall take away some of your sons who will descend from you, whom you will beget; and they shall be eunuchs in the palace of the king of Babylon.'"

In fulfilment of this prophecy, a ruthless pagan king takes King Jeconiah captive. Some of his sons and perhaps he himself were going to be castrated. There would have been widows and all sorts of tragic family situations that we can but speculate on as this was a major war scene and prisoners were not treated with any regard to our present day norms concerning human rights. Note also that the sons Hezekiah will beget, are in the distant future for that prophecy was not fulfilled until about a hundred years later, which is an example of the use of the term beget.

Along with the above prophecy effecting the situation we have this excerpt from the Law of Moses which shines some light on the question about the different fathers. Most of us consider this to be a strange custom, however, God had a purpose for everything He instituted into His Law.

Deuteronomy 25:5-6 NKJV

"If brothers dwell together, and one of them dies and has no son, the widow of the dead man shall not be *married* to a stranger outside *the family;* her husband's brother shall go in to her, take her as his wife, and perform the duty of a husband's brother to her. 6 And it shall be *that* the firstborn son which she bears will succeed to the name of his dead brother, that his name may not be blotted out of Israel.

This explains why we have both Shealtiel and Pedaiah recorded as the father of Zerubbabel. They are recorded as brothers and Pedaiah must have had to continue the inheritance on behalf of his brother.

Jeremiah 22:28-30

"Is this man Coniah a despised, broken idol— A vessel in which *is* no pleasure? Why are they cast out, he and his descendants, And cast into a land which they do not know? 29 O earth, earth, earth, Hear the word of the Lord! 30 Thus says the Lord: 'Write this man down as childless, A man *who* shall not prosper in his days; For none of his descendants shall prosper, Sitting on the throne of David, And ruling anymore in Judah.'" (Coniah is also called *Jeconiah* and *Jehoiachin.*)

This Scripture placed a curse on the descendants of Jeconiah that prohibits them from prospering on the Throne of David. He is also written down as childless, though he clearly had a number of children. However, due to all his sons becoming eunuchs, he effectively had no progeny and so it is only an adopted son who could pass on the inheritance to the throne.

Jeremiah 52:31-34 NKJV

Now it came to pass in the thirty-seventh year of the captivity of Jehoiachin king of Judah, in the twelfth month, on the twenty-fifth *day* of the month, *that* Evil-Merodach king of Babylon, in the *first* year of his reign, lifted up the head of Jehoiachin king of Judah and brought him out of prison. 32 And he spoke kindly to him and gave him a more prominent seat than those of the kings who *were* with him in Babylon. 33 So Jehoiachin changed from his prison garments, and he ate bread regularly before the *king* all the days of his life. 34 And as for his provisions, there was a regular ration given him by the king of Babylon, a portion for each day until the day of his death, all the days of his life.

With all the above giving us a look at the historical and prophetic context, we can now present what follows as the most likely scenario. At the age of eighteen after reigning for only three months, Jeconiah is taken to Babylon by King Nebuchadnezzar along with his wives, mother, sons and many others (2 Kings 24:14-15). (He must have started at a young age!) After thirty seven years Nebuchadnezzar dies and his son, Evil-Merodach lets Jeconiah out of prison (2 Kings 25:27-30). We presume he finds his sons were all made eunuchs according to the prophecy given to Hezekiah (2 Kings 20:18). Seeing his family neutered and perhaps at this stage a widower, Jeconiah then marries the widow of Neri and thus adopted her sons: Shealtiel and Pedaiah, thus conveying the right to the throne to them as their progeny would sooner or later have become the only surviving heirs. Or perhaps he just took another wife as it is noted that he already had "wives" (2 Kings 24:15) indicating that he was that way inclined. Thus Shealtiel would have both Jeconiah and Neri as his recorded fathers with Neri being a blood descendant of David from the line of Nathan. Note: any other bloodline sons of Jeconiah, if he had any that weren't made eunuchs, would never be able to prosper on the Throne of David because of the curse that was upon them. Jesus could not come from that bloodline.

Following through with this likely scenario we conclude that Shealtiel marries but dies childless. Pedaiah would then have stepped in as kinsman redeemer and taken his brother's wife to continue the heritage as per the Law and thus we have both Shealtiel and Pedaiah recorded as Zerubbabel's father. The whole story of Ruth, Naomi and Boaz is another example that is typical of this custom.

Zerubbabel has a number of children, two of which are only recorded in Matthew and Luke: Rhesa and Abiud, who begin two separate bloodlines leading to Joseph and Mary. Because Zerubbabel is not subject to the curse on Jeconiah's actual bloodline, both Joseph and Mary can pass the inheritance of the Throne of David to Jesus and He can prosper on it. This ensured a legal male all the way through for Joseph to legally adopt and be Jesus' step-father and convey the right of inheritance to the throne, whilst Mary has the actual bloodline from King David.

There is one more factor in this whole incredibly complex scenario that is added by the following prophecy which was spoken against Zedekiah. As mentioned above, he had been placed on the throne by Nebuchadnezzar when his nephew King Jeconiah was taken into captivity. It is to be noted that Ezekiel never called Zedekiah "king" but always referred to him as "prince", presumably because the actual king was still alive and ended up outliving him. Jeremiah also refers to Jeconiah as king of Judah when he came out of prison (Jeremiah 52:31-34). However, in this passage the Throne itself is spoken of:

Ezekiel 21:25-27 NKJV
'Now to you, O profane, wicked prince of Israel, whose day has come, whose iniquity *shall* end, 26 thus says the Lord God: "Remove the turban, and take off the crown; Nothing *shall remain* the same. Exalt the humble, and humble the exalted. 27 Overthrown, overthrown, I will make it overthrown! It shall be no *longer,* Until He comes whose right it is, And I will give it *to Him.*"'

The NIV and numerous other translations render the word "overthrown" as "ruin" so that it reads as follows:

Ezekiel 21:27 NIV
A ruin! A ruin! I will make it a ruin! The crown will not be restored until he to whom it rightfully belongs shall come; to him I will give it.

So then, whilst the curse of not prospering on the Throne of David was circumvented when the line of Nathan was joined to the kingly bloodline with the birth of Zerubbabel, this verse prohibited that restoration from happening until the coming of Messiah. Although Zerubbabel became governor of Judea when the Jews returned to the Promised Land, none of the descendants of David would ever reign as king on the Throne of David until Jesus came whose right it was and is to this day. This understanding effectively removes any claim by any other descendant of David to sit upon that Throne. The suggestion that the British Crown is presently inheriting that right is thoroughly debunked. They may indeed be descendants of King David, along with other kings and queens in Europe, but certainly not the inheritors of the Throne of David, for He whose right it is has already come and claimed it for Himself through His absolute obedience and is presently seated on that Throne on which He must reign until every power and authority is made subject to Him (1 Corinthians 15:25-28). God has absolutely and amazingly covered every single detail to fulfil both the Law and the Prophets. Hallelujah!

Judgment Day

Although this subject was touched on in the main body of this study, it's worthy of a fuller presentation. One of the foundations of our faith is the reality of eternal judgment (Hebrews 6:2). When this foundation is properly laid in our hearts it automatically empowers us toward righteous living and a healthy appreciation of the destination of all mankind which leads to compassionate evangelism when we remember that we all have an appointment with the Judge. In the following three passages from Matthew we see that the end of the age is also the time of the Judgment.

Matthew 13:40-43 NKJV
Therefore as the tares are gathered and burned in the fire, so it will be at the end of this age. 41 The Son of Man will send out His angels, and they will gather out of His kingdom all things that offend, and those who practice lawlessness, 42 and will cast them into the furnace of fire. There will be wailing and gnashing of teeth. 43 Then the righteous will shine forth as the sun in the kingdom of their Father. He who has ears to hear, let him hear!

Matthew 13:47-50 NKJV
"Again, the kingdom of heaven is like a dragnet that was cast into the sea and gathered some of every kind, 48 which, when it was full, they drew to shore; and they sat down and gathered the good into vessels, but threw the bad away. 49 So it will be at the end of the age. The angels will come forth, separate the wicked from among the just, 50 and cast them into the furnace of fire. There will be wailing and gnashing of teeth."

Matthew 25:31-46 NKJV
"When the Son of Man comes in His glory, and all the holy angels with Him, then He will sit on the throne of His glory. 32 All the nations will be gathered before Him, and He will separate them one from another, as a shepherd divides *his* sheep from the goats. 33 And He will set the sheep on His right hand, but the goats on the left. 34 Then the King will say to those on His right hand, 'Come, you blessed of My Father, inherit the kingdom prepared for you from the foundation of the world: 35 for I was hungry and you gave Me food; I was thirsty and you gave Me drink; I was a stranger and you took Me in; 36 I *was* naked and you clothed Me; I was sick and you visited Me; I was in prison and you came to Me.'

37 "Then the righteous will answer Him, saying, 'Lord, when did we see You hungry and feed *You,* or thirsty and give *You* drink? 38 When did we see You a stranger and take *you* in, or naked and clothe *You?* 39 Or when did we see You sick, or in prison, and come to You?' 40 And the King will answer and say to them, 'Assuredly, I say to you, inasmuch as you did *it* to one of the least of these My brethren, you did *it* to Me.'

41 "Then He will also say to those on the left hand, 'Depart from Me, you cursed, into the everlasting fire prepared for the devil and his angels: 42 for I was hungry and you gave Me no food; I was thirsty and you gave Me no drink; 43 I was a stranger and you did not take Me in, naked and you did not clothe Me, sick and in prison and you did not visit Me.'

44 "Then they also will answer Him, saying, 'Lord, when did we see You hungry or thirsty or a stranger or naked or sick or in prison, and did not minister to You?' 45 Then He will answer them, saying, 'Assuredly, I say to you, inasmuch as you did not do *it* to one of the least of these, you did not do *it* to Me.' 46 And these will go away into everlasting punishment, but the righteous into eternal life."

In the parable of the wheat and the tares, we learn that both the wheat and the tares come off the field at the time of harvest. Jesus explains to us that it is in this manner that He sends out His angels to separate the wicked from the righteous at the end of the age. In each of the illustrations Jesus gave we find a common theme: The wheat and tares are taken from their world to the place where they are separated from one another; In the parable of the dragnet the fish are taken out of their world to where they are sorted on the shore; Likewise with the parable of the sheep and the goats. When He comes in His glory, we are brought before the throne of His glory where the judgment is decreed. The tares are separated from the wheat, the bad fish from the good fish and the goats from the sheep. All are resurrected from the dead: the wicked to the resurrection of condemnation leading to eternal punishment; the righteous to the resurrection of commendation (well done good and faithful servant) leading to abundant eternal life.

John 5:26-29 NKJV
For as the Father has life in Himself, so He has granted the Son to have life in Himself, 27 and has given Him authority to execute judgment also, because He is the Son of Man. 28 Do not marvel at this; for the hour is coming in which all who are in the graves will hear His voice 29 and come forth—those who have done good, to the resurrection of life, and those who have done evil, to the resurrection of condemnation.

Most Christians understand that the righteous are not subject to the condemnation, but they generally overlook the fact that there is still a judgment for His servants. There are many Scriptures on this subject so let's look at the main passages that speak on this:

Matthew 25:14-30 NKJV
"For *the kingdom of heaven is* like a man traveling to a far country, *who* called his own servants and delivered his goods to them. 15 And to one he gave five talents, to another two, and to another one, to each according to his own ability; and immediately he went on a journey. 16 Then he who had received the five talents went and traded with them, and made another five talents. 17 And likewise he who *had received* two gained two more also. 18 But he who had received one went and dug in the ground, and hid his lord's money. 19 After a long time the lord of those servants came and settled accounts with them.

20 "So he who had received five talents came and brought five other talents, saying, 'Lord, you delivered to me five talents; look, I have gained five more talents besides them.' 21 His lord said to him, 'Well *done,* good and faithful servant; you were faithful over a few things, I will make you ruler over many things. Enter into the joy of your lord.'

22 He also who had received two talents came and said, 'Lord, you delivered to me two talents; look, I have gained two more talents besides them.' 23 His lord said to him, 'Well *done,* good and faithful servant; you have been faithful over a few things, I will make you ruler over many things. Enter into the joy of your lord.'

24 "Then he who had received the one talent came and said, 'Lord, I knew you to be a hard man, reaping where you have not sown, and gathering where you have not scattered seed. 25 And I was afraid, and went and hid your talent in the ground. Look, *there* you have *what is* yours.' 26 "But his lord answered and said to him, 'You wicked and lazy servant, you knew that I reap where I have not sown, and gather where I have not scattered seed. 27 So you ought to have deposited my money with the bankers, and at my coming I would have received back my own with interest. 28 Therefore take the talent from him, and give *it* to him who has ten talents. 29 'For to everyone who has, more will be given, and he will have abundance; but from him who does not have, even what he has will be taken away. 30 And cast the unprofitable servant into the outer darkness. There will be weeping and gnashing of teeth.'

Luke 12:42-46 NKJV
And the Lord said, "Who then is that faithful and wise steward, whom *his* master will make ruler over his household, to give *them their* portion of food in due season? 43 Blessed *is* that servant whom his master will find so doing when he comes. 44 Truly, I say to you that he will make him ruler over all that he has. 45 But if that servant says in his heart, 'My master is delaying his coming,' and begins to beat the male and female servants, and to eat and drink and be drunk, 46 the master of that servant will come on a day when he is not looking for *him* and at an hour when he is not aware, and will cut him in two and appoint *him* his portion with the unbelievers.

Luke 19:11-27 NKJV
Now as they heard these things, He spoke another parable, because He was near Jerusalem and because they thought the kingdom of God would appear immediately. 12 Therefore He said: "A certain nobleman went into a far country to receive for himself a kingdom and to return. 13 So he called ten of his servants, delivered to them ten minas, and said to them, 'Do business till I come.' 14 But his citizens hated him, and sent a delegation after him, saying, 'We will not have this *man* to reign over us.' 15 "And so it was that when he returned, having received the kingdom, he then commanded these servants, to whom he had given the money, to be called to him, that he might know how much every man had gained by trading. 16 Then came the first, saying, 'Master, your mina has earned ten minas.' 17 And he said to him, 'Well *done* good servant; because you were faithful in a very little, have authority over ten cities.' 18 And the second came, saying, 'Master, your mina has earned five minas.' 19 Likewise he said to him, 'You also be over five cities.'

20 "Then another came, saying, 'Master, here is your mina, which I have kept put away in a handkerchief. 21 For I feared you, because you are an austere man. You collect what you did not deposit, and reap what you did not sow.' 22 And he said to him, 'Out of your own mouth I will judge you, *you* wicked servant. You knew that I was an austere man, collecting what I did not deposit and reaping what I did not sow. 23 Why then did you not put my money in the bank, that at my coming I might have collected it with interest?'

24 "And he said to those who stood by, 'Take the mina from him, and give *it* to him who has ten minas.' 25 (But they said to him, 'Master, he has ten minas.') 26 'For I say to you, that to everyone who has will be given; and from him who does not have, even what he has will be taken away from him. 27 But bring here those enemies of mine, who did not want me to reign over them, and slay *them* before me.'"

Matthew 24:45-51 NKJV
"Who then is a faithful and wise servant, whom his master made ruler over his household, to give them food in due season? 46 Blessed *is* that servant whom his master, when he comes, will find so doing. 47 Assuredly, I say to you that he will make him ruler over all his goods. 48 But if that evil servant says in his heart, 'My master is delaying his coming,' 49 and begins to beat *his* fellow servants, and to eat and drink with the drunkards, 50 the master of that servant will come on a day when he is not looking for *him* and at an hour that he is not aware of, 51 and will cut him in two and appoint *him* his portion with the hypocrites. There shall be weeping and gnashing of teeth.

In these Scriptures we find the Lord rewarding His servants according to what they have done for His Kingdom. When the Lord said for us to store up treasure in heaven, He really means that there are rewards that we will treasure. Amen.

In Matthew 24:15 we note that each was given "talents" according to their ability. This is totally just and fair. You will not be judged by the performance of someone else, only for what you have done with what was given you. However we note that there are two types of servants who find themselves receiving their portion with the wicked: those who do absolutely nothing with that which was given to them and others who turn on their fellow servants to beat them and who make their fellowship with the drunkards.

The following Scripture is rather sobering . . .

Matthew 7:21-23 NKJV
"Not everyone who says to Me, 'Lord, Lord,' shall enter the kingdom of heaven, but he who does the will of My Father in heaven. 22 Many will say to Me in that day, 'Lord, Lord, have we not prophesied in Your name, cast out demons in Your name, and done many wonders in Your name?' 23 And then I will declare to them, 'I never knew you; depart from Me, you who practice lawlessness!'

These people were people of faith: casting out demons, performing miracles and prophesying. But they continued in sin. Obviously committing sins that lead to death. As we saw above, the real bad ones that beat up on their fellow servants are destroyed with the unbelievers. Here we see that those who continued in sin were obviously believing a Gospel that had no repentance and thus were "workers of iniquity" or "workers of lawlessness" depending on your translation. It's amazing how many times I've heard this verse quoted and almost always they leave out the last phrase. The condemnation is not upon miracle working, it's upon sinfulness and lawlessness.

The following verse is also sobering:

Luke 12:47-48 NKJV
And that servant who knew his master's will, and did not prepare *himself* or do according to his will, shall be beaten with many *stripes*. 48 But he who did not know, yet committed things deserving of stripes, shall be beaten with few. For everyone to whom much is given, from him much will be required; and to whom much has been committed, of him they will ask the more.

Here we see both the severity and fairness in the justice of God. A lot of people don't like these Scriptures for they speak of judgment being administered to His servants. Clearly they are punished (disciplined by a loving Father) for their unrepented sins that John spoke of as sins that do not lead to death (1 John 5:17). Paul also speaks a bit on this subject in the following verses:

1 Corinthians 3:9-15 NKJV
For we are God's fellow workers; you are God's field, *you are* God's building. 10 According to the grace of God which was given to me, as a wise master builder I have laid the foundation, and another builds on it. But let each one take heed how he builds on it. 11 For no other foundation can anyone lay than that which is laid, which is Jesus Christ. 12 Now if anyone builds on this foundation *with* gold, silver, precious stones, wood, hay, straw, 13 each one's work will become clear; for the Day will declare it, because it will be revealed by fire; and the fire will test each one's work, of what sort it is. 14 If anyone's work which he has built on *it* endures, he will receive a reward. 15 If anyone's work is burned, he will suffer loss; but he himself will be saved, yet so as through fire.

Let us be sober minded, for we must all give account for the things we have done. Thankfully, those things that we have confessed and turned away from will not be brought to mind. Let us be attentive to walk in the grace of God which teaches us to deny ungodliness.

Titus 2:11-13
For the grace of God that bringeth salvation hath appeared to all men, 12 Teaching us that, denying ungodliness and worldly lusts, we should live soberly, righteously, and godly, in this present world; 13 Looking for that blessed hope, and the glorious appearing of the great God and our Saviour Jesus Christ;

By the way, I do not believe one can lose their salvation. That said, I do believe it's possible to deliberately walk away from righteousness, which amounts to a rejection of the new creation and consequently a rejection of the Gospel. Thus it is that one does not lose their salvation, but they can by their actions and the intents of their heart come to a place of deliberate rejection of that which they had received. This does not come about by stumbling and weakness, but a complete wilfulness that one persists in over time. It is such a person who has so completely rejected righteousness that when they re-enter the state of unbelief, it is impossible to renew their faith and find repentance.

Matthew 12:36-37 NKJV
But I say to you that for every idle word men may speak, they will give account of it in the day of judgment. 37 For by your words you will be justified, and by your words you will be condemned."

Romans 14:10-12 NKJV
But why do you judge your brother? Or why do you show contempt for your brother? For we shall all stand before the judgment seat of Christ. 11 For it is written: *"As* I live, says the Lord, Every knee shall bow to Me, And every tongue shall confess to God." 12 So then each of us shall give account of himself to God.

2 Corinthians 5:10 NKJV
For we must all appear before the judgment seat of Christ, that each one may receive the things *done* in the body, according to what he has done, whether good or bad.

Philippians 2:12-13 NKJV
Therefore, my beloved, as you have always obeyed, not as in my presence only, but now much more in my absence, work out your own salvation with fear and trembling; 13 for it is God who works in you both to will and to do for *His* good pleasure.

Take heart my friends, God is at work in you both to will and to do. We are not in this battle against the flesh and powers of darkness alone. They may always be at work to ensnare us in sin, but we have the indwelling Holy Spirit at work in us to deliver us from evil. Hallelujah!

1 John 1:9 NKJV
If we confess our sins, He is faithful and just to forgive us *our* sins and to cleanse us from all unrighteousness.

1 John 2:1-2 NKJV
My little children, these things I write to you, so that you may not sin. And if anyone sins, we have an Advocate with the Father, Jesus Christ the righteous. 2 And He Himself is the propitiation for our sins, and not for ours only but also for the whole world.

If you stumble, or even if you have been stubborn and wilful for a time, God is always calling us turn to Him and avail ourselves of His boundless grace with which we can work out our salvation with holy reverence for our God is a consuming fire. And remember that the purpose of the commandment of God is love from a pure heart, sincere faith and a clear conscience. When we come to our senses, we will not want to reject these things and will cease from giving ourselves to evil.

One of the promises of God concerning the Judgment is that the righteous have a part to play.

1 Corinthians 6:3 NKJV
Do you not know that we shall judge angels?

Matthew 12:41-42 NKJV
The men of Nineveh will rise up in the judgment with this generation and condemn it, because they repented at the preaching of Jonah; and indeed a greater than Jonah *is* here. 42 The queen of the South will rise up in the judgment with this generation and condemn it, for she came from the ends of the earth to hear the wisdom of Solomon; and indeed a greater than Solomon *is* here.

Matthew 19:28 NKJV
So Jesus said to them, "Assuredly I say to you, that in the regeneration, when the Son of Man sits on the throne of His glory, you who have followed Me will also sit on twelve thrones, judging the twelve tribes of Israel.

These three quotes all have examples of the righteous having some kind of participation in the judging of the wicked. Matthew 19:28 has caused some confusion in some circles as the word translated "regeneration" has left the door of interpretation wide open to some speculation. The English word "regeneration" comes from the Greek word *palingenesia*. It's a compound word: *palin*; Strongs #3825 meaning again; and *genesia* Strong's #1077 a derivative of genesis #Strong's 1078 meaning: beginning; or birth. By itself, *genesia* is also translated "birthday"; twice referring to Herod's birthday celebration (Matthew 14:6 Mark 6:21).

In the context wherein this verse is found, Jesus was explaining the Kingdom of God (Matthew 19:23-20:16). He speaks of the new creation and the judgment with words that literally mean 'again' and 'beginning'; *palingenesia*: a re-genesis; a rebirth of creation; a new beginning where righteousness dwells. Hallelujah! Good times a coming for those who have been made righteous.

However, for those who remain in their wickedness, there is no good news. There is the resurrection of the just and there is the resurrection of the unjust (Acts 24:15). There is the promise of eternal life and there is the promise of an eternal fire.

It has been noted that there are many who do not believe that our God who is LOVE would punish people forever. It is appropriate that I address this matter both from Scripture and from reason. Firstly from Scripture:

Matthew 5:29-30 NKJV
If your right eye causes you to sin, pluck it out and cast it from you; for it is more profitable for you that one of your members perish, than for your whole body to be cast into hell. 30 And if your right hand causes you to sin, cut it off and cast it from you; for it is more profitable for you that one of your members perish, than for your whole body to be cast into hell.

In the above passage we note two things. Firstly Jesus is drawing our attention as to how seriously we are to regard the reality of hell. And in so doing He lets us know that it is the person's "whole body" that is cast into hell. You see, after the resurrection, no one will die. It's a matter of where you will live. Death is finished. Your body is restored to you and it's a matter of where you are going to spend eternity.

I believe Jesus even mixed a little humour in here. If anyone actually cuts off their hand or plucks out their eye they will discover that the issue is actually in their heart. What follows are a few verses describing the reality and nature of hell.

Matthew 3:12 NKJV
His winnowing fan is in His hand, and He will thoroughly clean out His threshing floor, and gather His wheat into the barn; but He will burn up the chaff with unquenchable fire.

Matthew 8:12 NKJV
But the sons of the kingdom will be cast out into outer darkness. There will be weeping and gnashing of teeth."

Matthew 13:42 and 50 NKJV
and will cast them into the furnace of fire. There will be wailing and gnashing of teeth.

Matthew 22:13 NKJV
Then the king said to the servants, 'Bind him hand and foot, take him away, and cast him into outer darkness; there will be weeping and gnashing of teeth.'

Matthew 25:46 NKJV
And these will go away into everlasting punishment, but the righteous into eternal life."

Mark 9:42-48 NKJV
"But whoever causes one of these little ones who believe in Me to stumble, it would be better for him if a millstone were hung around his neck, and he were thrown into the sea. 43 If your hand causes you to sin, cut it off. It is better for you to enter into life maimed, rather than having two hands, to go to hell, into the fire that shall never be quenched— 44 where

'Their worm does not die
And the fire is not quenched.'

45 And if your foot causes you to sin, cut it off. It is better for you to enter life lame, rather than having two feet, to be cast into hell, into the fire that shall never be quenched— 46 where

'Their worm does not die,
And the fire is not quenched.'

47 And if your eye causes you to sin, pluck it out. It is better for you to enter the kingdom of God with one eye, rather than having two eyes, to be cast into hell fire— 48 where

'Their worm does not die
And the fire is not quenched.

Luke 3:17 NKJV
His winnowing fan is in His hand, and He will thoroughly clean out His threshing floor, and gather the wheat into His barn; but the chaff He will burn with unquenchable fire."

Unquenchable fire: a fire that cannot be put out. It cannot be quenched and it will never be quenched. Having heard what Jesus said about it, here we have some verses from the Apostles:

2 Thessalonians 1:9 NKJV
These shall be punished with everlasting destruction from the presence of the Lord and from the glory of His power,

Jude 7 NKJV
. . . Sodom and Gomorrah, and the cities around them in a similar manner to these, having given themselves over to sexual immorality and gone after strange flesh, are set forth as an example, suffering the vengeance of eternal fire.

Jude 12-13 NKJV
These are spots in your love feasts, while they feast with you without fear, serving only themselves. They are clouds without water, carried about by the winds; late autumn trees without fruit, twice dead, pulled up by the roots; 13 raging waves of the sea, foaming up their own shame; wandering stars for whom is reserved the blackness of darkness forever.

It appears that the burning fire of hell burns in darkness. Some people look at these Scriptures and still reason in their hearts that a loving God will not torment people in an everlasting unquenchable fire.

An understanding of God's Love is needful at this juncture. God is indeed LOVE. And oh, that we might know the love of God in its entirety:

Ephesians 3:17-19
that Christ may dwell in your hearts through faith; that you, being rooted and grounded in love, 18 may be able to comprehend with all the saints what is the width and length and depth and height— 19 to know the love of Christ which passes knowledge; that you may be filled with all the fullness of God.

One of the things about the Love of God is that He actually hates evil. God hates evil with such a passion we can hardly imagine. He hasn't got one single nice thought about any kind of evil: He hates lies, He hates murders, He hates child abuse, He hates rape, He hates betrayal, He hates manipulative power and control, He hates greediness and selfishness, He hates thievery, He hates pride and arrogance and He hates that which has hatred of what is good. His hatred of evil knows no bounds. A zillion years from now and He will still hate evil. He hates it more than you or I. And yet, in His great mercy He is willing to forgive anyone who will turn from the evil of their heart, giving each one sufficient revelation and time to repent.

You will not find God thinking, "Oh, sin isn't that bad. I'll think I'll let them off now. Turn the heat down, or switch the pain off. Remove them from their just punishment." At some point in time in eternity, He may send someone to the edge of the eternal fire of torment where the ungodly are suffering and ask for a report. "Are they still evil?" the Lord asks. "Yes Lord, they are still evil." Then the Lord would say, "Then let the fire burn. I still love righteousness and I still hate evil."

There are not going to be any nice people in hell. We look at the outward appearances of people, but God looks on the heart. God knows that the heart of mankind is deceitfully wicked beyond all imagination (Jeremiah 17:9). Evil people can do a lot of good and kind things, but inwardly the 'nice' people are really hypocrites putting on a good front for their own sense of self-righteousness. All the people who will end up in hell are people who would not repent from evil and turn to righteousness. I wasn't saved because I was a good person. I was a wretched sinner that deserved to roast in an everlasting fire. But because I believed in His mercy and grace and responded with repentance and faith, I will inherit eternal life. God's love is shown to us in that He has granted sinners repentance and for this we are eternally grateful. It is His kindness that leads us to repentance (Romans 2:4). He delights in mercy and takes no pleasure in the soul that perishes.

Everyone in hell will have rejected Christ Jesus somehow and their heart will have rejected the mercy and grace of God. This means they have rejected goodness, kindness, faithfulness, honesty, mercy, justice, compassion etc. etc. People who reject these things are absolutely evil. They love darkness rather than light (John 3:19).

We must reject the idea that Jesus is looking for good people to save. There is no such thing. Jesus said of His own disciples that they were evil (Matthew 7:11). Let us get this clear. Jesus is looking to save sinners (Matthew 9:13).

Judgment Day. If the awareness is properly sown into our hearts it will produce both a gratefulness and a soberness in our walk with God, and as mentioned above, it will produce compassionate evangelism as our hearts will be moved by His Love. Amen. By way of reminder, here's what Paul had to say on the matter:

Acts 24:15-16
I have hope in God, which they themselves also accept, that there will be a resurrection of the dead, both of the just and the unjust. 16 This being so, I myself always strive to have a conscience without offense toward God and men.

He Who Now Restrains

I present this study for your perusal. To call it a study may be slightly misleading. Perhaps a discovery would be more accurate. This phrase, "He who now restrains", you may well know, is found in 2 Thessalonians 2:7 and it has generated much discussion as to who the "He" is. To put it in its context I'll quote the whole passage where this phrase is found.

2 Thessalonians 2:1-12 NKJV
Now, brethren, concerning the coming of our Lord Jesus Christ and our gathering together to Him, we ask you, 2 not to be soon shaken in mind or troubled, either by spirit or by word or by letter, as if from us, as though the day of Christ[a] had come. 3 Let no one deceive you by any means; for that Day will not come unless the falling away comes first, and the man of sin[b] is revealed, the son of perdition, 4 who opposes and exalts himself above all that is called God or that is worshiped, so that he sits as God[c] in the temple of God, showing himself that he is God. 5 Do you not remember that when I was still with you I told you these things? 6 And now you know what is restraining, that he may be revealed in his own time.

7 For the mystery of lawlessness is already at work; only He[d] who now restrains will do so until He[e] is taken out of the way.

8 And then the lawless one will be revealed, whom the Lord will consume with the breath of His mouth and destroy with the brightness of His coming. 9 The coming of the lawless one is according to the working of Satan, with all power, signs, and lying wonders, 10 and with all unrighteous deception among those who perish, because they did not receive the love of the truth, that they might be saved. 11 And for this reason God will send them strong delusion, that they should believe the lie, 12 that they all may be condemned who did not believe the truth but had pleasure in unrighteousness.

Below are the common textual variants

a 2 Thessalonians 2:2 NU-Text reads the Lord.
b 2 Thessalonians 2:3 NU-Text reads lawlessness.
c 2 Thessalonians 2:4 NU-Text omits as God.
d 2 Thessalonians 2:7 Or he
e 2 Thessalonians 2:7 Or he

This portion of Scripture has been the subject of much discussion of which I became aware of many years ago. So at some point in time, so long ago I can hardly remember, I did some study on this passage.

Whenever I find a passage that is disputed as to its meaning, I get out Strong's Concordance and Vine's Expository of New Testament Words (hereto referred to as Strong's and Vine's) to check on the translation of the words used. Sometimes I refer to an obscure version of the Bible called The Concordant Literal which has also been helpful from time to time. Fortunately, I have found very few translation problems, and those that I have found have usually been minor, concerned with shades of meaning. And as far as the Gospel is concerned, not one problem have I found.

But in this passage you will be astounded by what I have discovered. You will be able to see for yourself for the evidence is available to all.

Come, look and see what I have found about "He who now restrains."

2 Thessalonians 2:7 NKJV
For the mystery of lawlessness is already at work; only He who now restrains will do so until He is taken out of the way.

The first thing to note is the use of the upper case for the word "He". As you can see by the foot notes above, and my Bible at home has it as a centre column reference; "he" rather than "He", is an alternative. To be sure, there is no upper or lower case in the original Greek. This is an arbitrary decision of the editors and not a matter of translation, though it does have problems grammatically speaking which I will come to later. However, it is the last phrase that is a real eye opener: ". . . taken out of the way".

The word translated 'taken' is Strong's #1096. The Greek word is *ginomai*. Its meaning is: to cause to be, to become, to come into being. This meaning is confirmed in Vine's under the word 'take', Note #34. Etymologically it is the root to such words in English such as generate, Genesis, begin, etc.

This same Greek word *ginomai* is translated 29 times in the New Testament as 'to become' and only once is it translated 'taken' and that is in this verse. This is a remarkable departure from the normal usage. It makes no sense. Conversely, I further discovered that the English word 'taken' is found about 60 times in the New Testament and only once is the Greek word *ginomai* the originating word, and that is also in this verse. Astounding. How could this be? To my simple believing mind, this is indeed a mistranslation.

But there is more. In the very same phrase, look at what I found.

The word translated "way" is Strong's #3319. The Greek word is *mesos*. It means: in the middle; in the midst of; or between. This translation is also confirmed in Vine's under the word 'midst'. An example of the use of *mesos* is found in the word Mesopotamia which means: the land in the middle, the land between the Tigris and the Euphrates rivers.

Now let's just analyse what has been discovered. We have Vine's and Strong's, both well respected reference books for Bible research and we have the etymology of our English language also bearing witness as to the true meaning of these two Greek words and somehow repeated translators and or editors have failed to get it right. WOW. To me this is one out of the box. (Don't ask me the origin of that saying lest I get side tracked)

Here is how this phrase reads when translated according to the consistent usage of these two words: ". . . until he becomes in the midst", or ". . . until he comes to be in the midst".

Here is how the whole verse should read:

2 Thessalonians 2:7 My Version
For the mystery of lawlessness is already at work; only he who is now restraining will do so until he comes to be in the midst.

Now here is how the whole passage should read:

2 Thessalonians 2: 1-12 My Version
Now, brethren, concerning the coming of our Lord Jesus Christ and our gathering together to Him, we ask you, 2 not to be soon shaken in mind or troubled, either by spirit or by word or by letter, as if from us, as though the day of Christ had come. 3 Let no one deceive you by any means; for that Day will not come unless the falling away comes first, and the man of sin is revealed, the son of perdition, 4 who opposes and exalts himself above all that is called God or that is worshiped, so that he sits as God in the temple of God, showing himself that he is God. 5 Do you not remember that when I was still with you I told you these things? 6 And now you know what is restraining, that he may be revealed in his own time.

7 For the mystery of lawlessness is already at work; only he who is now restraining will do so until he comes to be in the midst.

8 And then the lawless one will be revealed, whom the Lord will consume with the breath of His mouth and destroy with the brightness of His coming. 9 The coming of the lawless one is according to the working of Satan, with all power, signs, and lying wonders, 10 and with all unrighteous deception among those who perish, because they did not receive the love of the truth, that they might be saved. 11 And for this reason God will send them strong delusion, that they should believe the lie, 12 that they all may be condemned who did not believe the truth but had pleasure in unrighteousness.

Now take note that I also used the lower case for the word "he" in verse 7. The reason is that it follows the normal laws of grammar common to all languages that use pronouns. Whenever a pronoun is used, it always has an antecedent. It always refers to a character or subject previously mentioned in the sentence or paragraph.

Historically, there is untold dispute over this verse, so settle in while I get pedantic and give a basic English grammar lesson to sort this one out once and for all.

Let's go back to the beginning of the paragraph and see this grammatical law in action. In verse 1, Paul addresses the brethren and begins to speak of the coming of our Lord Jesus Christ. Thus Jesus becomes the antecedent for the use of the word "him" later in the sentence. No further pronouns referring to Jesus are used through verse 2 or 3. At the end of verse 3, another character is introduced into the paragraph who is called the "man of sin", the "son of perdition". The paragraph continues and of course, the pronouns now refer to the latest character who serves as the antecedent for all the following: . . . who exalts himself . . . he sits as God . . . showing himself . . . that he is God . . . that he may be revealed . . . in his own time.

The pronouns: himself, he, himself, he, he, his, continue to be the man of sin as no other character has been introduced to the passage. In verse 7, when the translators or editors chose to use "He" instead of "he", they were breaking the most basic laws of logic and grammar because another character to be the antecedent for the use of "He" has not been introduced. In the real world, we can all see that it's the same character, that there has been no other character introduced and it's still the man of sin being talked about.

2 Thessalonians 2:7 My Version
For the mystery of lawlessness is already at work; only he who is now restraining will do so until he comes to be in the midst.

It's not until the next verse that another character is introduced into the paragraph:

8 And then the lawless one will be revealed, whom the Lord will consume with the breath of His mouth and destroy with the brightness of His coming.

Because the Lord is re-introduced into the paragraph, the pronouns that follow now refer to Him: . . .it is His mouth and . . . His Coming. The use of the upper case is now justified.

Correctly used pronouns always refer to the last antecedent, the last character or subject in the sentence or paragraph. The only exception to that rule is found when two simultaneous characters are interacting with each other such as in a sentence that might say, "He said to him" and that does not apply in this instance. The conclusion this author has come to is that the capitalization is unwarranted and confusing and probably done to support a doctrine held by the editors or translators.

As they say in Old King James language, "Here endeth the lesson."

Now the whole passage makes sense. There is no change of subject in the middle of the paragraph. It follows the normal rules of grammar. The antecedent for "he" is not some other character artificially inserted to support some spurious doctrine. Apart from the introduction and concluding comments, the paragraph is speaking about the lawless one all the way through. One does not have to juggle with the phrase about the restrainer, nor use the imagination to put in the Holy Spirit, or the Church, or Michael the archangel or whatever one can come up with to try and make sense out of a grammatical error.

As to the meaning of the disputed verse, we again must take it in its context. Paul says that the coming of the lawless one is according to the power of Satan. It is Satan that wants to be worshipped as God (Ezekiel 28, Isaiah 14). This verse is saying that when the time is right for him, according to the working of Satan, with all power and signs etc., the man of sin will be revealed. In the meantime, the mystery of lawlessness is already at work and Satan is restraining himself like con men do, who do not reveal their motives but wait for the opportune time to do their dirty deed. No mystery, just plain talk.

And what is more, you don't have to take my word for it. Anyone can go to the reference books and check it out for themselves.

After writing all the above, a friend of mine called to let me know he had come across another translation that supported my findings. Here it is in the Institute for Scripture Research version (ISR). By the way, I do not necessarily endorse the entirety of this particular translation, but at least they got this verse correct.

2 Thessalonians 2:7 ISR
For the secret of lawlessness is already at work – only until he who now restrains comes out of the midst.

Just get your pen and make the necessary update in your Bible and "She'll be right, Mate!" Hope you find this enlightening.

However, it does throw a spanner into the works of some popular end-time theories. Well . . . we need a spanner in the works when there are loose nuts that need tightening. Hallelujah! (To my North American friends, a spanner is a wrench)

A Time, Times and Half a Time

The above phrase is found twice in the writings of Daniel the prophet in most modern Bibles. Many commentaries interpret this phrase as meaning three and a half years and a growing number of translators of recent versions have incorporated the idea of three and a half into their text as Scripture in conformance with a huge convoluted end time theory that will need a little pedantic attention to unravel. With that in mind, here are the two verses in four different versions of the Bible which we will now examine carefully. Firstly we have the King James Version:

Daniel 7:25
And he shall speak great words against the most High, and shall wear out the saints of the most High, and think to change times and laws: and they shall be given into his hand until a time and times and the dividing of time.

Daniel 12:7
And I heard the man clothed in linen, which was upon the waters of the river, when he held up his right hand and his left hand unto heaven, and sware by him that liveth for ever that it shall be for a time, times, and an half; and when he shall have accomplished to scatter the power of the holy people, all these things shall be finished.

Here are the same verses in the New King James:

Daniel 7:25 NKJV
He shall speak pompous words against the Most High, Shall persecute the saints of the Most High, And shall intend to change times and law. Then the saints shall be given into his hand For a time and times and half a time.

Daniel 12:7 NKJV
Then I heard the man clothed in linen, who was above the waters of the river, when he held up his right hand and his left hand to heaven, and swore by Him who lives forever, that it shall be for a time, times, and half a time; and when the power of the holy people has been completely shattered, all these things shall be finished.

And here they are again in the International Children's Bible which is representative of eight other translations that use the phrase "three and a half years":

241

Daniel 7:25 ICB
This king will say things against the Most High God. And he will hurt and kill God's people. He will try to change times and laws that have already been set. The people that belong to God will be in that king's power for three and one-half years.

Daniel 12:7 ICB
The man dressed in linen who stood over the water raised his hands toward heaven. And I heard him make a promise. He used the name of God who lives forever. He said, "It will be for three and one-half years. The power of the holy people will finally be broken. Then all these things will come true."

Here it is also from the Common English Bible:

Daniel 7:25 CEB
He will say things against the Most High and will exhaust the holy ones of the Most High. He will try to change times set by law. And for a period of time, periods of time, and half a period of time, they will be delivered into his power.

Daniel 12:7 CEB
I heard the man clothed in white linen, who was farther upstream, swear by the one who lives forever as he raised both hands to heaven: "For one set time, two set times, and half a set time. When the breaking of the holy people's power is over, all these things will be over."

Of the above four versions, the NKJV is representative of the majority of modern English Bibles which present this phrase from these two verses with identical or very similar words so that many commentaries now equate the two verses as speaking of the same event.

The ICB is an example of a more recent trend in later Bible versions to render the phrase as "three and a half years" and consequently to connect the two verses to the phrase in Daniel Chapter 9:27 which speaks of the "middle of the week" which is also understood to mean three and a half years.

In this study we will examine these two verses in order to show that they are not to be equated or conflated. To do this we will first look at the original language of Daniel 7:25 and Daniel 12:7 and then we will look closely at the context of these two verses along with Daniel 9:27 and we shall see what we shall see.

Daniel 7:25
. . . until a time and times and the dividing of time

By way of reminder, this portion of Scripture was written in Aramaic which is a 'sister' language to Hebrew with many words being identical or similar. The word rendered 'time' is the Aramaic word *iddah* and refers to menstruation and it corresponds with the Hebrew word *iddan*, which is variously translated, moment, period of time, situation, appointed time etc.

To suggest this word means year in this verse is most unfortunate for there is a distinctly different Aramaic word for year and that word is *shena* or *shenah*. The corresponding Hebrew word for 'year' or 'years' is *shana*, which is used about 800 times throughout Scripture. The KJV's use of the word 'time' is at least literal if not fully understandable.

As noted above, the Common English Bible renders "time and times" as follows:

Daniel 7:25 CEB
. . . period of time, periods of time . . .

In this they got it accurately. However, along with most Bible versions, they render the KJV word "dividing' as "half a period" or "half a year", though a few versions agree with the KJV. The Aramaic word that is translated "dividing" is *pelag*. The Hebrew rendition of this word is *palag*, or *Peleg*, which is also translated 'divide' or 'divided' and refers to the land being divided by water; as in canals or rivers or streams. Peleg, the first man recorded to die after the flood was named after the event that divided the earth, probably when the melt back from the ice age divided the continents and made many islands (Genesis 10:25). So it is that *Pelag* or *palag* more literally means the dividing of time, in particular between this age and the age to come, in other words: the end of the age.

Here it is in its context and as you will see, this literal translation fits:

Daniel 7:21-27
I beheld, and the same horn made war with the saints, and prevailed against them; 22 Until the Ancient of days came, and judgment was given to the saints of the most High; and the time came that the saints possessed the kingdom.

23 Thus he said, The fourth beast shall be the fourth kingdom upon earth, which shall be diverse from all kingdoms, and shall devour the whole earth, and shall tread it down, and break it in pieces. 24 And the ten horns out of this kingdom are ten kings that shall arise: and another shall rise after them; and he shall be diverse from the first, and he shall subdue three kings. 25 And he shall speak great words against the most High, and shall wear out the saints of the most High, and think to change times and laws: and they shall be given into his hand until a time and times and the dividing of time.

26 But the judgment shall sit, and they shall take away his dominion, to consume and to destroy it unto the end. 27 And the kingdom and dominion, and the greatness of the kingdom under the whole heaven, shall be given to the people of the saints of the most High, whose kingdom is an everlasting kingdom, and all dominions shall serve and obey him.-

Do you see it? The last earthly kingdom is persecuting the saints until the dividing of time when the judgment is made and the saints then inherit the everlasting Kingdom. In the light of that which I have discovered, here's a paraphrase of how I believe this verse should be rendered:

Daniel 7:25 My Version
And the saints shall be given into his hand from time to time until the dividing of time at the end of the age.

Now let us look at the similar phrase in English in Daniel 12:7 which reads, ". . . a time, times and an half" in the KJV and "time, times and half a time" in the NKJV.

The Hebrew words are completely different from the words used in Daniel 7:25: "time" originating from the Hebrew word *mo'wed*; and half from *wahesi*. *Mo'wed* means "appointed time", most commonly used of a meeting of the congregation. Also of appointed feasts or any set period of time, so on rare occasions it could mean a year. And *wahesi* actually does mean "half", though not specifically that of time as it is used in terms like "half a cubit" etc.

Again the KJV is literally more correct, even if the meaning is not so clear, so we shall look at the context in both the KJV and the NKJV:

Daniel 12:6-7
And one said to the man clothed in linen, which was upon the waters of the river, How long shall it be to the end of these wonders?

7 And I heard the man clothed in linen, which was upon the waters of the river, when he held up his right hand and his left hand unto heaven, and sware by him that liveth for ever that it shall be for a time, times, and an half; and when he shall have accomplished to scatter the power of the holy people, all these things shall be finished.

Daniel 12:6-7 NKJV
6 And one said to the man clothed in linen, who was above the waters of the river, "How long shall the fulfillment of these wonders be?"

7 Then I heard the man clothed in linen, who was above the waters of the river, when he held up his right hand and his left hand to heaven, and swore by Him who lives forever, that it shall be for a time, times, and half a time; and when the power of the holy people has been completely shattered, all these things shall be finished.

The context reveals that this "time, times and an half", or "half a time", is immediately before the complete scattering of the "holy people" as the passage is speaking of that period of time that included the Abomination of Desolation (Daniel 12:11). The KJV has "scattered" and the NKJV has "shattered" and on this rendering scholars and translators are divided, understandably as the word is used both ways throughout Scripture. However, when I looked through the examples of its use, when it referred to people groups or nations it almost always meant "scattered". When used of a clay jar that is struck and is shattered, the imagery includes the scattering of the pieces.

"Time, times and an half" is part of the answer to the question "How long shall the fulfillment of these wonders be?" Therefore it is reasonable to assume it is speaking of a period or periods of time. "How long?" We take note that the question mentions "these wonders" which alerts us to look and see what the "wonders" are as they form an important part of the context and have significance with regard to the meaning. All the historical oppressions of the King of the North and the King of the South are not in mind here. The wonders Daniel had just heard of was the deliverance of his people whose names were in the Book of Life, the people being awakened unto everlasting life, the wise shining and turning many to righteousness (Daniel 12:1-3). When, or how long till the fulfillment of these wonders? How about three and a half years.

Daniel 9:27 NKJV
Then he shall confirm a covenant with many for one week;
But in the middle of the week
He shall bring an end to sacrifice and offering.

The three and a half years of the remainder of the seventieth week of Daniel 9:27 was when many of Daniel's people would enter the New Covenant. And then the people were scattered. They went everywhere preaching the Word. Hallelujah! When we remember that these prophecies of Daniel are to be viewed synoptically, it is easier to join the dots and see that this scattering of the holy people was accomplished in the New Testament. We certainly cannot make this verse fit the description of the Jews destroyed by the Romans who were described as having reached the fullness of their iniquity and consequently are not considered holy.

So then, Daniel 7:25 is speaking of the end of the age, but Daniel 12:7 and Daniel 9:27 are synoptically speaking of the second three and a half years of the 'seventieth week'.

Hope you have found this enlightening.

How to Find the Lost Ten Tribes

For centuries the mystery of the whereabouts of the Ten Tribes of Israel has generated controversy. Opinions vary greatly: They are lost forever, never to return; They all died off; They have become so assimilated through intermarriage with the nations wherein they were scattered, that they are no longer an identifiable people group; They have already returned and are totally assimilated and intermarried with the Jews; They are identifiable, but they will never return; They are identifiable and they will return when they come under Rabbinical authority having come back to the teachings of the Torah; And lastly, they are identifiable and they will return when a remnant of them that truly repents joins with the rest of Judah (the Jews) who also repent and acknowledge Yeshua as their Messiah. Whilst this chapter is focused on the Lost Tribes of Israel, it necessarily has some comments about the Jews too.

Increasingly during the Nineteenth and Twentieth Centuries, and continuing to this day, a vast amount of archaeological and historical research has been added to the pool of knowledge. With the advent of the Internet in recent times, more and more scholars have been exploring this topic and are finding that there is information now readily available to anyone who is even partially computer literate. It is now possible to study almost any subject and discover in a matter of hours what would have previously taken years of painstaking research.

In this short presentation I will approach the subject from four different angles; firstly from Biblical Prophecy; secondly from Biblical History; thirdly from Secular History; and last but not least from the writings of the Jews. By way of summary we will do some connecting of dots from which we will draw some rather obvious conclusions.

From Biblical Prophecy

It is in the early chapters of this book that most if not all of the biblical prophecies that would help us identify the Ten Tribes have already been mentioned. From those passages of Scripture we can confidently make the following observations:

Because they were under the Law of God, all the curses of the Law came upon them when they were deported from the Promised Land by the Assyrians. Taken into slavery, they experienced many years of oppression and suffered terribly at the hands of their captors. Ezekiel Chapter 4 gives us a prophecy foretelling that the suffering for their iniquity would be for a specific time. It was portrayed symbolically as 390 days, possibly calculated as a day for a year. If taken from Ezekiel's time, this coincides with the Roman's defeat of Antiochus who was ruling the Seleucid Greek Empire in the area of Syria. This major weakening of the Greek dominion may have been the final end of the Israelite's time of being utterly dominated and the beginning of their main migration north and west outside of the dominion of Rome, though it is possible and probable that at the change of each empire's rule, some may have already escaped through the Caucasus Mountains beforehand.

Therefore, we should look through history for a people who migrated, as there was going to be a time when they would be "wanderers among the nations" (Hosea 9:17). They may still have an obsessive propensity to travel willy-nilly to and fro.

They would at times have name derivatives of Abraham and Isaac. "In Isaac your seed is called" (Genesis 21:12). "Let my name be called upon them, and the name of my fathers Abraham and Isaac, and let them increase to a multitude in the midst of the earth" (Genesis 48:16).

In spite of the traditional Christian belief and response to the subject, we should not consider the Ten Tribes of Israel forsaken (Jeremiah 51:5) or having died out or assimilated into oblivion among the nations of the earth (Amos 9:9).

Whilst they would be primarily of one race due to their custom of marrying within their respective tribes, we should look for a people with whom it is common to find a significant portion of them that inter-marry with many races. "For they have begotten pagan children" (Hosea 5:7). "Ephraim has mixed himself among the nations" (Hosea 7:8).

The Northern Tribes were condemned as "the drunkards of Ephraim" (Isaiah 28:1). One of their negative characteristics is their inclination to excessive alcohol.

Another of their negative characteristics is a propensity toward drug addiction. God's judgment against Israel in the latter days includes sorcery (Micah 5:12). The word translated to sorcery from either Greek or Hebrew is the word we also translate as pharmacy or drugs. This is not to be confused with medicinal drugs for the treating of physical ailments. It is drugs that affect the soul: the mind, will and emotions of the individual. This is what God is prohibiting in His Word, for these kind of drugs are known to open up a person to the demonic realm (many people don't know what they are playing with). Thus it is that sorcery is often closely associated with witchcraft, as drugs are often purposely used to facilitate contact with the spirit world in order to obtain spiritual power; another negative trait of the apostate Israelites.

We should not necessarily look for Jewishness or Jewish customs within their cultures because Israel no longer embraced the Torah during the period before their exile, but instead they embraced lives of idolatry and pagan worship, which was the central impetus for removing them from the Land of Israel in the first place (Daniel 9:7).

We can identify Israel by identifying the nations that are hosting Judah (the Jews) in the last days (Jeremiah 50:4, 20, 33-34). These verses all indicate that they (Israel and Judah) will be walking TOGETHER and will return to Zion TOGETHER. "In those days the House of Judah shall walk with the House of Israel, and they shall come together out of the land of the north to the land that I have given for an inheritance unto your fathers" (Jeremiah 3:18). Also see Isaiah Chapter 11.

We should look for a people who have historically possessed "the gates" of their enemies, the strategic military vantage points (e.g. major sea ports, narrow but significant sea channels, major trade routes, mountain passes, etc.). "And they blessed Rebekah and said to her, 'Let our sister become the mother of thousands of ten thousands, and let your seed possess the gates of those who hate them'" (Genesis 24:60). The "gates" also referred to the seats of power within cities and states.

We should look for a nation and a company of nations that are similar and that inhabit the ends of the earth and have pushed the peoples (nations) to the ends of the earth and have become a dominating world power.

Numbers 24:8
God brought him forth out of Egypt; he hath as it were the strength of an unicorn: he shall eat up the nations his enemies, and shall break their bones, and pierce them through with his arrows.

Micah 5:8-9
And the remnant of Jacob shall be among the Gentiles in the midst of many people as a lion among the beasts of the forest, as a young lion among the flocks of sheep: who, if he go through, both treadeth down, and teareth in pieces, and none can deliver. 9 Thine hand shall be lifted up upon thine adversaries, and all thine enemies shall be cut off.

Isaiah 41:15
Behold, I will make thee a new sharp threshing instrument having teeth: thou shalt thresh the mountains, and beat them small, and shalt make the hills as chaff. 16 Thou shalt fan them, and the wind shall carry them away, and the whirlwind shall scatter them: and thou shalt rejoice in the Lord, and shalt glory in the Holy One of Israel.

Deuteronomy 33:17
His glory is like the firstling of his bullock, and his horns are like the horns of unicorns: with them he shall push the people together to the ends of the earth: and they are the ten thousands of Ephraim, and they are the thousands of Manasseh.

We should look for a nation and nations where they are called "sons of the Living God", nations that have been known and or are known now as having a predominantly Christian heritage. For "the number of the children of Israel shall be as the sand of the sea, which cannot be measured or numbered. And it shall come to pass in the place where it was said to them 'You *are* not My people,' *There* it shall be said to them, '*You are* sons of the living God '" (Hosea 1:10).

We should look for nations that have been prominent in proclaiming the truth about God and that have been His witnesses unto the nations (Isaiah 43:1-13). Nations that have sent out many evangelists and missionaries to the rest of the world.

Although they would be scattered in all directions, we should look primarily to the North and the West from Jerusalem. Also to "the coastlands" and "the isles of the sea". "Behold, I will bring them from the north country, and gather them from the coasts of the earth" (Jeremiah 31:8). "They shall walk after the LORD: he shall roar like a lion: when he shall roar, then the children shall tremble from the west (Hosea 11:10). "Behold these shall come from far, and lo these from the north and from the west; and these from the land of Sinim" (Isaiah 49:12). "I am a father to Israel, and Ephraim is my firstborn. Hear the word of the LORD, O ye nations, and declare it in the isles afar off, and say, 'He that scattered Israel will gather him and keep him, as a shepherd does his flock'" (Jeremiah 31:10).

From Biblical History

In Chapter Three where we chronicled Israel going into exile, we found that they were deported from their land to areas that we now identify as Mesopotamia in modern Turkey (2 Kings 17 and 1 Chronicles 5:26). We also noted that the Assyrians replaced the deported Israelites with people from other lands to occupy that portion of the land known as Samaria. We also discovered that a small remnant found opportunity to return to Samaria and along with the pagans dwelling there, they also became known as Samaritans (John 4:1-42).

When the Assyrians were preparing to attack Judah with the intention of doing unto them as they had done to Israel, in response to the prayers of His people, the army of the Assyrians was struck down and 185000 soldiers died in the night (Isaiah 37:36). This event dramatically weakened the ruling powers and presented an opportunity to the Israelites by which many would have been able to escape from under the Assyrian oppression.

In Ezekiel Chapters 16 and 23 we find that Israel had been mixing with the Assyrians for some time before the pagan nation turned on them. It seems that during this time many Israelites were living among the Assyrians, having adopted their evil ways. These Assyrian Israelite mixture is the likely origin of a people group known as Cimmerians that emerged in that area around that time. It is thought that Cimmerian is a transliteration of Samarian, which of course is easily connected to the portion of the Promised Land known as Samaria. Ezekiel was directed to take his message to them, so although in this passage their exact location was not mentioned, it was within Ezekiel's ability to go to them as directed by the Lord. Presumably they were still in the proximity of where they had been deported to which was in Upper Mesopotamia, south of the Caucasus Mountains.

Apart from Ezekiel's final words to them calling them to repentance and his prophecy mentioned above delineating the limits of the punishment for their iniquity, we hear no more history from the Word of God, though perhaps the Jews questioning among themselves in response to a comment that Jesus made is an indication that some were among the Greeks at the time of Christ (John 7:35).

From Secular History

As just mentioned, history records the presence of a people group called Cimmerians who established a powerful presence near the Caucasus Mountains in the land that is presently called Georgia. Later Cimmerians or Samarians were also found north of the Caucasus Range. Most secular scholars have scant idea as to where they originated from and this is not surprising from a Christian perspective, for we would expect unbelievers to have a natural aversion to confirming or giving any credence to biblical history. Why would we expect secular historians to be willing to explore possibilities that would support information contrary to their world view? When confronted with evidence that totally refutes evolution, from secular scholars we hear crickets. For this reason, when searching through information on the migrations of the Ten Tribes of Israel, we start with the sure Word of God as our foundation and from secular historical sources we are often left to make conjectures from scant evidence, a little bit here and a little bit there, most of the time having to fill in the gaps by joining the dots.

In approximately the same area, north of the Caucasus Mountains, historians also note the presence of yet another nation rising to power, an empire that became known as the Scythians. The secular historians also consider these people to be a mystery when it comes to their origins. The Scythians are also mentioned in the New Testament without any indication as to who they were (Colossians 3:11). Earlier in our study, we took note of the Jewish historian Josephus, writing in the first century AD, who recorded that there were *"but two tribes under the dominion of the Romans"*, and that *"the Ten Tribes are beyond the Euphrates and have become a multitude that none could count"* (*Antiquities of the Jews*, 11.5.2).

This area that Josephus describes as being beyond the Euphrates is easy for us to identify. Beyond the headwaters of the Euphrates we find the Caucasus mountain range which is the prominent geographical feature between the Black Sea and the Caspian Sea. It is the very same part of the world where these two people groups show up in history. Thus the Cimmerians and the Scythians are certain candidates for the label Ten Lost Tribes. For more on this go to: britam.org/cimmerians-scythians.html

Another people group that arose a few hundred years later in that area and formed an empire is the Khazars. Again the secularists declare they are of unknown origin. They too are very likely the remnants of the Scythians and Cimmerians who remained after the majority had embarked on mass migration to the north and to the west, some by sea and others by land. Many of the Khazars ended up converting to Judaism and consequently intermarried with those from Judah to become the ancestors of the Ashkenazi Jews who are the majority of European Jewry to this day. Now that is interesting . . .

So then, from the same area we have the Cimmerians, the Samarians, the Scythians and the Khazarians and they can all be identified by the term Caucasian as this area is where we find the Caucasus Mountains. As the Caucasian people spread north and west they colonised and conquered and to a certain degree they intermarried. Some scholars consider Germany to be a mixture of Assyrian descent and sons of Isaac; the Saxons, which would also link their heritage to the Cimmerians. When Babylon defeated the Assyrian Empire, the Cimmerians would have had opportunity to escape through the Caucasus Mountain passes, or by boat on the Black or Caspian Seas at either end of the mountains. Likewise when the Babylonians were overrun by the Medes and Persians.

Whilst secular historians are unlikely to see any Ten Tribe connections, those with a Biblical bent have noted that the Iberian Peninsula (also known as Spain and Portugal), was referred to as Iberia by both the Greeks and the Romans. Iberia was also the ancient name they gave for a country located between the Greater and Lesser Caucasus Mountains that is now known as Georgia which is the very area where the Ten Tribes were known to have dwelt. Whilst the etymology is contested, Iber (pronounced eeber) from which we get Iberia, is derived from one of Abraham's ancestors who was called Eber or Heber (Genesis 11:14-16) from which we also get the term Hebrew (Genesis 14:13).

Whilst there are lots of speculations as to the identity of the Ten Tribes, this particular historical document is of considerable interest: The Scottish Declaration of Independence dated 6th April 1320, also known as The Declaration of Arbroath which is stored in the National Archives of Scotland at Edinburgh. Available online.

In the preamble of the document, which was originally written in Latin, it briefly mentions events of their history, including Israel's crossing of the Red Sea, their migration from Scythia to Spain and eventually to their "home in the west". At the time and place of writing it is to be noted that "west" in the document is relative to Europe and the letter was being written to the Pope. What follows is a translation of the first paragraph:

Most Holy Father, we know and from the chronicles and books of the ancients we find that among other famous nations our own, the Scots, has been graced with widespread renown. It journeyed from Greater Scythia by way of the Tyrrhenian Sea and the Pillars of Hercules, and dwelt for a long course of time in Spain among the most savage peoples, but nowhere could it be subdued by any people, however barbarous. Thence it came, twelve hundred years after the people of Israel crossed the Red Sea, to its home in the west where it still lives today. The Britons it first drove out, the Picts it utterly destroyed, and, even though very often assailed by the Norwegians, the Danes and the English, it took possession of that home with many victories and untold efforts; and, as the histories of old time bear witness, they have held it free of all servitude ever since. In their kingdom there have reigned one hundred and thirteen kings of their own royal stock, the line unbroken by a single foreigner.

The document continues with a plea for the Pope to intervene and prevent war between the Scots and the English, charging him with responsibility for much bloodshed if he does nothing. This appeal was apparently successful. Note: The "Tyrrhenian Sea" is off the west coast of Italy and the "Pillars of Hercules" is an ancient term for the Straits of Gibraltar, in particular referring to the prominent peaks on either side that navigators could easily get their bearings from.

From this statement written to the Pope, we find the Scottish Elders making mention of their history and they traced their heritage all the way back to Israel crossing the Red Sea, and noted their sojourn in "Greater Scythia". We also note that they "*dwelt for a long course of time in Spain*". Probably this was when the name Iberia was given to that land.

Another very interesting historical and etymological connection that scholars have brought to light is the similarity between the Hebrew and Gaelic Languages. This particular web-page is of considerable interest:

https://archive.org/stream/affinitybetweenh00stra/affinitybetweenh00stra_djvu.txt

Here is a quote from the study on this page which was originally written by Thomas Steatton back in 1872.

In the following pages there are given about twelve hundred and seventy Hebrew words, which in meaning and sound are like words in Gaelic. This is four hundred and fifty-two words having a non-Celtic prefix, and eight hundred and twenty other words.

I have not reckoned the whole number of words in Hebrew (to be found in the Hebrew Old Testament); it is only a random guess that the twelve hundred and seventy Hebrew words akin to Gaelic are perhaps about one-fourth, or it may be one-third, of all the words in the Hebrew language.

In 1833 I noted several words with a syllable prefixed; so that I was then nearly making the discovery which I did not make till 1871. In 1833 I gave but a very cursory attention to the subject, being then about to attend medical classes.

In this comparison of Hebrew with the Celtic, only one branch of the Celtic is referred to; namely, the Gaelic, now spoken in the Highlands and Western Isles of Scotland. The words quoted may be found in the Gaelic Dictionary by Macleod and Dewar. (Glasgow, 1831; and, second edition, Edinburgh, 1833.) Any remarks here about the Gaelic or Scoto-Celtic apply equally to the Irish language, and to the Manx.

There is so much information on this subject to digest that for the sake of brevity I shall limit myself to the above link, but if you type "The similarity between the Hebrew and Gaelic

253

Languages" into your browser you will find a wealth of validated research available for your perusal.

The Writings of the Jews

The Jewish historian Josephus, whose quote we mentioned above, gives us the clearest and most authoritative statements available. Therefore it deserves being repeated: *"there are but two tribes under the dominion of the Romans"*, and *"the Ten Tribes are beyond the Euphrates and have become a multitude that none could count"* (*Antiquities of the Jews*, 11.5.2).

The Roman Empire never expanded north of the Caucasus Mountains. This natural barrier served to protect the Israelites from the dominion of the Romans. Another Jewish writing from late in the first century AD says this of the Ten Tribes:

2 Esdras Chapter 13:39-45
And whereas thou sawest that he gathered another peaceable multitude unto him; 40 Those are the ten tribes, which were carried away prisoners out of their own land in the time of Osea the king, whom Salmanasar the king of Assyria led away captive, and he carried them over the waters, and so came they into another land. 41 But they took this counsel among themselves, that they would leave the multitude of the heathen, and go forth into a further country, where never mankind dwelt, 42 That they might there keep their statutes, which they never kept in their own land. 43 And they entered into Euphrates by the narrow places of the river. 44 For the most High then shewed signs for them, and held still the flood, till they were passed over. 45 For through that country there was a great way to go, namely, of a year and a half: and the same region is called Arsareth.

Whilst the accuracy of this particular document is questionable seeing as it is considered to be among the books designated apocrypha, it does indicate some Jewish belief in the in the knowledge of the whereabouts of the Ten Tribes at the time of writing.

Not long after the Josephus' historical recording, a great debate is documented between two famous Rabbis which we find in the Jewish Mishnah: Rabbi Akiva and his opponent, Rabbi Eliezer ben Hyrcanus. What follows are their core statements:

"The Ten Tribes shall not return again, for it is written (Deuteronomy 29:27) *'. . . and He cast them into another land like as this day.' As this day goes and returns not, so do they go and return not."* So says Rabbi Akiva.

But Rabbi Eliezer says, *"Like as this day"*: *'as the day grows dark and then becomes light, so also with the Ten Tribes; now they are in darkness, but in the future there shall be light for them.'"*

The setting of this debate is around the time of when Bar Kochba was being proclaimed as Messiah among the Jews, around 130-132AD. Rabbi Akiva, who was strongly advocating support for this 'Messiah', argued that the Ten Tribes would not return and he sought to dismiss the revelation of Scripture with his interpretation in order to encourage the Jews in their uprising against Rome with Bar Kochba as their general. At that time, the Ten Tribes were showing no inclination of returning and because Rabbi Eliezer's understanding was that Messiah had to come before their return, he was therefore not in support of proclaiming Bar Kochba as Messiah. For a more complete analysis of the Rabbinical stance on this subject, type *Will the Lost Tribes Return? By Dennis Jones* into your search engine. However, the main point is that the debate was not about their existence. That was positively assumed by both sides of the argument. It was about whether or not they would return. All the evidence points to the reality that the Jews knew where the Ten Tribes were at that time.

It's time to join the dots. One of the difficulties in assembling all the information is the complicating factor of the Ten Tribes having mixed themselves with the pagans. This verse gives us some hope in the task of identification:

Amos 9:9 NKJV
"For surely I will command, And will sift the house of Israel among all nations, As *grain* is sifted in a sieve; Yet not the smallest grain shall fall to the ground.

Here the Lord gives us assurance that despite them being among the nations, He will bring them through the nations like grain in a sieve. In the metaphor of this verse, the nations are the sieve and Israel is the grain.

Putting it all together now, it becomes clear that if we travel north and west from Jerusalem and keep going to the coastlands and the far off isles we end up in North and Western Europe and the British Isles. If we look at the history of these nations we find that the European people have absolutely dominated the world over the last few centuries and in recent times the English speaking nations have risen to prominence with the United States of America becoming the world super power. American military might, though somewhat depleted in recent times, still spends more on defence than the next 28 nations combined. This would make the English speaking people the most likely candidate for being identified as at least one of the sons of Joseph if not both Ephraim and Manasseh.

Identifying Manasseh is a little difficult, many scholars have suggested the USA with Great Britain being Ephraim. Others have opined that it is the other way around, pointing out that Britain truly only permanently fully colonised Canada, Australia, New Zealand and parts of Southern Africa, even though their dominion included many more countries. Whereas America went on to establish 50 individual states, each with their own Governor and laws; that maintained a unifying body over the breadth of an entire continent; and have become much more dominant in the world. They truly became a multitude or "company of nations".

That Ephraim was going to be greater than Manasseh (Genesis 48:19-20; Deuteronomy 33:16-17) is a factor in tracing who is who. Also, Manasseh was the actual firstborn and just as they received part of their inheritance first on the east side of the Jordan and the tribe was geographically divided, it is thought that the final fulfilment of their promised greatness would be similar. Maybe . . .

Another possibility is that Russia is Manasseh. They too have become a great nation. Although they are nowhere near as influential as the USA, they are without doubt the second greatest nuclear power and are thus a force to be reckoned with. Isaiah 9:21 NKJV says, "Manasseh will devour Ephraim, and Ephraim, Manasseh; both are against Judah." The animosity that exists between Russia and the rest of the west could be the fulfilment of this verse from Isaiah, with the tension between Russia and the USA being a significant indicator.

Perhaps it is the Spanish and Portuguese that are candidates for Manasseh. Their power is much diminished these days, yet they were once a great world power that also had some conflict with the English speaking nations, even in recent times with the Falkland Islands conflict with the Spanish in Argentina. So there is much to be said in favour of the idea that Manasseh could refer to the Spanish. Their influence over the vast majority of the South American continent cannot be denied. Angola and Mozambique on the African continent were also Portuguese colonies. Though the idea of Israelite heritage is held by a minority in English speaking nations, it appears that the Spanish and Portuguese have no recollection within their culture, even though as mentioned above, Iberia is the name by which the Spanish Peninsular has been known for centuries. Well, Manasseh's name was given because Joseph had been made to forget His father's house and forget his heritage. Glad that ultimately it is up to God to sort this all out and not me.

An analysis of the dispersion of the clans of Scotland reveals that they have been scattered equally throughout both the USA and all the British colonies along with almost all the other people groups found on the British Isles, whether Welsh, Irish or English. This would seem to indicate that all the English speaking Caucasians are probably from the same Israelite tribe of Joseph, most likely from Ephraim. This would give support to the idea of Russia or perhaps Spain being Manasseh.

Another possible identifying factor is the study of their beginnings in Genesis. Most people agree when we are identifying Ishmael and Esau that the characteristics that generated the hostility toward Israel and Judah back in biblical times are being repeated in our generation. Likewise with the tribes of Israel. Joseph was separated from his brothers. So we should look for Joseph to be somewhat separated from the other Israelites. Joseph rose to prominence in Egypt so we should expect Joseph to rise to prominence in the world. Again this points to the Spanish and the English speaking nations as they are both somewhat separate from Europe, England by the English Channel and Spain by the mountain range known as the Pyrenees. Spain even remained neutral in World War Two. Isaiah 9:21 says that Ephraim and Manasseh would be against one another yet both would be against Judah. There is no doubt that both the

English speaking and Spanish peoples have had times of giving Judah a hard time. Both have had times when they banned all Jews and drove them to exile. In the latter days that tendency will end as the Lord has said that their antagonism towards one another will finish (Is 11:13). In recent times Spain has apologised to the Jews for their historical prejudice and have opened their doors to Jewish immigration.

Without being able to be absolutely certain of any particular individuals tribal identity due to the mixed marriages that have somewhat blurred the picture, the promise of God is that they would not be unknown to Him. Nevertheless, because of the many identifying factors and the biblical prophecies to assist in our search for understanding, we can with a reasonable amount of surety eliminate most of the world's nations from our probability list.

When we look at the English speaking nations of the world and their respective histories, their colonizing, their military dominance, their constant rebellions and yet their many revivals toward God, it is not hard to see that they are indeed the descendants of Joseph, probably Ephraim, and that the European nations are most likely predominately Israel and the Spanish most likely are Manasseh, though some scholars have suggested that the Spanish are descendants of Benjamin which would allow for Russia to be identified as Manasseh. One word that describes them all is Caucasian.

The one nation that is totally fulfilling the predictions concerning Ephraim at this point in time is the United States of America. No other nation at this point in time has qualified to fit the Biblical description. The European nations and Russia probably mostly being the other ten tribes. Many scholars have identified the Scandinavians as being descendants of the tribe of Dan. No doubt there is a lot of mix and match. Interestingly about Dan, though they had land allotted to them in the South of the Promised Land, some of them ended up taking over cities and establishing themselves north of Galilee thus the tribe was somewhat scattered even before they left the Promised Land. Various scholars have identified Danites being scattered from Ireland through to Scandinavia.

There is no doubt in my mind that these above mentioned nations have fulfilled much of the prophesied destiny of Israel and they are fast approaching the time when they will fulfil their final destination. They are descending into deep apostasy at this very point in time, even to the point of cultural suicide. Many are praying for a revival for these nations. Perhaps it is in response to the prayers of the saints that judgment is stayed. May the church of God get its act together and cast off the traditions of man and 'get in there' with God. One day, sooner or later, God will bring a remnant of Israel back to the land promised to Abraham, Isaac and Jacob and they shall be joined together with Judah into a kingdom that shall never be divided again.

A couple of Jewish websites (Eat the fish; spit out the bones) are now actively promoting this understanding; britam.org and hebrewnations.com, so it looks like God is beginning the work of reconciliation. This will be accomplished, not because of their righteousness, but for His Holy Name's sake. It is going to be one of the major events of the latter days preceding the coming of our Lord Jesus Christ. However, we have covered that topic fully already in the chapter on the Second Exodus.

A great cloud of delusion has kept the majority of believers blinded to the Two House Reality and a new replacement theology has emerged that replaces Israel with Judah. Whilst the descendants of the Kingdom of Judah are children of Abraham, Isaac and Jacob, they are NOT descendants of the Kingdom of Israel who are also children of Abraham, Isaac and Jacob. We have some interesting times coming. Here's a reminder of what the Lord says in the middle of that long passage in Jeremiah Chapters 30-31 concerning the great regathering: "In the latter days ye shall consider it" (Jeremiah 30:24). Obviously, before the great regathering there will be a great awakening that brings the 'Lost Ten Tribes' to consider their heritage and destiny. This book may be one of the instruments God will use to bring this awakening about.

Any attempt by any person who believes they are a descendant of Joseph or one of the other Ten Tribes, to return to the Land of Israel, is unlikely to be successful at this point in time (2017AD) unless it is God Himself that has so declared for them personally. Those who have been accepted and granted immigration rights have all been people that have kept the Jewish traditions, have a Rabbinical conversion certification or have a proven ancestry. Until the Jews have an encounter with their Messiah, they are just not going to have their nation invaded by a Non-Kosher-Crowd.

But I believe that when the time comes there will likely be prophets arise within the populations of these nations and the true believers will hear what the Spirit is saying when it comes time to go. It might also be that there is simply no other place on earth where they will be welcome. If it comes about because of nuclear war, it might be that evacuation because of radiation contamination forces the issue. God will also have prepared the hearts of the Jews. In the meantime, we've got love to pursue and a Gospel to preach so let us be about our Father's business.

The Revelation of Revelation

In my introduction to this book I made the following comment:

"The student of eschatology is presently confronted with a multitude of end-time theories: pre-tribulation, mid-tribulation, post-tribulation, pre-millennial, post-millennial, a-millennial, futurist, historicist, full or partial preterist, hyper-literal or allegorical interpretations and the list goes on . . . With variations within each particular school of thought we probably find that there are over a hundred different scenarios offered up as truth, if not more. Therefore, if you happen to align yourself with any one of the eschatological viewpoints, you will automatically find yourself in disagreement with over ninety percent of the Christian Community. This ought not to be."

All through the writing of this study I have been totally focused on presenting the prophecies that can be readily understood from the plain reading. In the beginning I presented the Twelve Rules for Handling God's Word and have been diligently holding fast to those principles. My motivation was and is to extract from the Scriptures what God has actually said rather than give an interpretation which would really only be my opinion. In so doing I discovered that the Word of God was constantly pulling down the private interpretations of man, including some that I had taken on myself.

It is acknowledged that most end-time Bible teachers are genuinely attempting to make biblical sense out of the symbolism found in the Book of Revelation. But the very fact that there are sooooo many different ideas floating around brings us to the inevitable conclusion that they cannot all be correct. And I am loathe to add yet another opinion to the plethora of prophetic pontifications. Yet the Book of Revelation by its very nature demands to be understood.

Along with many others, I observed that although there are countless interpretations of the various visions found in the writings of John of Patmos, they can all be arranged into seven basic perspectives from which the various interpretations spring forth and they are: The Idealist; The Historicist; The Preterist; The Futurist; The Literalist; The Universalist and The Doctrinalist. The Idealist, Historicist, Preterist, and the Futurist are the more commonly known viewpoints. If you type Four Views of Revelation into your browser, you will find many books and articles attempting to explain these different approaches to the Apocalypse, usually but not always favouring one view over the others. Some of these books have invited writers of the different persuasions to present their point of view.

The Literalist, Universalist and Doctrinalist viewpoints are minority views possibly not heard of by many, but I have included them in order to completely cover all the known variations of perspective that are used to interpret this most controversial book. The following is a brief summary of each of the different views that the eschatology pundits have put forth:

The Idealist Viewpoint

Basic Premise: The Book of Revelation is a non-historical and non-prophetic drama about spiritual realities. This method of interpretation has its origins among the ancient theologians of Alexandria, who spiritualised and allegorised much of the Bible to the extent that the many historical events were not treated literally at all but as symbolic stories from which we may learn.

The Historicist Viewpoint

Basic Premise: The Book of Revelation is a prophetic picture of the church history from the time of its writing to the end of the age. Historicists believe the events in Revelation are symbolic of historical events throughout the church age and they usually interpret Mystery Babylon and the Beast as being the apostate church with the Papacy as the Antichrist. Many also interpret the letters to the seven churches as descriptive of seven eras of church history.

The Preterist Viewpoint

Basic Premise: The Book of Revelation is primarily prophetic of the imminent events that were to happen in 70AD with the fall of Jerusalem and the destruction of the Temple, though some accept the last chapters as pertaining to the end of the age. With both Full and Partial Preterists there is some dispute, with Full Preterists insisting Revelation 19 was only spiritual and also occurred in 70AD. They typically interpret the millennium as being a symbolic number only and that it represents the church age. (Preterist: from the Latin *praeter* meaning 'past')

The Futurist Viewpoint

Basic Premise: The Book of Revelation is primarily prophecy about the final days leading to the end of the world. Apart from those who hold a historical view of the letters to the seven churches, the Futurists believe the prophecies of Revelation are yet to come. They generally believe in a literal thousand year reign of Jesus Christ who will return to rule in His physical resurrected body from Jerusalem. They also believe in a rapture of believers before a seven year tribulation that comes before Jesus' millennial rule, though some believe the rapture is after that tribulation or in the midst of it. Thus we have Pre-tribulation, Mid-tribulation and Post-tribulation end-time theorists among those who hold to the Futurist point of view.

The Literalist Viewpoint

Basic Premise: The Book of Revelation is fully prophetic and is to be taken literally all the way through, even those portions that seem clearly symbolic. It is somewhat similar to the Futurist viewpoint, but attempts to overcome the vagaries of interpretation by taking the plain meaning to its fullest extent. Often denigrated as being hyper-literal by its detractors.

The Universalist Viewpoint

Basic Premise: All of the above views of the Book of Revelation are legitimate. In the Universalist mind-set, there is no contradiction between Idealist, Historicist, Preterist, Futurist, or Literalist. This viewpoint assumes that the Apocalypse has multiple fulfillment of each of its prophecies and can also be taken completely literally whilst still having an allegorical meaning. In this view God has performed a miracle by giving a five in one prophecy. This viewpoint is thought by its detractors to be the result of a worldly post-modern concept coming into the church expressed in the following phrase: What is true for you is true for you and what is true for me is true for me. In other words, whatever you make of it is okay.

The Doctrinalist Viewpoint

Basic Premise: The Book of Revelation cannot be understood without a comprehensive understanding of the Gospel AND a thorough appreciation of the prophecies of the Apostles and the Prophets. The Doctrinalist subjects the Apocalypse and its various interpretations to the scrutiny of that which has already been revealed in plain language from the Word of God and rejects that which cannot be substantiated from the rest of the Bible. The Doctrinalist therefore advocates understanding Revelation from the frame work of all that has been written in the Scriptures before it came into being.

The Apocalypse of John of Patmos is so saturated with symbolism that it has provoked many authors to present hundreds of pages pulling these various views of Revelation apart and assembling plausible proofs of support for their own preferred viewpoint, only to find that others have attacked their ideas with equal plausibility. At different times throughout history the different views have all had their day of being more prominent than the others. Presently the Futurist view seems to be riding high, though in early church times the Idealist was more prominent. During the Reformation, the Historicist perspective rose to prominence, and after the prognostics of the Historicist views at that time failed to manifest, along came the Preterists and later the Futurists, though both of them claim support from early church times. Little is known of the origins of the Literalists, the Universalists or the Doctrinalists, whose views I stumbled upon in the course of my research.

However, for me to properly address this subject is more than can be accomplished in a small chapter. The subject is huge, and it has become obvious that it will require me to present my discoveries in another book. Besides, it really is another subject and somewhat off topic from this present study. However, those of you who have apprehended the reality of the Kingdom of Judah, the Kingdom of Israel and the Kingdom of God will be well prepared to receive what I have discovered about the writings of John of Patmos. The title of this chapter you are presently reading will be the title of my up and coming publication. If you have been enlightened with The Lion and The Unicorn on the Road to Zion, you will certainly enjoy The Revelation of Revelation. Look for more details in this Appendix under Recommended Reading.

In my treatise I will be presenting a more complete overview of each of the seven different viewpoints and their various pros and cons along with some very interesting historical and archaeological discoveries, including some astounding information about the number 666 and the name of the beast (exposed by ancient documents), all now made available online for all to see. This study also brings into question most contemporary eschatological theories and actually overturned a number of my own beliefs about the end times.

Whilst I will be giving each of the different viewpoints their due consideration, I will be giving particular attention to the Doctrinalist Viewpoint. Their basic premise caught my attention as their exegesis methodology aligns with the Twelve Rules for Handling God's Word that I presented in my introduction. The Doctrinalist approach to the Book of Revelation advocates using Scripture as the ONLY interpreter. I have found this to be the key that unlocks the door to the truth behind this mysterious book. No more Scriptureless interpretations. (Scriptureless: not yet found in English dictionaries) (: -)

The Revelation of Revelation will allow you to finally build a spiritual understanding of the Apocalypse that destroys the eschatological confusion, builds faith and confidence in the promises of God, and does not require you to jettison your intelligence, although it may require an unexpected paradigm shift. In the meantime, leave Revelation alone. Without a revelation, it is not a revelation. And look forward to reading The Revelation of Revelation. Amen.

Love, joy and peace to you in Jesus Mighty Name.

Recommended Reading

I mentioned the writings of the Jewish 1st century historian Josephus many times and **The Complete Works Of Flavius Josephus** should, in my opinion, be in every Christian's Library along with a couple of small books that are now considered as apocrypha, **1st and 2nd Maccabees.** I would never consider either of these as Scripture, but they are very useful in understanding some of the history of what is otherwise known as the silent years before the New Testament. The Josephus account of the fall of Jerusalem is also of considerable interest.

Not sure about all of his end-time theology, but Jack Smith's **Islam: The Cloak of Antichrist** is a very good insight into the belief system of this religion that is growing rapidly throughout the world.

James Farquharson's book: **Daniel's Last Vision and Prophecy** written back in 1838 has been electronically digitised & edited by Dr Peter Bluer 2007 and is available online as a PDF. I stumbled upon it when I was looking for a quote of his. I haven't read the whole thing, but what I saw confirmed the understanding and conclusion I had come to in my studies regarding the latter part of Daniel Chapter Eleven and Chapter Twelve. It looked like a very thorough presentation.

The Torch of the Testimony by John W. Kennedy gives an account of Christians down through the ages that have maintained their faith outside the institutional church that has historically and periodically persecuted them.

Look for my web page **www.livingandlovingbyfaith.com** for other interesting and informative articles that remove confusion and build up the Body of Christ. You will also find links to other helpful ministries, especially in the realm of equipping the saints for their personal evangelism and their walk of love. It is on this website that you will find details on the publication of my treatise of the Book of Revelation which will be entitled **The Revelation of Revelation**, along with information on how to obtain a copy.

About the Author

In the South Island of New Zealand there is an elusive character whose pen name is Elihu Ben Ephraim: pastor, teacher, evangelist and a disciple of Jesus Christ; who never thought he would ever find himself writing a book on prophecy and has only given himself to this project because he believes God has laid it on his heart. His primary focus in life is to proclaim Him and His Word, with an emphasis upon knowing who you are in Christ and who He is in you, leading to a life of love and power in the Holy Spirit. Consequently he is unwilling to be forthcoming concerning details of himself as he is not particularly interested in becoming well known. If you ever get to meet him, he'll welcome you with a smile, put the kettle on, and very soon you will be talking about the things of God over a cup of tea or coffee, or perhaps a ginger beer.

Printed in the United States
By Bookmasters

Printed in the United States
By Bookmasters